THE AMERICAN HERESY

Thomas Jefferson

From his last portrait, by Thomas Sully, now in the Library
of the United States Military Academy at West Point

THE AMERICAN HERESY

By
CHRISTOPHER HOLLIS

ST. AIDAN PRESS, LLC
Morning View, Kentucky

The American Heresy.

First published in 1927 by Sheed and Ward, London. Reprinted from 1930 Minton, Balch, & Co. edition.

Typesetting, layout and cover design copyright 2024 St. Aidan Press, LLC.

Cover images are:
  Thomas Jefferson, painted by Rembrandt Peale.
  Portrait of John C. Calhoun, (1782–1850), by Rembrandt Peale.
  Abraham Lincoln, by George Peter Alexander Healy.
  Official Presidential Portrait of Woodrow Wilson, by Frank Graham Cootes.
  A drawing of the imprint made by the 1782 Great Seal of the United States, by Walter Manton in 1892.

All rights reserved.

ISBN-13: 978-1-962503-09-9
ISBN-10: 1-962503-09-7

For more information, contact:
www.staidanpress.com
staidanpress@gmail.com

We have made no intentional change from the original text except to correct mistakes in spelling and punctuation.

TO
DOUGLAS WOODRUFF

CONTENTS

	PAGE
THE JEFFERSONIAN STATE	1
THOMAS JEFFERSON	4
JOHN CALDWELL CALHOUN	84
ABRAHAM LINCOLN	153
WOODROW WILSON	225
THE NEW STATE	308
APPENDIX A. THE DECLARATION OF INDEPENDENCE	311
APPENDIX B. THE VIRGINIA STATUTE OF RELIGIOUS LIBERTY	315
APPENDIX C. THE BILL OF RIGHTS	317
APPENDIX D. THE FOURTEEN POINTS	319
INDEX	324

ILLUSTRATIONS

	PAGE
THOMAS JEFFERSON	*Frontispiece*
JOHN CALDWELL CALHOUN	85
ABRAHAM LINCOLN	155
WOODROW WILSON	227

MAPS

		PAGE
I.	THE UNITED STATES—TO ILLUSTRATE:	321

    THE MISSOURI COMPROMISE.

    THE MEXICAN WAR.

    THE OREGON SETTLEMENT.

    THE COMPROMISE OF 1850.

II. THE UNITED STATES—TO ILLUSTRATE: 322

    THE WAR OF INDEPENDENCE.

    THE WAR OF 1812.

III. THE SOUTHERN STATES—TO ILLUSTRATE: 323

    THE CIVIL WAR.

In revising this work for its American edition I have profited from the advice and criticism of many friends. In especial I should like to express my thanks to Mr. D. W. Brogan, who, while by no means agreeing with my interpretation of American history, was yet kind enough to put his large learning at my disposal.

C. H.

November, 1929.

THE
AMERICAN HERESY

The Jeffersonian State

"WE HOLD THESE truths to be self-evident, that all men are created equal, that they are endowed by their Creator with certain inalienable rights, that among these are life, liberty, and the pursuit of happiness."

The two marks of the Jeffersonian state were freedom and equality. Let us examine the meaning of these marks.

Freedom, in Jefferson's mouth, was a very negative thing, even as the functions of government were, to his mind, very negative. Freedom meant simply "absence of interference." Man should be interfered with as little as possible by the laws. The laws had the right to interfere with liberty only in order to increase liberty—to interfere with such conduct as would, if permitted, violate the liberty of others.

By equality, on the other hand, he meant something much larger than that each man should have a vote. Equality was, in Jefferson's eyes, rather social than political. He demanded that no prestige of rank should prevent any one citizen from freely speaking his mind to any other citizen. And this virtue of outspokenness is perhaps, even today, the largest special virtue of the Americans. It has survived the ruin of the Jeffersonian state.

The American Heresy

If a state was to remain free and equal, Jefferson thought that it must be agricultural and property-owning. It must be agricultural because the complexity of factory organization made it necessary that men should be divided into masters and servants. Only in an agricultural society could property be so distributed that all men might possess a little and therefore only in such a society could equality be preserved. An agricultural society also was the only free society. For such a society, being economically self-sufficient, could live its own life, regardless of the rest of the world. An industrial society, dependent for its existence upon its capacity to exchange its surplus products against those of other countries, would, as we in England know, continually have to allow its policy to be dictated by commerce.

The Jeffersonian state had, from the beginning, two main obstacles to its realization—a large population of black slaves in the South and, in the North, a growing, though not yet dominant, spirit of commercialism, whose demand was that the object of policy should be not to give the citizen this or that sort of life, but simply to give him as high a material standard as possible.

The Jeffersonian state soon had to meet two attacks.

On the one hand, it had to face the subtle perversion, by those who claimed to be his followers, of Jefferson's teaching upon slavery. He had accepted slavery as a necessary evil. The generation which followed, having discovered that, owing to the invention of Eli Whitney, a slave was a vastly more valuable commodity than it had previously imagined, claimed that slavery was good in itself. Slavery had existed in Jefferson's Virginia, but it did not exist in his Utopia. It existed both in Calhoun's South Carolina and in his Utopia.

On the other hand, Jefferson's state had to face the growing hostility of the commercial classes of the North, who were not content that commerce should play that restricted rôle of supplier of the needs of agriculture, which was the most that Jeffersonian

The Jeffersonian State

philosophy would allow to it. The first attack from this quarter was that of Hamilton, who attempted to impose on the Jeffersonian state a plutocratic government. It was defeated. But the Federalist party re-emerged as the high-tariff party, as the Republican party, captured the government, fought the Civil War and eventually smashed the Jeffersonian state.

The Jeffersonian state was, as has been said, a state primarily agricultural. The independence of the agricultural interest was safeguarded, in the Constitution, by the doctrine of state rights— by the guarantee of a real independence to the agricultural state, which would prevent Washington or New York from becoming the master of her life. That state-life the Civil War killed. It is the thesis of this book that the United States, which were previously a reality, have since been only a name. They have been Hamiltonian rather than Jeffersonian, if one must search out for them an ancestor among the American Fathers.

Thomas Jefferson

I

THOMAS JEFFERSON was a sandy-haired man, an architect, a market-gardener and the author of curious works—one, to refute the Comte de Buffon, on American animal life, and another, also on American animal life, called the Declaration of Independence. In his republican veins ran the royal blood of the Princess Pocahontas and the noble blood of "the bonny Earl of Murray" of Scotland. He wrote once to a friend "to search the Herald's office for the arms of my family. It is possible there may be none. If so, I would with your assistance become a purchaser, having Sterne's word for it that a coat of arms may be purchased as cheaply as any other coat." Nor through all his life did he ever forget that all men were born equal—particularly himself. He was no snob but was, what is much rarer, a conscious citizen, a republican, a member of the Public Thing.

The modern American cannot understand this English gentleman, feels uncomfortably that he was unique, is ignorant why. Yet the key is simple, and, because of it, after a hundred and fifty years, he is still worth a student's study. For he was the only man in English history who was both a democrat and a republican. The lesson of England is that the liberal has never been the democratic side. By the accident of living in Virginia, Jefferson did not find this out. Not until old age did he discover of Bolingbroke, in curious research, that "he was indeed called a

Tory; but his writings prove him a stronger advocate for liberty than any of his countrymen, the Whigs of the present day." And even then he did not suspect the reason.

II

The causes of the American War are, in some casual way, known to every schoolboy. It is not necessary to do more than repeat here a summary. After the Seven Years' War England found herself saddled with a considerable debt. The war had been fought largely for American benefit and had freed the Americans from the French menace, which they feared. Now Grenville, the English minister, had discovered that the Continent of America lived by smuggling. This discovery was his fatal blunder. For it raised against him a powerful vested interest. "One quarter of all the signers of the Declaration of Independence," Professor Barnes[1] has discovered, "were bred to . . . the contraband trade." When, therefore, Grenville added that he thought it only fair that the Americans should pay a contribution of a third towards the expenses of the standing army, which had to be maintained in the colonies in order to protect them from Indian aggression, the trade was already suspicious. Grenville cared nothing how America raised the money. He gave the colonists a year to find a method convenient to themselves. But they, intelligent enough to understand that British owners of American property would prefer that that property should be defended by American money but, if such money were not forthcoming, would at the last resort defend it with their own, refused any suggestions. Grenville therefore attempted to enforce upon the country the Stamp Act. The American reply was a boycott of all Government stamps.

---

[1] *History and Social Intelligence*, by Harry Elmer Barnes. A. A. Knopf, New York, 1926.

Proving futile of revenue, the Act was repealed by the next Government—that of Lord Rockingham.

The second attempt to tax the Americans was made by Townshend, who placed duties upon tea, glass and paper. Again the American reply was a boycott and the British Parliament repealed the duties on glass and paper but kept that on tea. Thence through a jaded whirl of massacres and tea-parties emerged a Declaration of Independence.

It is well to examine the sides to this controversy.

The conventional American case is expressed in the slogan, "No taxation without representation." "Man," it was argued, "had a natural right to freedom." Therefore it was wrong that he should be taxed except by the votes of an Assembly, in the electing of one member of which he had himself a vote—and it was stupid of George III not to understand this.

It raises two questions. What could George III be expected to think of the American slogan? And what was its real truth? On the first, at any rate, only a little imagination is needed to see how fantastic is the common blame of George. In his England, out of about seven millions only 300,000 had a parliamentary vote at that date. Yet all the seven millions were taxed. The other peoples of Europe lacked even these rudiments of representation. They, too, were taxed. Moreover, in the opinion of George III, the very strength of England's representative system was the main menace to her freedom. The honest object of his domestic policy was to break that strength. If George III neglected a truth, he neglected it with all his age. If every other country had "taxation without representation," was it monstrous tyranny to ask America to accept it, too? Was it sensible to expect a humane King to strengthen in America that institution, from which he was struggling hard to set England free?

The second question let us divide again. Are there any natural rights? Certainly there are. Aristotle and the schoolmen settled that. Jefferson, Rousseau and the rest only copied out such parts of the scholastic teaching as they could understand. Is there a natural right to liberty? Yes. Has "no taxation without representation" a necessary connection with liberty? None in the world.

The representative system may be better or worse than other forms of government in practice. It shares the nature of government. Government is force—an interference by force. The Government taxes the citizen by force. To pretend that in a Parliamentary country the voter really taxes himself is a silly playing with words. Mr. Hirst[1] proudly claims that "Jefferson stripped loyalty and royalty of all their mystic properties." It is a pity that he did not go on, like Rousseau, to perform a similar service for representation.

Consider how tenuous is the thread which in a large country connects a representative and his elector. For nineteen-twentieths of the votes which he casts, my representative has no sort of mandate from the constituency, of which I am one among twenty thousand electors. And, if he has none, what have the other six hundred-odd members, in whose election I had not even this small share? In what sense am I a freer man, if I am taxed thus, than if I live under the personal rule of a Charles I or a George III—kings to whom I have probably at least taken an oath of allegiance?

The word "representative" had, it is true, more meaning in the time of Jefferson than it has today. For the Member for Old Sarum at least did represent somebody, its owner who put him there. The very success of the system made Jefferson's argument partly valid. For, with all its defects, the Parliament of England, in the eighteenth century, did represent, if not the people of England, at least Englishmen. Once therefore that the American became conscious that he was of a different nationality from the Englishman, he was clearly degraded if he allowed himself to

---

[1] *Life and Letters of Thomas Jefferson*, by F. W. Hirst. Macmillan and Co.

be ruled and taxed by a body of Englishmen. At the same time, the existence of a realm implies that a single sovereignty resides somewhere. Otherwise, there is, as Seabury[1] said, "an Empire without a Government"—a contradiction in terms. Jefferson's theory that England and America had "the same executive chiefs but no other necessary political connection," was clearly mere words. The pre-Revolution Whig was willing to take an oath of allegiance, provided that there went with it a promise that he would never be called upon to act on such an oath. Was there, if England was not willing to be taxed for the military defense of America, as she is today willing to be taxed for the naval defence of Australia, no alternative but that the two should

"Union in disunion find,
In separation peace?"

The American cry was "No taxation without representation." But the Americans had no intention of obtaining representation in a British Parliament, nor would such a plan have been practicable. Their cry was therefore really the cry of the modern French peasant: "No taxation with (or without) representation," in which, it is true, there is a certain noble freedom. Yet through that cry, "so paltry a sum as threepence in the eyes of a financier, so insignificant an article as tea in the eyes of a philosopher," as Burke said, "were able to shake the pillars of a commercial Empire that circled the whole globe."

"Commercial" is there the important word. If the Empire was only a commercial contract for buying in cheapest markets and selling in dearest, then, if the Americans thought that they could drive bargains more successfully outside it, there was no

---

[1] Samuel Seabury (1729–96), Rector of St. Peter's, Westchester, New York, and afterwards Protestant Bishop of Connecticut; author of the *Farmer's Letters* and *An Alarm to the Legislature of the Province of New York*; the ablest Loyalist pamphleteer in America.

argument which could restrain them. True, they owed their position to the past defense of Britain, but gratitude does not figure in a Benthamite vocabulary. Yet Empires are of two kinds. They may be commercial, or, like the Roman or Spanish, cultural, imposing upon their territories a certain way of life and only incidentally bringing commercial gain to the mother-country. It was not at the first certain of which class this British Empire was to be. The cultural Empire has a missionary nature and in it a much stronger central authority will be admitted than in the former. The Stuarts might have stood for such an England. Not until 1688 was the commercial state from which a weaker Imperial policy was required definitely established. Yet it must not be forgotten that George III, with Bolingbroke's *Patriot King* in one pocket and a Jesuit's defence of James II in the other, had dedicated his life to the overthrow of that commercial state.

Is it not true that the Americans without indignity could have borne much from a King that they could never bear from a Parliament? Americans could not tolerate to be ruled by Englishmen. Either a democracy or an aristocracy is numerous enough to be national. A single ruler alone can transcend nationality. The King was, as Jefferson himself said in his pamphlet, "A Summary View of the Rights of British America," "the only mediatory power between the several states of the British Empire." From the Kings, James I and Charles I, had come the first challenge to the British Parliament's right to tax America. "It was not fitting," James had said, "that Parliament should make laws for those countries" (*i.e.* the American colonies), and Charles that "the colonies were without the realm and jurisdiction of Parliament" (for which—and for one or two other things—they cut off his head). Would not the true American policy, if the Americans had known their business, have been to strengthen the hands of the King so as to make him independent of the King's Friends? Franklin, alone of Americans, seems sometimes to have suspected this.

The fallacy of the Americans was then to argue throughout on those assumptions of 1688, which George was throughout questioning. Yet Jefferson's debating answer was a good one. Seabury used to maintain that it was impossible for a subject to have rights against the sovereign. But, said Jefferson, England was, rightly or wrongly, living under the settlement of 1688. The justification of that settlement was that the sovereign had violated the rights of the subject. If such a thing was not possible, George III was not King of England. And indeed in such an answer lies all the truth and tragedy about George, all the case for him as George Guelph, all the case against him as George III. He was a Jacobite who did not quite possess the courage of his convictions.

The Americans met the offensive of the royal Government by a boycott. This was a weapon in itself reasonable and legitimate. There was no compulsion upon anybody to use a stamp, nor to buy tea. If he preferred to go without, the British Government had no just cause of complaint. But a voluntary boycott, if unexceptionable, would have been also futile. Only about two-thirds of America were in sympathy with Whig policy. Unless it was generally obeyed the boycott would never bring the British Government to make concessions, and it was not possible to enforce it upon the unwilling except by methods which led people to wonder which was the worse tyranny, the distant or the near at hand. Only a very philosophic radical found it self-evident that every man had the right to life, liberty, the pursuit of happiness and tar and feathers.

III

In Massachusetts desultory preparations proceeded. But, at that date, Massachusetts was of less importance than Virginia. Jefferson was a member of the second Virginia Convention, which was sitting throughout 1775. The older and landed classes had hopes even now of reconciliation. A resolution was passed, "that it is the most ardent wish of this colony (and, they are persuaded, of the whole Continent of North America) to see a speedy return to those halcyon days, when we lived a free and happy people." All might have passed off in peace, had there not sprung up a young man, a certain Patrick Henry, a barrister and a Presbyterian, who had gained some reputation from his violent attacks upon the clergymen of the Established Church. He cried out: "Why stand we here idle? Is life so dear, or peace so sweet, as to be purchased at the price of chains and slavery? Forbid it, Almighty God! I know not what course others may take, but as for me, give me liberty or give me death."

Such language is intolerable. War is so great an evil that, when it and peace are in the balance, no man has the right to use rhetoric, whose whole purpose is to rob its hearers of the use of reason. Even at this distance of time an honorable reader must feel shamed when he comes across such speech. Yet, because of it, Virginia, by a vote of sixty-five to sixty and the advice of Jefferson and Washington, committed herself to preparations for war. The die was cast. In the next month war broke in Massachusetts; at Lexington the first blood was shed.

A last attempt at conciliation was made by Lord North. He promised to exempt from taxation any colony which would, of its own accord, make a contribution to Imperial needs. The difficulty of such a plan is clear. A single power must have the ultimate responsibility. Then, as today, that power would have been the British Government. Therefore, even under Lord North's scheme, the American would still have been taxed. The method of raising money, indeed, would have been of his own choice, but he would still have had to contribute it for British spending. Yet how could such a difficulty be avoided? If you would have an Empire, it needs an Emperor.

The American Heresy

If such then was the feeling of America, or, at least, of vocal America, separation was inevitable. And yet Franklin told Chatham in 1774 that he had never heard from anyone "drunk or sober, the least expression of a wish for separation." Certainly he had not. The American Whig wished England to shoulder the burden of the defense, America to accept its shelter. Of this service in the past Jefferson admitted that "the aids granted were doubtless valuable." Yet to suffer its continuance was unworthy of a free nation. And an Englishman may feel proud that, in 1776, his ancestors rose up against this American tyranny and freed their country from it for ever in 1783.

After taking his part in the rejection of Lord North's proposals by the Virginia Assembly, Jefferson travelled off to Philadelphia, to witness their rejection by the general Continental Congress. He was one of a Committee of Four, whose task it was to draft a reply to that proposition.

Having resolved to appeal to arms Jefferson wisely determined to pitch the American demands as high as possible. In his answer to Lord North, the provocations under which the British suffered are entirely neglected. To claim any right of taxation was, he shouted, "to leave us without anything we can call property." And the foaming of a half-witted and very private Member of Parliament, called Vane, who had said of Massachusetts, "Delenda est Carthago," was solemnly paraded as the opinion and intention of the British Ministry. It was both masterly and abominable.

Yet America needed not only rhetoric, but philosophy. Tom Paine, the first of a long and happy band of trans-Atlantic lecturers, had settled in Philadelphia, rightly confident that he could make a living out of the Americans by inventing for them noble reasons for doing whatever they might wish to do. On 10th January, 1776, appeared his pamphlet, "Common Sense," the reasoning of which a certain Washington found "sound" and "unanswerable." In it was set forth the absurdity of submission to the arbitrary rule of a tyrant.

In the word "arbitrary" lies the whole strength of the American metaphysics. To submit oneself to the rule of a single man is no degradation, provided that upon the principles of government there is original agreement and the ruler is answerable for his application of those principles to a person, independent of his own creation. But to submit oneself to the rule of the English monarchy was a degradation. For it was in the very nature of the English monarchy, built not only upon the Hanoverian settlement in politics but upon the Elizabethan settlement in religion, that it, alone among European monarchies, openly repudiated this duty of answering for its conduct. The King was Head of the Church as well as the State. To such a monarch's power it was no doubt necessary to invent some check. This, though George III could not understand it, nor, it is fair to say, could Tom Paine, nor Tom Jefferson, is the one really overwhelming argument for the Americans—and the one argument for the Americans that no American has ever used.

IV

Jefferson's first concern was to make final the independence from Great Britain both of America and of Virginia. For this purpose he drafted a constitution for Virginia. It is the document of a man trying to turn 1688 into a victory for democracy, nor do the details of this model republic need repetition. Only by one clause is its author raised for a breathless moment to the company of the great political reformers. "Every landless citizen," he says, "is entitled to fifty acres of unappropriated land." A man, that is, by his very manhood, has a title to property. The shallow skeptic has died. A brave philosopher, forced by reality to speculate upon the ultimate nature of man, has come to birth. Man is a property-owning animal.

Jefferson, as if captured by his new passion, was anxious to push on and give a metaphysic to a Continent. There was debate whether it were wiser to issue at once a Declaration of Independence or to wait for a more nearly unanimous opinion. The braver side rightly won the day. Jefferson was of it and was elected Chairman of the Drafting Committee. Thus did he come to be the author of that Declaration, through which he is remembered as a philosopher and his reputation as a prophet is wholly in the dust. One or two of his clauses were afterwards struck out or altered. That, for instance, which condemned the slave-trade, since it was offensive alike to the delegates of the South, who owned the profitable slaves, and to those of the North, who owned the profitable ships in which the slaves were carried, had to be omitted. Nor was the whole passed, until a swarm of stinging flies from a neighboring livery stable, straying in through the window, created among honorable members an anxiety to cut the debate as short as possible. Yet substantially his work remained. Such are the services to civilization of the stinging fly.

A handful of slave-owners met together and declared it to be self-evident that all men were born equal. Man's natural right to life they made the excuse for a bloody war, in which many innocent men would be done to death. From such paradoxes were the United States born. Yet they were paradoxes of which it would be unfair to imagine their authors ignorant, or to blame them because they were not afraid to state their theory in its fullness, although the application of it could be immediately only partial. These first builders of independent America were in many ways five hundred years behind their times. It was greatly to their credit. The twilight of death of the last four centuries has produced little that was more medieval than the Declaration of Independence.[1]

---

[1] *See* Appendix A.

Thomas Jefferson

"If," as Mr. Hirst truly says, "praise of the Declaration is superfluous, criticism is vain." It is more valuable to grasp clearly the religious metaphysic upon which it is based. This metaphysic is that of the natural rights of man. The Declaration begins then, as is reasonable, with a statement of faith in the existence of God. If there is no God, clearly there can be no natural rights. For natural rights depend upon obligation. Obligation depends upon a God, to Whom the debt can be owed.

Jefferson goes on to assert that God, having created Man, had created him of a certain nature, or, as he puts it, possessed of certain rights. Of this teaching the summary is in the two famous sentences: "All men are created equal." "They are endowed by their Creator with certain inalienable rights. Among these are life, liberty and the pursuit of happiness." These truths Jefferson held to be self-evident.

First let us consider whether they are true. It is sometimes solemnly demonstrated, with some statistical erudition, that all men cannot be equal since one is taller, or another uglier, than his neighbor—a most difficult observation, of which apparently Jefferson was thought to have been incapable. It is as if one were to argue that all men cannot have immortal souls, since some like artichokes and others like Wagner.

What is your evidence, it is asked, for the existence of natural rights? The words of the question are reasonable, but the thought is most unreasonable. For the questioner means, on what historical date was it laid down in a charter, which no professor is clever enough to prove a forgery, that natural rights exist? Or, in other words, when were these God-granted rights man-granted?

Now these truths are metaphysical, not historical, and a pragmatic mind, which has thrown over metaphysics and therefore thrown over thinking, naturally cannot rise to their comprehension. Yet they must be proved. Jefferson is wrong when he calls them "self-evident." They are not postulates, things unthinkably not, like a man's knowledge of his own existence, or of other existence, or his knowledge that a thing cannot at the same time be both *A* and not *A*. That the soul of a St. Francis or a Napoleon or a Shakespeare is equal to that of some criminal imbecile—no truth could well be less self-evident. It is a profound metaphysical mystery, and the great majority of the human race which has lived and died, would have agreed with Alcibiades, that such talk was ὁμολογουμένη ἄνοια, "confessed folly." And, according to their lights, they would have been right.

For the equality of man is the conclusion of a considerable train of deduction. And one to whom the steps in the deduction have not been pointed out has no reason to grant the conclusion. Briefly, the equality of man rests on the possession by every individual of a soul to be saved or damned—and on that alone. Those who do not hold the one have no reason to hold the other.

Algernon Sidney, to whom, after Locke, Jefferson owed his largest debt, had written that "the common notions of liberty are not from the school divines, but from Nature." And Jefferson, in his own copy of Sidney, has marked this passage. Yet it is almost childish in stupidity. All metaphysical truths, it is clear, are necessarily derived from Nature—that is to say, from God. St. Thomas Aquinas did not pretend that men were unequal, until he made them equal by writing the "Summa Contra Gentiles." Sidney had not, perhaps, any conscious intention of casting discredit upon one to whom credit was due, but his mind was not one at all capable of appreciating such a distinction. Jefferson copied out Sidney.

Every nation is built upon a philosophy. America was built by Jefferson upon a true philosophy. But, enunciating right principles for his society, he justified those principles sentimentally, where they should have been justified rationally. The rationalist can answer his opponents; the sentimentalist cannot. The rationalist can argue: "All men are born equal, because God created them so, equal before His altar, equal in His sight. If you cannot see this, it does not become the less true, nor does it make the difference of a pin to anything, except perhaps the state of your soul." The sentimentalist can only say: "I, at least, feel all men to be equal. And, if you do not, you must, I suppose, be made differently from me." America, the sentimentalist, was soon to be challenged for her reasons. She was unable to give them.

The Declaration of Independence is an intensely interesting exposition of the metaphysical opinions of Thomas Jefferson—and, in many ways, the metaphysic of Thomas Jefferson is more important than the history of America. Yet it would be a mistake to imagine the two very closely connected. "History," a great American has said, "is bunk," and, when Alexander Hamilton came anxiously to inquire how it might be possible to get his tea for threepence in the pound cheaper, he was little edified to find a sandy-haired man on a mountain, perorating out of the works of a fourteenth-century Prince-Bishop of Geneva.[1]

Hamilton himself, it was true, had said that "the sacred rights of mankind . . . are written, as with a sunbeam, in the whole volume of human nature, by the Divinity itself." "Sunbeam" is good. So is "itself." It is so much less superstitious to put things like that into the neuter—and then it was the fashion to use such language; but Jefferson actually seemed to mean it. At first it was even disturbing. But, having discovered, as he thought, that Jefferson, when he claimed that all men were equal, did not mean that they should all have votes, or equal wealth, but merely that they were equal in the sight of a God, Whose existence, as an entirely respectable skeptic, he admitted to be extremely doubtful, Hamilton, in the end, unconcernedly let him be. The future was to show his mistake, and never again was the

---

[1] Adhémar Fabry, who, in 1387, made with the citizens of Geneva a compact, according to which the government of the state was regulated both by him and by his successors.

American people to run the desperate risk of choosing for their President a man acquainted with metaphysics.

Jefferson, having been brought face to face with the evils of monarchy, identified his doctrine more completely with representative democracy than was at all necessary. If there is agreement between ruler and ruled on the moral law, equality in a large state is probably best guarded by an absolute monarch. To a heterogeneous society the *pis aller* of some sort of representative system is perhaps necessary. Yet equality does not in itself imply one method of legislation rather than another. It concerns itself only with the object of legislation, to which it applies a Kantian formula that every subject of the State must be treated as an end in himself, not merely as a means to others' happiness, or, as Algernon Sidney wrote and Jefferson quoted, "the mass of mankind has not been born with saddles on their backs, nor a favored few booted and spurred, ready to ride them legitimately by the grace of God."

This, if it does not necessarily imply democracy, does at least, it has been argued, condemn slavery. And it does imply, it is true, that in a slave state every man must look forward to and work for an eventual emancipation, if only because nobody ought to be found willing to accept the moral responsibilities of slave-ownership, but it is very possible that in a particular society equality might be hindered rather than helped by an immediate emancipation. For the doctrine is always faced with the paradox, that, if all men are equal, then the man who sees that truth is superior to the man who does not. It might be ruinous to a society to trust a group of men with the responsibilities of freedom, when they have not yet been able to learn the responsibilities of equality. For this reason Jefferson sensibly did not emancipate his slaves.

V

After drafting the Declaration of Independence, Jefferson attempted to foist upon the new nation a coat of arms, representative, on the one side, of the children of Israel in the wilderness, George III, somewhat unconvincingly disguised as Pharaoh in the distance, and still farther in the distance "clouds radiant with the hidden glory of God"; on the other, "Hengist and Horsa, the Saxon chiefs, from whom we claim the honor of being descended, and whose political principles and forms of government we have assumed." The nation, careless of its Nordic origins, unceremoniously rejected the plan, and Jefferson, retiring from Congress, took a seat for the County of Albemarle, in the Assembly of Virginia. Virginia was the center of American resistance. His wife was ill and at Monticello. For these two reasons, he thought that he was better employed at Williamsburg than at Philadelphia.

In the Assembly he busied himself with the introduction of a variety of humanitarian reforms into the educational and judicial systems of his state. They were mostly good and useful, but *"le roi philosophe de Virginie"* met for them with only a moderate success. His main work in these years was the introduction into the state of religious toleration. Colonial Virginia had been of the Established Anglican religion, and uniformity had been rigidly enforced. This uniformity Jefferson set himself to destroy, and we may be grateful to the old Virginia Establishment, if for nothing else, that it forced from its opponent two extremely interesting statements of the principles of eighteenth-century Free Thought. These statements Mr. Hirst passes by with unqualified praise. Let us prefer examination.

In his *Notes on Virginia*, published in 1781, before the passage of his "Statute of Religious Freedom,"[1] Jefferson includes an essay on toleration. The case for it he bases on four arguments. "It

---

[1] For the "Statute of Religious Freedom" *see* Appendix B.

does me no injury for my neighbor to say there are twenty gods or no god." "Error alone needs the support of government. Truth can stand by itself." "Difference of opinion in religion is advantageous." ". . . a thousand systems of religion. . . . Against such a majority we cannot effect this (*i.e.* uniformity) by force."

Of these propositions the first two would, I suppose, be today accepted by the majority of people without question and as truisms. But of that majority the majority again would accept them as such only because they do not bother at all about religion. They are carelessly willing that the world should be filled with temptations to their own or their children's faith, because the faith that they profess they profess only with a quarter of their heart. Religion does not interfere with their conduct anyhow, and they start with the preconception that it does not matter what religion a man believes. They are too indolent to think out their religion. The tolerance, upon which they pride themselves, is only sloth.

Put before such people some philosophy which patently interferes with conduct, and you will soon see how large is their tolerance. They will allow free speech to Fifth Monarchy men, but they will allow none to Bolshevists. Supposing that I arise in Hyde Park and say "I am a man of peace myself, and have no intention of practicing what I preach, but, on purely metaphysical grounds, it seems to me that most red-headed men would be all the better for a garrotting," where would the tolerant red-headed men be found? Jefferson himself, when he had to appoint a Professor of Law to the University of Virginia, cared nothing about his religion, but a great deal about his politics.

It is argued that the business of the state is to preserve the freedom of everyday life, and that that freedom is violated by social custom, but not by religious belief. Now it is the fashion to pretend that morality does not depend upon religion, but this clearly cannot be true, nor is it reasonable. To certain actions the

Thomas Jefferson

name "good" is applied. A man may often find himself called on for such an action and be disinclined to it. To the man who believes in a religion, a God, a system of rewards and punishments and the rest, there is a reason why he should overcome his disinclination. To the man who does not believe, there is no such reason.

The argument that there are plenty of good agnostics is superficial. There are, indeed, many men, lacking religious faith, whose instincts lead them to behave with social responsibility. The reason for that is that they are the inheritors of religious generations; they live in a society predominantly religious. They are reaping what they have not sown, but they go about calling themselves rationalists, and boasting that they do good "without hope of reward," or, in other words, without reason. They do good, because they want to. Other agnostics do harm because they want to, and the number that do harm rather than good increases with each generation that they are removed from religion.

It is not, therefore, true that it does me no injury that my neighbor believes in no God. No more is it true that it does me no injury that he believes in twenty. For, if the belief that there is a right and a wrong comes from a belief in God, the belief in the details of right and wrong comes from the nature which a man believes God to possess. The Free Thinker, when it suits his thesis, argues that it makes no difference to a man whether he be a Catholic or a Protestant, Buddhist or agnostic. At another moment he will discredit the Catholic religion by pointing to the backwardness of Catholic countries, saying that this comes of their Catholicism. It is not possible to have it both ways. And to say that my neighbor's religion has nothing to do with me, nor mine with his, is a glib and dishonest half-truth.

Then, says Jefferson, "truth can stand by itself." This has a fine ring about it. "Magna est veritas et prævalebit" is a motto to conquer the centuries, and it is annoying to have such words

The American Heresy

mouthed about by people who mean no more than that they do not care in the least what opinion prevails and will not be bothered with the business at all. Is it not fair to say that that is often the real meaning of people who use such language today? Jefferson, though he used it, certainly did not believe it. For in his Bill for Establishing Religious Freedom he writes—what clearly must have been his true opinion—that men "have maintained false religions over the greatest part of the world and through all time."

Yet truth in the end does prevail. But each new heresy, though it finally die, may do immense harm before its death. Nobody today apostatizes because of Voltaire. The influence of Herbert Spencer is very small. Yet such men, possessed of a certain capacity to reproduce the ideas of their day, impotent when their day is passed, may in it do enormous harm to the half-educated, into whose hands their writings fall. If one faces the truth instead of sheltering from it behind some mid-Victorian generalization, it is impossible to deny this. What policy should be pursued towards such men? By what excuse does society evade its duty of protecting those who cannot protect themselves?

The orthodox Liberal answer is, I suppose, that the believer also should state his case, that such a man should be presented with the two and allowed to think it out for himself. But, as everybody knows, he cannot think. Certainly the believer is able to answer the attacks of Spencer or of anybody else. But he is not necessarily able to answer them so as to appear to such a man to come out of the controversy victorious. For the chief effect of half-education is to contract the imagination, to cause a shrinking back from the mysterious. To this shrinking the popular writer appeals. He does not justify it by argument, but assumes it and flatters it. The contest is not between reason and reason, but between reason and glibness, and before many judges glibness will gain the verdict.

There arises then the question whether truth matters. Certainly those who are in error but good faith and live up to their principles have as large a hope of salvation as any. Yet a right ethical system is one which bids a man accomplish those purposes for which he was created; a wrong ethical system bids him accomplish some other purposes. The neglect of truth is not immediately disastrous, but a man suffers for it in the end.

Jefferson's third proposition is most interesting. It opens the whole picture of his mind. "Difference of religion," he says, "is advantageous." Why? It is Mill *On Liberty* fore-run. He likes a society of persons, eagerly inquiring. There is more variety of character; life is fuller. In other words, inquiry is more desirable than truth. In much of life this is certainly so. From the point of view of the soul, it is perhaps better to have a nation of people who tinker about with motor-cars, than a nation in which the motor-cars go. It is certainly important that some people should be running around, guessing whether there are mountains on the moon; it is of very little importance that they should guess right. There seems only one necessary condition for the playing of such delightful games—that people should be quite sure, before they begin, of their fundamental truths, from which they can learn on which fields they can and on which they cannot safely play. In religion alone truth is more important than inquiry.

Jefferson's fourth reason for toleration—the incapacity of force to produce uniformity—every sane man would accept where it is true. Force that fails of its purpose is merely cruel. Nor has the claim been made, as he imagined, that coercion should be used to "propagate" a religion, but only to defend from attack a society whose life has been built upon one particular religious system. The citizen of the liberal state, whatever his beliefs, must recognize that in that state they are only personal beliefs. But to the curious it should surely occur that, if it was necessary for Jefferson to use the argument that coercion would be immoral in Virginia, because it would be ineffective, then there must be a great deal to be said for it in, say, Spain, where it was certainly most effective.

No one is ambitious to light again the fires of Salem. Any one who has deduced such an ambition from the preceding pages can have understood very little of their argument. We ought certainly to tolerate to the last tolerable limit. But at the same time it is only wise to admit that, if we face the question honestly, the limits of the tolerable are very hard to find. Such a question has a thousand difficulties, which are not popularly faced. Those difficulties should be faced, if our tolerance is to stand a strain. And I believe that, if a time of persecution should come, men will find a more certain refuge among those who have thought out the difficulties than among those who have been content to repeat the catchwords of the Victorian market-place and languidly, between lunch and tea, thank the Great Unknowable that they are not such men as Torquemada. "Must I shoot a simple-minded boy for deserting," Lincoln was afterwards to ask, "and spare the wily agitator, whose words induce him to desert?" If one professes an absolute belief in Free Speech, the obvious answer is "Yes!" Yet it cannot be pretended that that is an easy answer, or even necessarily a merciful one.

It would be unfair to complain of Jefferson for granting religious toleration. George III was the head of the Established Church of Virginia, as of England. It was an obvious move in a war against him to weaken his power by weakening its power. Nor did Jefferson lack his larger, somewhat misty principles. Toleration had indeed been refused in Virginia for quite a good reason. The Catholics in Maryland had allowed some Puritans to take refuge in their state from persecution at the hands of the Virginians and the Puritans, who hated religious freedom in America even more than they did in England, had repaid the hospitality by capturing the political machinery and using it to deprive Catholics of their civil rights. Virginia Episcopalians were strengthened in their determination not to run the risk of such very conscientious guests. Yet it is probably true that the life of eighteenth-century Virginia was not so essentially bound up with an especially Episcopalian theology as to justify its preservation by coercion. Toleration was right.

Yet, if Jefferson did a good thing, he did it for a collection of very unsatisfactory reasons. He repeats in groveling superstition the *ex cathedra* pronouncements of some infallible irreligious authority, of whom he has forgotten even the name. At the back of his mind, as at the back of most Free Thought, is a contradiction. He cannot remember whether he was told to defend toleration because man's mind was so free that it was a blasphemy to shackle it, or because it was so conditioned by environment that it was a cruelty to punish it for reaching conclusions, for which it was hardly responsible. The Bill for Establishing Religious Freedom begins with the words: "Well aware that the opinions and beliefs of men depend not on their own will, but follow involuntarily the evidence proposed to their minds; that Almighty God hath created the mind free, and manifested His supreme will that Free it shall remain by making it altogether insusceptible of restraint. . . ." There are limits to the rapidity with which even a rationalist, drafting an Act of Parliament, can decently contradict himself.

Jefferson, writing the inscription for his own tombstone, took praise as the author of "the Statute of Virginia for Religious Freedom." Great harm is done by allowing men to play about with their own epitaphs.

VI

The Declaration of Independence cast upon each State the duty of organizing its own civil government. Native governors had to be appointed to perform the functions of the old royal governors. The first governor of Virginia was the verbose Henry, who accepted the promotion, preferring, on the whole, liberty to death. In this, as in all tasks, he was incompetent and, when his term came to an end, Jefferson was one of the two candidates nominated to succeed him.

By a few votes Jefferson was elected over his friend and opponent, John Page, and from June, 1779, to June, 1781, he was Governor of Virginia. The central Government, unable to meet its expenses by taxation, had taken refuge in the printing of paper money. In spite of French assistance, this inflation led to a virtual declaration of bankruptcy, and Jefferson, one of the first, saw that stability could only be restored by a return to a currency of real value. He was a most orthodox economist.

Yet it is hardly possible to understand American financial difficulties except as a part of the general story of the war. This story is made needlessly complicated by the attempt to bang the truth into the similitude that the war was one in which the Americans beat the English. The Americans did not beat the English, nor could they have possibly done so, nor was there ever any question of their doing so. If the war had been allowed to drag on, as a contest between England and America alone, English incompetence might have betrayed to the Americans isolated victories. These victories, like the victories of the Boers, could only have delayed the inevitable end. By superior sea-power and man-power England would have been certainly victorious. The certainty was mathematical.

This the Americans clearly saw. Their object, in the first phase of the war, was not to defeat the English, but to fight well enough to make it appear worth the while of the French to have them for allies. Only the French, at that date, could possibly have beaten the English. Only the French did beat the English.

The first phase of the war consisted of the campaign of Saratoga. By it the English hope was to detach the New England

States from the American side. The American hope was to defeat this plan, not for any military purpose so much as for that of advertisement before France. General Burgoyne laid down his arms at Saratoga. The advertisement was sufficient. The French accepted their ally. The first phase was finished.

After Saratoga the Americans were soon joined, not only by France but also by Spain and Holland. The second phase was thus very different from the first. It was the French revenge for the Seven Years' War. The combined French, Dutch and Spanish fleets were, on the whole, able to hold the command of the sea against the English. The English hope lay, not any longer in lopping off from the alliance an extraneous American province, but in paralyzing the very center of the resistance, Virginia itself. At the time that England adopted this strategy, Jefferson became Governor of Virginia.

The English were at New York to the north and at Charleston to the south. Washington's policy was not to attempt to defend Virginia against casual raids. He felt that the spirit of the people was such that it was not to be thus broken. Instead she must denude herself for the reinforcement of the real fighting fronts to the south and north and trust for her own salvation to the poorly supported leadership of Jefferson's friend, Lafayette, who, because of his "zeal, illustrious family and connections" (but principally the two latter), "held the commission of Major-General of the United States."

Because of this policy and his loyalty to it the two years of Jefferson's government were years of hard trial for his state. Some part or other of his territory was continually in enemy occupation. The most prominent of the raiders was Benedict Arnold, still warm from his treachery. Once at least Jefferson himself was almost captured. General Tarleton, at the head of a company of dragoons, determined on a raid upon Charlottesville and Monticello, whose object was to be the capture of the Legislature and the Governor. His plan might well have succeeded, had it not been for one Jouitte, who happened to be sitting in the Cuckoo Tavern, at Louisa, when Tarleton rode through. Jouitte took to horse and by hard riding and the use of a short cut was able to reach Monticello and Charlottesville before the dragoons. He gave warning and the Legislature met and hastily dissolved itself on a resolution to assemble again in four days' time "west of the Blue Ridge at Staunton."

Jefferson had climbed, with a telescope in his hand, up Carter's Mountain, whence he could get a good view of Charlottesville. Unable to see anything astir in the town, he had already dismissed the warning as that of a false rumor and was descending the hill in order to return to his ordinary business when he noticed that he had left his sword on the hill-top. Going back to pick it up, he took one last look through the telescope, and now saw that all Charlottesville was swarming with dragoons. Jumping on his horse he rode off to Enniscorthy. Five minutes later the party sent to kidnap him ascended the hill from the other side.

Jefferson has been much criticized for the misfortunes of Virginia during his governorship. Colonel Henry Lee, "Light Horse Harry," an officer in command of the troops in North Carolina, collected and gave form to these criticisms in his *Memoirs of the War in the Southern Department of the United States*, and they have, from time to time, been repeated by modern writers, notably Dr. Eckenrode.[1] To the student of Jefferson's ideas and their influence it cannot very much matter whether such criticisms are just or unjust. Yet, on the whole, Mr. Hirst seems to have proved his point that they have been made by persons ignorant or forgetful that Jefferson denuded Virginia in obedience to the strategy of Washington. The Legislature of Virginia held an inquiry into

---

[1] *The Revolution in Virginia*, by H. J. Eckenrode. Houghton Mifflin Company. Boston, 1916.

Jefferson's conduct at the close of his period of office. It unanimously decided that "the sincere thanks of the General Assembly be given to our former Governor, Thomas Jefferson, Esq., for his impartial, upright and attentive administration when in office." There seems no reason to reverse its verdict.

A month after Jefferson's retirement, General Cornwallis surrendered at Yorktown and the second phase of the war was ended. England's inability to reconquer America was now undisputed. The expletives of Lord North are the evidence.

VII

For the next two years Jefferson held no public post. They were not happy years for him. His wife's health was growing worse and he himself lacked the occupation which might have prevented this worry from being continually before his mind. Probably it was from such a hope of distraction that he undertook the writing of his book, the *Notes on Virginia*.

The name gives too niggard a conception of its scope. The book, in origin, was indeed but the answers to a *questionnaire*, upon the geographical and social conditions of Virginia, sent out from the French legation at Philadelphia, and it contains much most strictly relevant information, both interesting and accurate. Yet under Jefferson's ample hand it grew to be a collection of *obiter dicta* upon all things, human and divine—a marvelous monument to the many-sidedness of his extraordinary character. He had Voltaire in the soul. The great merit of Voltaire is that he attacked religion, not as the ponderous modern attacks it, but with the weapon of ridicule—a weapon which, if well used, can be enjoyed, however poor the occasion of its use. Jefferson's humor, on the other hand, was not strong. Something must have been lacking to the humanity of a man who "could not bear the novels of Scott, because of his detestation of the institutions of medieval times." In both Jefferson and Voltaire all is marred by a proud and horrid glibness. Yet, on the whole, the disciple, by far the inferior writer, was a nobler man than the master. For he could forget his reader, which Voltaire never could. The *Notes* show us their author, not merely anxious to acquire sufficient of the patter upon every subject to lay down the law concerning it, but one of those strange and most rare beings, a lover of truth.

Jefferson was clearly much worried about the future of this America that he had unloosed. He had come across the curious speculation upon American degeneracy of the Abbé Raynal.[1] The Abbé had observed that "*l'Amérique n'ait pas encore produit . . . un homme de génie dans un seul art, une seule science.*" And he accounted for this deficiency by the greater humidity and cold of the American Continent. Why such an effect should follow such a cause, he did not at all explain. And Jefferson, rightly, demanded the evidence even for the cause. It appears, indeed, that America is drier and hotter than Europe. It is certainly drier and hotter than England, but that, I suppose, it would be difficult to avoid.

The climatic patter was, of course, merely the psycho-analysis of its day. Yet somehow or other the Abbé had struck on a truth—a truth that can be overstated but cannot honestly be denied. The proportion of great men to population is far smaller in America than in Europe. Jefferson had forcibly replied by comparing America of his day with three million, to France with its twenty and England with its ten. Today the whole advantage in that comparison is on the other side. America has grown from three to a hundred millions, yet still she is faced with the alternative of barbarism or cultural dependence upon Europe. America

---

[1] Raynal, Guillaume (1713-96), an unfrocked priest; author of *Histoire philosophique et politique des Établissements et du Commerce des Européens dans les Deux Indes.*

was born (Jefferson himself was more responsible than any other) the child of European ideas and thus incapable of producing an independent culture of her own. Americans are not Englishmen but they are Europeans, half-conscious always of their origins, half-conscious therefore of their exile.

It was, indeed, the great error of the Fathers to simplify too much the problem and to fail to see that, if they broke the political link, inevitably they would also enormously weaken the cultural link with Great Britain and, through Great Britain, with Europe. Neglecting this, in the name of freedom they divorced themselves from the fountain of all freedom.

Perhaps the experience of Congress had opened his eyes. Jefferson was still an ardent democrat, but by now he had learned to be anxious lest all power in the new state should be concentrated in the legislature. "An elective despotism," he wrote, "is not what we fought for." And he foresaw that in time the American would follow the British legislature into corruption. There was, it seemed to him, but one ingenious safeguard. For he shrewdly thought that democracy was less liable to corruption than oligarchy, not through any sentimental belief in the infallibility of the General Will, but simply because, under it, political power is so widely distributed that there are not enough bribes to go round. Somebody, therefore, having been omitted from the distribution, will have an interest in exposing the system. It is a fundamental motto of economics that you cannot bribe all of the people all of the time, while the eighteenth-century oligarchy of England could comfortably be managed upon the principle of One Man— One Bribe.

Yet even this consolation of Jefferson has proved vain. The experience of Congress had taught him much about representative institutions. He had learned that they might become corrupt, but he had not yet learned that they might become undemocratic. Rousseau, alone of the eighteenth-century writers, wanted democracy and yet contemptuously dismissed representation as a fraud. He foresaw, as others did not, that representative institutions would, in practice, hand over all the power in the country to the wealthy. There is but one test of who is master in the land. To whom do you give the bribe, if you want to get a thing done? In parliamentary countries you give it to the richest man that you can see.

Jefferson is not to be blamed because he did not prophesy and guard against this. Many do not see it even now that it has happened. Only the other day a Professor, not doing it for a joke, described England in the *Times* newspaper as "an ultra-democratic country," and presumably was paid for doing so. Nor had Jefferson any illusion at all that democracy could stand against plutocracy, if the country became industrialized. "Our government," he thought, "will remain virtuous . . . as long as they are chiefly agricultural. When they get piled upon one another in large cities, as in Europe, they will become corrupt, as in Europe." If the American could not be content with the simple life and must use manufactured goods, let him use those of other countries, obtaining them by exchange against the product of his own agriculture. The American himself must remain on the land. For an agricultural society is a stable, free society, not dependent for its prosperity upon the chance that some foreigner will wish to buy its products.

Because of this opinion Jefferson was a strong Free Trader. He has been hailed of the company of Cobden. And, indeed, it is not company which any man need be ashamed of keeping. Yet Jefferson's argument for Free Trade was different from and, perhaps, stronger than that of Cobden. In the England of Cobden's day, the agriculturalist was protected at the expense of the manufacturer; in the America of Jefferson's, the manufacturer was to be protected at the expense of the agriculturalist. A case for Protection can only be made out if it can be shown that the protected class is for some social or moral reason of such importance to the country that it is to her interest thus artificially to keep it alive. Those who read the speeches of Disraeli and Lord George Bentinck against Cobden must see that at the time of the Repeal of the Corn Laws there was much to be said for this special preservation of the agricultural interest in England. But in America Jefferson was careful to show that Protection was doubly damnable. The special class, which it would create at the expense of the rest, could only be a menace to the rest. Money would be taken out of the good man's pocket and put into that of the bad. Happy is the man who is born into a country where the lucidity of Cobden and the thunder of Cobbett can be used in the same argument and lead to the same conclusion.

VIII

On 6th September, 1782, Jefferson's wife died. Anxious now for an excuse to leave the memories of Monticello, he accepted a nomination to Congress, and, the next month, set out for Philadelphia and Annapolis. Throughout a stormy session he worked at the establishing of America's new coinage. In a masterly memorandum he recommended the adoption of the dollar system, for which blessing his country is therefore indebted to him.

In 1784 Jefferson was sent by Congress to Europe as a plenipotentiary to negotiate, with John Adams and Benjamin Franklin, Treaties of Commerce with European countries. In the next year Franklin resigned the Paris Ministry and Jefferson was appointed to succeed him. Thus, during the interesting period that preceded the year 1, Jefferson was in Europe, traveling from place to place and country to country, observing pleasure-gardens, vegetable hot-pots, Cochin-China seed and whatever other sign of the coming destruction might stray within sight of his most careful eye. In Italy he was disgusted to find that the authorities forbade him to take rice-seed out of the country. But, invoking, as he said, "the higher law," he stuffed his pockets full of it, and, by diplomatic immunity, evaded the customs.

The tumbrils were preparing for the streets and Jefferson was busy buying ladies' corsets, "wondering if they would suit. Mr. Jefferson has the honor to present his compliments to Mrs. Smith and to send her the two pair of corsets she desired. He wishes they may be suitable, as Mrs. Smith omitted to send her measure. Times are altered since Mademoiselle de Samson had the honor of knowing her: should they be too small, however, she will be so good as to lay them by a while. There are ebbs as well as flows in this world."

The prominence of Jefferson's friend, the Marquis de Lafayette, in the early days of reform and his "canine appetite" for popularity brought Jefferson more closely in touch with French politics than it is common for an immune ambassador to be. Once, at any rate, such intimacy created difficulty. The whole Patriot party, "inadvertently," as he writes, "to the embarrassment under which it might place me," both in his official capacity, one presumes, and in his larder, descended upon him for dinner. After dinner "the cloth being removed and wine set on the table after the American manner" (oh, times and morals) they proceeded to a six-hour debate upon the party program, with which they should face the King. The next day, poor Jefferson had to go to the Minister, Count Montmorin, with an apology for the use to which his house had been put, for he had been torn hopelessly between the duties of an ambassador and a host. The apology was most graciously accepted.

The summoning of the States General, the early debates, the Tennis-Court Oath, the charge of the German mercenaries, the Bastille, Louis' donning of the tricolor—in all these, where, for good and ill, our new Europe was reborn, Jefferson was present as a spectator—reserved, opinionated, interested, intelligent and with, one fancies, a certain half-conscious feeling of superiority that he alone, or almost alone, in Paris had seen this sort of thing before and knew how the best men made a revolution. Had he seen this sort of thing before?

Certainly in at least two senses the French Revolution was made by America. The expense of the American War, wrecking Turgot's schemes of reform, emptied the royal treasury and made necessary the summoning of the States General. And the young men came back from America with their heads full of large talk. Yet this large talk did not make the Revolution. The Revolution, the real Revolution that came, was not made by the young men from America. All that they did with their large talk, or rather all that their large talk did with them, was to make certain that, when the People challenged them, by what right did they exist, they would not be quite sure, until they had looked it up in Paine, whether they could answer.

Their philosophy did not give them the courage of their convictions, but it took away from them the courage of their privileges.

The American Revolution may, if you care to argue so, have been for the people. Those who made it certainly honestly believed that it was. Yet certainly it was not by the people. All the thought, all the leadership came from men who, according to the old Greek advice, "first got an independent income and then practiced virtue." Only persons of independence, the eighteenth-century American felt, should be allowed to sign declarations of it.

Jefferson's opinions were that Marie Antoinette was at the bottom of all the trouble, that the desirable end for which a sane patriot should work was an Anglo-Montesquieu Constitution, that the King would willingly accept this and that the Queen alone prevented it. The experience of a hundred years largely confirms his advice. The Revolution brought enormous benefits and great horror. One who looks back must applaud a man who would have given to France the benefits and spared her the horror. Traditionally the French monarchy was the friend of the people. The monarchy played upon itself a tragic trick when it threw itself into the hands of the aristocracy. The people played upon itself a tragic trick when it destroyed the natural protector of equality. Yet one cannot help feeling that Jefferson's advice, even when it was most wise, was a little futile. He seems unconscious that forces had been unloosed incalculably larger than any that America ever knew. In America a few gentlemen had put on fancy-dress, in order to throw some tea into a harbor. They had shocked but they had not ended the eighteenth century. But in France a whole world was dying and was coming to birth. Danton, the bull, Robespierre, Carnot of iron, and the Little Corporal, in whose mind the visions of Cæsar and of Charlemagne danced—all these were at that day abroad in France. There were no such men in Philadelphia, and Jefferson, pardonably perhaps, did not seem to recognize the difference. It did not occur to him that, however long he stayed in Paris, there would ever be an evening when Lafayette would not be at all free to come and dine.

He sneered at Burke as a man "of some smartness of fancy but no sound sense." Burke, as Paine said, "pitied the plumage but forgot the dying bird." Much of his *Reflections on the French Revolution* is nothing but magnificent sentimentality. Yet at least he, alone of Englishmen or Americans, saw from the first that here was a wholly larger business than any that there had been in England in 1688 or in America in 1776. The other glad Whigs disliked crowned heads, and, before the execution of a King, split the party upon the question, whether at a pinch they were more of a nuisance on or off a body.

IX

While Jefferson was at his post in Paris, American politicians were busying themselves with a Constitution for their new country. Previous to the war, the States, which had now gained their independence, had had no official connection with one another. For military reasons during the war, they had, often most unwillingly but of obvious necessity, submitted to some central control. After the war it was soon clear that there was no agreement among Americans concerning the future government which they desired. At the extreme left was Patrick Henry and a small knot of his supporters, who saw no need for a Federation at all. On the right was Alexander Hamilton, the friend of a strong executive, and, if he dared be, even of monarchy; an immigrant from the West Indies who therefore lacked the local loyalty, which was at that date the normal possession of every American, he was for crushing the States by the preponderant strength of the central Government. Between Henry and Hamilton were men of every variety of middle opinion.

Yet there was all but general agreement that some sort of union was desirable. Jefferson himself, though jealous now, and to become yet more jealous, for the rights of the State, was persuaded of this. A Convention had met at Philadelphia in May, 1787, and, after long debate, produced the present Constitution of the United States. There was much opposition to it. "That among the opponents of the Constitution," wrote Charles Francis Adams,[1] "are to be reckoned a great majority of those who had most strenuously fought the battle of independence against Great Britain, is certain." On the other hand, Hamilton,

---

[1] Charles Francis Adams (1807–86), American Minister in London during the Civil War, Editor of the *Works of John Adams, Second President of the United States, with a Life of the Author*, and the *Memoirs of John Quincy Adams*.

hopeless of monarchy, had even been compelled to abandon his substitute of a President and Senate, elected during good behavior—that is to say, unless they were convicted on impeachment, for life. Yet, even if he were defeated in this, the result was generally considered a victory for him and his party. The modern orator of Independence Day speaks no more than the truth when he says that the Constitution was "built as a bulwark against Bolshevism."

Hamilton was content to support the Constitution because he was confident that, once a central government was established, it would be able at each crisis, or pretended crisis, to filch from the States such powers as might seem to it convenient. In this he has been proved disastrously right. Jefferson, also foreseeing the danger, thought to guard the liberty of the individual by the addition to the Constitution of a series of Amendments.[1] Many others doubted and were induced to support ratification only by the argument that there could be no danger in giving the Constitution a trial, since any State could always secede again if it wished to do so. What a sorry joke have their descendants made of poor Jefferson and his friends. How Alexander Hamilton must grin from his grave!

The Constitution, wrote the *Centinel*[2] at the time, "is the most formidable conspiracy against the liberties of a free and enlightened nation that the world has ever witnessed." Yet it is not, as one looks back, fair to blame Jefferson for being content with the safeguards of the Amendments. He could not be expected to foresee the history of the next seventy-five years. It was important, as he saw, that the State should remain the unit of sovereignty. Only with such a unit would genuine experiments at democracy be possible. It was no fault of his if strong men were to come and trample on the safeguards which he laid down.

---

[1] Commonly called *The Bill of Rights*. *See* Appendix C.
[2] A Boston newspaper.

Jefferson landed at Norfolk, in Virginia, on the 23rd of November, 1789. When he had set sail from France he had imagined that he would only be absent from that country for a short time and that, after a few months' leave, he would return to his post. But at Norfolk a newspaper was put into his hands, in which it was reported that Washington intended to appoint him Secretary of State in the Cabinet of the first President of the United States. Soon after a letter arrived confirming the report and with some reluctance Jefferson accepted it as his duty.

He first paid a visit of two months to Monticello and was effusively welcomed by all—especially by the negroes of his estate. "When the door of the carriage was opened, they received him in their arms and bore him to the house, crowding around him and kissing his hands and feet—some blubbering and crying—others laughing." What the negro blubbered is perhaps not evidence. Still in an estimate of Jefferson's character it is well to remember this and a few similar scenes. He had developed the knack of pointing morals and adorning tales to a fine art and it is easy to get the impression of him that he, as are so many friends of the human race, was impeccably inhuman, too proud to soil philosophic benevolence by individual friendship. And there must certainly have been many moments when friends longed for him to forget for an hour that all men were born equal. But there were others when he did forget it in treating them as such.

X

The party system in American politics had not, at that date, developed. Washington was the first and the last of her Presidents to be elected without opposition, and men of all opinions were collected in his Cabinet. Of these the two protagonists of its divisions were to be Jefferson and Hamilton, who had been appointed Secretary of the Treasury. Hamilton was there already, prepared for battle, and on a certain large day in history—on 24th March, 1790—appeared in the *Daily Advertiser* the seemingly harmless paragraph: "On Sunday last arrived in this city Thomas Jefferson, Esq., Secretary of State for the United States of America." The sniff of battle was in the air.

Jefferson's position made him responsible for two policies to which Alexander Hamilton was willing to lead opposition. In foreign politics all men were agreed, or pretended to be agreed, with the principle of George Washington that America should take no part in the quarrels of European countries. Yet, so far as she was to seek a foreign friendship, Jefferson insisted that it should be with France, Hamilton with England. In fiscal policy Jefferson was a Free Trader, Hamilton a Protectionist.

Alexander Hamilton is one of the most interesting and most able figures in American history and, if wrong-headed, not the less interesting nor the less able for that. Indeed, Jefferson's inferior in versatility, he was his superior in that capacity for intellectual skepticism concerning political remedies which is the certain mark of a strong mind. There were many, who played a gallant part in the late war, asking, like Hector, "no omen but their country's cause," and who felt great resentment that they should be told at the eleventh hour that they had all along been fighting for a variety of Wilsonian ideals, of which they had not previously heard, and which, so far as they understood them, they disliked. Hamilton's position was not unlike that of such men. A West Indian, he had understood and shared the American's desire to be free from Great Britain. The metaphysics which Jefferson imported into the struggle seemed to him both irrelevant and false. He disliked such language. He disliked it the more, because he had sometimes been himself compelled to use it.

Unlike Jefferson, he hated the British Government, not because it had been tyrannical, but because it had been incompetent.

Thomas Jefferson

The British Constitution was, to his mind, the best in the world. For the checks and balances, by which liberty is preserved, he had small use. He believed in no philosophy of rights. Efficiency and stability were the objects of Government and these were best secured by making it as easy as possible for wealth to obtain power.

To imagine that such means would attain such an end is as if a man were to believe that the capitalist system encouraged private enterprise. And Hamilton was certainly led to it, not by pure reason, but by a peculiar taste. He had a nose for baseness, which, at a distance at least, is to all but the prig, fascinating, if not attractive. He liked to think of men taking bribes. It pleased him, that sort of thing. At Jefferson's table Hamilton and John Adams were once guests. The talk was of the British Constitution. "Purge that Constitution of its corruption," said Adams, "and give to its popular branch equality of representation and it would be the most perfect constitution ever devised by the wit of man!" Hamilton was horrified. "Purge it of its corruption," he answered, "and give to its popular branch equality of representation and it will become an impracticable government."

Jefferson's great fear was that this new democracy of America would become a plutocracy. It was Hamilton's ambition to make it so. His policy was therefore to establish a strong National Bank and to make permanent a national debt which would be held mainly by the bankers. These men would thus be masters of the country's credit and would be able, at convenience, to control President, Senate or Congress and dictate the policy of the central government.

Meanwhile, by an ingenious device, which Jefferson deleted, he had calculated to be able to concentrate more and more power in the hands of the central government. Jefferson's friend, Madison, and Jefferson himself, on Madison's advice, had accepted the Constitution as a compromise, intending loyally to work it. Hamilton, as has been already explained, saw that if once a central government was established, whatever the conditions of its establishment, it would be able with patience and cunning to make itself omnipotent over the States. The wedge, the thin end of which Hamilton attempted to insert, was the power given by the Constitution to the central government to collect taxes to provide for "the general welfare" of the United States. In Jefferson's opinion, "the general welfare" meant those purposes—defense, diplomatic services and the rest—which, later in the Constitution, were assigned to the central government. Hamilton argued a Congress might levy taxes for any purpose which it considered to be for the general welfare of the United States and proposed the granting of bounties for the encouragement of manufactures. The double purpose of this scheme was clear. Such an interpretation would, in effect, destroy the Federal nature of the United States, while the application of it would create strong vested interests, no doubt judiciously distributed over the country, determined to prevent any other interpretation for the future.

The differences between Hamilton and Jefferson date from Jefferson's opposition to Hamilton's scheme for the establishment of a National Bank in 1790. This scheme Jefferson thought unconstitutional. Fiscal and foreign politics fanned the flame. Beneath the subtleties of personal insult it grew to a blaze. In April, 1791, the American edition of Tom Paine's *Rights of Man* appeared, and, without leave, the publisher printed upon the cover the private commendation of Jefferson. "Something is at length to be said against political heresies, which have sprung up here among us. I have no doubt that our citizens will rally a second time round the standard of Common Sense." It was an indiscretion and was interpreted as worse than an indiscretion.

During all these years the two were colleagues in the Cabinet and it was therefore impossible for them to attack each other publicly and by name. Jefferson, indeed, as research among papers

Thomas Jefferson

after his death revealed, wrote frequently of his grievances to French friends with a frankness which it must be rare to find in foreign secretaries in correspondence with distinguished foreigners. But at home the battle between the two was fought in the columns of two newspapers, the *National Gazette* and the *United States Gazette*. The protagonists lurked behind these newspapers as vague and disaffected shadows. The controversies were carried on by hirelings, named Fenno and Freneau, names which suggest a couple of music-hall comedians rather than the high confidants of weighty statesmen.

To these two writers, assisted only by an occasional and unofficial prod, all scurrility was reserved until July, 1792. But at that date Hamilton, incapable of longer restraint, took up the attack himself. He wrote to criticize, not any policy of statesmanship, but the conduct of Jefferson in paying to Freneau the salary of a pound a week as translator of foreign despatches in the Department of the Secretary of State.

It is not possible to applaud very loudly Hamilton's methods of newspaper controversy. Instead of attacking his colleague over his own name (which would, of course, have required his resignation), he preferred to do so under a variety of pseudonyms—a soiled and silly dodge, whose purpose is to produce the impression that what is really only the grievance of one man has filled with indignation the breasts of thousands in every quarter of the country. Thus "T. L." first leveled the charges of corruption against Jefferson. "American" read of them in his paper and was much shocked. "Amicus" was painfully unable to accept Freneau's explanation. "Catullus" had even more disturbing revelations which a sense of duty compelled him to make to the world. "Metellus," too, must add his word and, last but gloriously not least—it is almost too good to be true—the series were concluded by none other than "A Plain Honest Man." All this nonsense is reprinted in Lodge's *Works of Alexander Hamilton*.

The American Heresy

Mr. Hirst is surely justified in the scorn which he pours on such puerility. Yet the idiocy of Hamilton's methods of controversy does not prove that Jefferson was guiltless. That Jefferson's administration of his department was a model of economy is true but irrelevant. Equally true and irrelevant is it that Hamilton's methods of exposing corruption was hardly that which one would look for from a loyal colleague. Perhaps, too, Jefferson was right, when he "did not think that there was any harm in the Government having a critic in Freneau's paper as well as a flatterer in Fenno's." Most governments, probably, are the better for criticism but it is not for that reason necessarily desirable for a leading member of the Cabinet to use public funds, in order to make the utterance of that criticism possible, nor for a prominent Civil Servant to make of himself an irresponsible and most unofficial leader of an opposition.

Of "American's" third charge against him—that of setting up a paper to slander the Government—Jefferson was certainly guilty. He had looked forward, he said, at the paper's first setting-up to the chastisement of aristocratic and monarchical writers and he "knew well that there were such in the Government." The other two charges are more flimsy. He was accused of writing letters from France to oppose the present Constitution and of being against the payment of the public debt. To the first charge his defense was convincing. He had indeed been concerned at the absence of guarantees of individual liberty from the original Constitution and supported the plan for adding to it the Amendments of the Bill of Rights. He had not concealed this conduct, nor was there in it anything either treacherous or improper. The American nation had supported him. And, of all people, Hamilton had least reason to bring against him such charges—Hamilton, who openly mocked at the Constitution and whose policy was to work it only in order to pervert it.

Thomas Jefferson

Nor was the accusation that he was opposed to payment of the public debt better founded. He was far too good an economist not to be sensible of the blow to national credit which repudiation would deal. If his own intelligence had not been able to teach him such a lesson, the story of the American financial policy during the war would have shown him the evils of repudiation, and the financial negotiations in which, during his European trip, he was engaged in Amsterdam, the importance of good credit. It is true that he did not at all share Hamilton's curious opinions upon the value of a permanent debt and had argued that the country should free itself from debt as soon as possible. But pure malice alone interpreted his words to mean "free by defalcation" rather than "free by payment." As Jefferson, not unfairly, if waspishly, wrote: "I would wish the debt paid off tomorrow. He" (that is, Hamilton) "wishes it never to be paid but always to be a thing wherewith to corrupt and manage the legislature."

Washington suffered from his desire to have the benefits of representative and yet avoid the evils of party government. It is impossible. The very architecture of an assembly-room invites faction. Yet he was unable to see that, because the quarrel between his two leading subordinates was carried on largely by petty means, it was not therefore a petty quarrel. The quarrel, when Fenno and Freneau and Metellus and Catullus and A Plain Honest Man are forgotten, was whether America should be a free country or should be enslaved for fun.

Hamilton was Secretary of the Treasury from 1789 to 1795. During that time there were, apart from that of the Bank, three financial questions of first importance. It was his purpose to solve them all in such a way as to make more easy the establishment of that plutocratic government of which he was so fond. The first was that of the redemption of the internal loans which had been raised during the war. These loans had originally been largely bought by private and patriotic citizens, farmers or soldiers. During the war the Government had defaulted in its payment of interest. The value of the shares had therefore dropped to a very small figure. The policy, which Hamilton concocted for the benefit of his financial friends, was to allow them to buy up the shares at the low figure of, perhaps, a quarter or one-fifth and then to announce that he would redeem the debt at par plus the accrued interest. In this, during the time that Jefferson was still absent in France, he succeeded. It was his first victory. By it he spread ruin among the original holders, simple people and with no friends-in-the-know, who had sold out and the value of whose land had fallen, as he himself admitted, by from twenty to fifty percent.

His second financial problem was that of the debts incurred during the war by individual States. He proposed that the responsibility for all these debts should be assumed by the Treasury. The broad, if somewhat woolly, argument of justice which his friends put forward was that, since all had been contributors to a common cause, it was hard that those who had contributed most should have to suffer most. Yet on Hamiltonian principles it was sheer gain for a Government to possess an internal debt. Why should the State Governments be deprived of this inestimable blessing? Was it lest they become too powerful and too stable? And why, above all, should citizens of States such as Virginia and Pennsylvania, who had already made an attempt to meet their obligations, be forced as a reward to bear a share in the obligations of their less conscientious neighbors?

Hamilton had far more difficulty in securing the adoption of this than of the previous measure. The feeling for State rights was awake in the South. He was beaten in Congress by thirty-one votes to twenty-nine. In despair he appealed to Jefferson to call off the opposition, walked him up and down outside the President's house for half an hour, besought him to preserve the unity of the administration. In the end Jefferson agreed and induced his friends to allow Hamilton's scheme to pass. Only afterwards did he discover that Hamilton had assumed the obligation, not in order to meet it, but simply to increase the volume of shares to hand, which he might use as counters in his fascinating game. Jefferson said: "I was most ignorantly and innocently made to hold the handle." He had, one feels, only himself to blame for his ignorance. Men do not walk up and down for nothing.

Yet the Southern Congressmen only withdrew their opposition in return for a strange concession, which was afterwards very nearly found to be more important than any can at the time have foreseen. It was that the future capital of the United States should be built on the Potomac. In seventy years' time a gaunt humorist from Illinois was to look out from a new President's house and see the Confederate flag flying at Alexandria, across the river, and to wonder to what purpose at the end of all was Hamilton's so great walking up and down.

The third financial problem fell to Jefferson's rather than to Hamilton's department. Independence left the United States with two large classes of foreign debt—debts of individual Americans to individual Englishmen, and debts incurred by the loans of her European allies during the war. Between Jefferson and Genêt for the French Government, between Jefferson and George Hammond for the British, there was great argument. In general, no pages of history are more valueless than those in which bewildered statesmen try to explain to courteous foreigners the reasons why their country must postpone the meeting of impossible obligations, until such a date as their political opponents are almost certain to have succeeded to office. But here our Clio, a Muse, has, in a hundred years, played a clever little trick, and it is almost impossible for one whose sense of humor is partly mixed with malevolence, not to examine, with some amusement, the philosophical and financial wriggles of Thomas Jefferson in

The American Heresy

the days when the United States were debtors, and France and Great Britain their creditors.

The debt was not being paid off. Jefferson's business was to explain why, and this explanation he gives in a letter of almost a hundred pages to the British Minister.

The explanation is in two parts. Into the first, in which Jefferson accuses the British Government of various infractions of the peace treaty, by which American trade, and consequent capacity to pay, had been hindered, we need not enter. The second contains his philosophy of international debt. On this he lays down three principles, which, whether they be valid or not, are, at the least, well worth consideration.

First, he maintains that, if the creditor imposes a prohibitory tariff or some similar commercial regulation, then manifestly the debtor is freed from obligation, or at least immediate obligation, since the creditor is virtually, whether he sees it or not, refusing payment—a very pertinent principle. Second, to the objection that payment should then be made in hard coin, he replies with the principle of Vattel[1] "*nul n'est tenu à l'impossible.*" And, thirdly, he maintains that interest is not a part of the debt, but "something added to the debt by way of damage for the detention of it," and that therefore the debtor has no reason to pay interest on his debt for a period during which the creditor has refused, or virtually refused, by his commercial system, to accept the debtor's payment.

The morals of international debt are clear. Between two individuals there are two relations—the social and the economic. Where they clash the social must be recognized as superior to the economic and Solon is rightly praised for refusing to allow a man to sell himself into slavery for debt. So, too, between nations there are two relations—the political and the economic. The

---

[1] Emeric de Vattel (1719–87), Swiss jurist, author of *Droit des Gens, Questions de Droit Naturel*, etc.

political is superior to the economic. A government's first duty is to preserve the special form of life of the people for whom it is responsible. If it can only meet an obligation of debt by accepting such terms as would force it to abandon its free sovereignty in domestic affairs, it ought to reject those terms. As a man has no right to sell himself into slavery, even less has a government the right so to sell its people.

This thought Jefferson expressed in a letter which he wrote in 1813, after his retirement, to his son-in-law, John Eppes. He laid down the proposition that "the land belongs to the living, not to the dead," and asked whether, if a new generation finds its soil virtually alienated by the borrowings of its predecessors, now dead, it is bound to acknowledge the debt. He answers: "Everyone will say 'No,' . . . the laws of nature impose no obligation on them to pay this debt," and argues from this that no government has a moral right to accept debt-settlement which would impose upon a future generation of its citizens such an obligation. Jefferson speaks with no infallible authority either on morals or economics. Yet there are men in Washington today to whom it would not perhaps be an unreasonable impertinence to commend his ingenious pleadings.

Apart from his financial negotiations, Jefferson had only two problems of foreign policy with which to deal. The one was of major, the other of minor importance. The latter was that of the rights of exclusive commerce on the Mississippi which the possession of Louisiana gave to Spain. The controversy dragged languidly on until Spain escaped from it only by selling Louisiana to France by the Treaty of San Ildefonso, in 1800. The other—the more important problem—was that of the American policy towards the Anglo-French War which broke out in 1793. There was a Treaty with the old French monarchy by which, in the event of war, the United States guaranteed the safety of the French West Indian islands. France's declaration of war had almost coincided with the establishment of the Republic. Hamilton was anxious that advantage be taken of this change of government to repudiate the Treaty. For justification he quoted an *obiter dictum* of Vattel that a Treaty of Alliance is no longer binding on one party, when the other has so changed its form of government since the signature as to "render the alliance useless, dangerous or disagreeable." The principle is clearly valid but Jefferson was able to persuade Washington that France, by changing her government from monarchy to republic, could not have rendered herself dangerous or disagreeable to another government, already republican. The Treaty was therefore adjudged to be still binding.

Yet Jefferson was determined, in spite of it, that the United States should not be involved in war. In this he set himself no easy task. The feelings of the people were strongly pro-French and were fanned by the calculated indiscretions of Genêt, the French Minister to the United States. Genêt went everywhere, was toasted, greeted by the Marseillaise, spoke proudly of freedom, even assumed the right to fit out privateers, to sell prizes in America and to grant to American citizens licenses to prey on British commerce. It was intolerable to the American Government, which had at last to demand his recall. To this demand the French agreed. But Genêt, preferring the prospects of an American farmer to those of a half-pay diplomat, settled in New York State, became naturalized, married, and lived a quiet and unpolitical life until well on in the next century. How some men succeed in spite of all their strivings! He had dreams of being some sort of silly, splashing, political yahoo or other, and God laughed at him and turned him into a farmer.

He is, I think, often stupidly blamed. It is assumed that he did not foresee how embarrassing his conduct would be to the American Government. There is, I believe, no evidence for that assumption. He was—not to put the point too finely—paid to embarrass the American Government. His purpose was hopelessly to compromise it with Great Britain. But for his recall he might well have succeeded.

At the end of 1793 Washington was persuaded at last to agree to Jefferson's often repeated request to be allowed to retire. With nothing but joy in his heart, the man of the country turned his back, as he hoped, for ever upon the dirt of high politics. Those who represent Jefferson as ambitious and avid of power, it seems to me, largely misread his character. He abandoned power "at a moment when," as even his enemy, Chief Justice Marshall, admitted, "he stood particularly high in the esteem of his own countrymen," and only the inventions of malice can doubt that he imagined that he was abandoning it for good.

It is the habit of the English to be more indulgent towards a lust for power than towards other vices. Henry V is thought to propound a respectable conundrum when he speculates,

> "If to covet honor be a sin."

Yet in many ways ambition is the most repulsive of all the vices. It separates a man from his fellows and from the normal human life. It makes him gird against that equality in which God placed him. It kills joy. It is a part of pride. The aim of most education today is to fit the pupil to climb high on the ladder of life—to send him into the world properly equipped for the commission of mortal sin. Yet the certain stamp of the superior mind is its ability to rise above that code of the schoolmaster. Jefferson had that stamp. A man who holds a true philosophy concerning ambition may, in certain circumstances, feel it his duty to take part in public life. To his conscience some privilege, which he holds, implies that obligation. Thus a great man, such as George Wyndham, though his soul loathed all the scum of it, yet felt that "the gentlemen of England must not abdicate." A great man, such as Cardinal Mercier, condemns the violation of the moral law, utterly careless whether the violator be some poor and unknown street-woman or a German general at the head of a million men. Yet any man of imagination and a decent philosophy would rather, for his own pleasure, not have the responsibility of power than have it. Where he feels able to satisfy his own pleasure, he will abstain. Like Wordsworth's Warrior, he—

> "Though endued as with a sense
> And faculty for storm and turbulence,
> Is yet a soul, whose master-bias leans
> To homefelt pleasures and to gentle scenes."

Only a miserable and stunted imagination longs for power. "Power," said Napoleon, "is never ridiculous." It would be more true to say that it was never anything else. Plato was nobly right when he foresaw that in his republic of good citizens it would be necessary to force men to rule, since the philosopher would never of himself wish to do so.

Jefferson was therefore glad to escape from politics to farming, as would one whom the world had called bastard be glad to discover at length his true birth. He was glad, too, to return from Philadelphia, as are all wise men to return home. He preferred turnips to politicians, for, though, as he wrote, "I do not believe with the Rochefoucaulds and Montaignes, that fourteen men out of fifteen are rogues. I believe a great abatement from that proportion may be made in favor of general honesty," yet, in his opinion, among politicians, from whom after all Montaigne and La Rochefoucauld drew their morals, the proportion was larger than among other men. For rogues "nestle themselves into places of power and profit." Jefferson, though it is true that he never in his life refused a political honor, was yet more than content to retire from such company. He occupied his energy in farming, his talent for experiment in architecture and the invention of an improved plow.

His lighter moments he could now give to that seeing of shows, which was the odd, main passion of his life. Even in his busy days of Secretaryship he had found time to pay sixpence to see an alligator, a shilling to see "a learned pig," and the same sum—so stern was the republican's faith in equality—to see "a wax figure of the King of Prussia." In leisure he was willing to pay no less than twenty-five pence for a peep at "Caleb Phillips, a dwarf," the same for one at a painting.

XI

Washington was not a man of much theoretical understanding of political problems. He had personality and immense influence with the people. Whatever he said they would repeat. Yet what he said depended very largely upon the last possessor of his private ear. Jefferson at the end of his time in office had succeeded in establishing his influence with the President, who had usually sided with him. When Jefferson retired, Hamilton was easily able to seize his opportunity, and it soon became necessary to count the President as upon the Federalist side. He supported a Hamiltonian treaty with England, of which Jefferson disapproved. He denounced the Democratic clubs which had sprung up throughout the country as dangerous and subversive, while the Cincinnati, the Hamiltonian organization, whose object was almost declared to be the overthrow of the Constitution, went unrebuked. Yet Jefferson's disappointment only confirmed his resolution to abstain from public life. So large, he thought, was Washington's hold on public opinion that to oppose him would be useless.

For two years Jefferson remained thus in peace. But in 1796 Washington's second presidential term expired and he refused to accept a third. He had faced the troubles of the world for eight years with a calm and stately dignity of feature, which he owed chiefly to the shape of his false teeth, and he retired to the well-earned leisure of a Virginian country gentleman. A few years later he was to meet his death—and one can hardly wonder—from drinking a mixture of "molasses, vinegar and butter."

Meanwhile all Republicans felt that it was necessary that the party contest the Presidency. Jefferson had hoped that Madison would be the candidate. But it was soon clear that the party would not have Madison and would have Jefferson. With a heavy heart Jefferson consented. "My name was brought forward without concert on my part," he said. "I have no ambition to govern men, no passion which would delight me to ride in a storm." Jefferson and Aaron Burr, not as yet notorious, were the Republican candidates; for the Federalists, whose confidence Hamilton had by this time lost, John Adams and Thomas Pinckney.

The arrangement, by which today electors choose a President from a list of candidates for the Presidency, a Vice-President from another list of candidates for the Vice-Presidency, is an innovation since Jefferson's time. The votes were at that date not cast separately. Each elector wrote two names on his paper. He whose name occurred most frequently was declared President, the next candidate Vice-President.

The division between Republican and Federalist was almost geographical. The Republicans were dominant in the South, the Federalists in the North. The only exceptions to this rule were that Maryland was expected to support Adams, principally because of its rivalry with Virginia, and Pennsylvania Jefferson, because of its rivalry with Maryland. If the result was to be according to these expectations, Jefferson would be elected President with seventy-one votes and Adams second with sixty-eight.

But no good was done to Jefferson by the open support which he received from Adet, the new French Minister, and the Federalists were able to detach from him one of the electors from Virginia, one from Pennsylvania, one from North Carolina.

This exactly reversed the expected figures. Adams received seventy-one votes and was elected President. Jefferson was elected Vice-President with sixty-eight.

XII

Jefferson set out from Monticello for Philadelphia in March, 1797, traveling in company with "Certain Bones of an Unknown Quadruped," which he was taking to Dr. Wistar for classification and which Dr. Wistar identified as those of a giant sloth and christened Megalonyx Jeffersonii.

The Vice-President is no part of the Executive. His duties are those of presiding in the Senate and he exists that some one may be ready to step into Presidential shoes, if anything should happen to the President. Jefferson was well content to hold this "honourable and easy" post rather than "the splendid misery" of the first place. Yet he took seriously his Chairman's duties and, to fit himself for their performance, wrote a book, *A Manual of Parliamentary Practice*, which became the recognized guide of public bodies in the United States.

It was impossible that a man of his principles would find much to applaud in the policy of Adams' administration. The Federalists felt that their principles need no more be translated into the language of tedious decency, in order to satisfy a Washingtonian priggishness. Their policy was—it is not an unfair caricature—war abroad and tyranny at home. Government was to be carried on, in the delicious phrase which Alexander Hamilton used in a letter to Dayton, "for the purposes of a salutary patronage."

Jefferson's object was in some way to check these schemes and to give instead to his country the peace and freedom which he loved. The designs of France had been absurdly exaggerated.

The American Heresy

The country rang with the slogan of "Millions for Defence and not one Cent for Tribute." Hamilton was the master of every dodge with which Disraeli was afterwards to debauch an English music-hall. The country was preposterously arming and meanwhile Hamilton conducted an obscure and ludicrous correspondence with Miranda, the Venezuelan patriot. His vague and brilliant imagination seemed to be dazzled by the idea of forming an alliance with England and then setting off, at the head of a *grande armée du nouveau monde*, for the liberation of whatever countries might happen to exist from whatever governments might happen to be governing them. The first and necessary step in such a scheme was to destroy all liberty in his own country.

Just in time—on 18th February, 1799—Adams awoke to his senses. In defiance of his party and cabinet, he insisted on the reopening of negotiations with Talleyrand and one of the most silly and unnecessary of wars was easily averted. To Jefferson, Adams' conversion was "the event of events." Pickering, Hamilton's friend, was "shocked and grieved." As for Hamilton himself, "the little man wrought himself up to a degree of heat and effervescence."

But if it was found impossible to obtain war abroad, tyranny at home was more easily established. To "busy giddy minds with foreign quarrels" was to run too large a risk. It was safer to hunt down an alien. So two strong acts—the Alien and Sedition Acts—were passed, and there began what John Randolph called "the American Reign of Terror." The Alien Act gave power to the Executive to expel undesirable aliens, the Sedition Act to interfere with the freedom of speech and of publication.

In Jefferson's opinion, in passing these two acts, the central government had taken upon itself powers which the States had never delegated to it. The acts were therefore "unauthoritative, void and of no force." His policy was to get introduced into the Kentucky Legislature a series of resolutions declaratory of this interpretation of the Constitution and of a refusal to allow the enforcement of the laws within the boundaries of Kentucky. In his opinion the Union was a contract, and "as in all other cases of compact among parties having no common judge, each party has an equal right to judge for itself as well of infractions as of the mode and measure of redress."

Similar resolutions were afterwards introduced by Madison into the Virginia House and were passed, in spite of the opposition of George Washington and the fantastic Henry, who, from a belief that there should be no central government at all, had changed to one that its rightful power was almost unlimited. On an appeal to the electorate the resolutions were approved by an overwhelming majority.

This page of history was afterwards to have large importance. For to the precedent of the Virginia and Kentucky Resolutions Calhoun was to appeal in support of his policy of nullification. Madison, who was then still alive, denied that his doctrine was one of nullification, and Andrew Jackson, professedly a Jeffersonian Democrat, violently suppressed South Carolina's attempt. It is true that Calhoun, the leader of the attempt, expounded a process of nullification in more detail than had Madison. Yet it is hard to see what meaning Madison's theory can have had, other than that of nullification which Calhoun gave to it. The only difference, to which Madison could point, was specious and minute. Calhoun's argument was that the State must itself interpret which of its powers it had surrendered. Else it was not sovereign. This was also the language of the Kentucky Resolutions.

In 1801 Adams' Presidential term came to an end. The condition of the country was desperate and Jefferson, when asked to do so, felt that it was his duty to stand again. The four chief candidates were those of four years before—Adams and Pinckney against Jefferson and Burr. Jefferson was neither eager for election nor hopeful of his chances. Violent attacks were made upon him, because he was not a believer in the Christian religion. For, although his opinions upon that antiquity were not very different from those of Adams, the agnosticism of the latter was at least combined with those sound conservative principles, which, in the opinion of many believers, rob even agnosticism of nine-tenths of its dangers. Libels were also published concerning Jefferson's sexual life. A mulatto woman, born at Monticello, claimed to be his daughter. But he, always very careful about such things, produced a book in which were recorded the dates of all births on his estate. By comparison with his well-known public movements he was able to show that he had not been at Monticello at a time which would have made possible paternity on such a day. In reply to one libel perpetrated by a clergyman, he wrote, "If Mr. Smith thinks the precepts of the gospel intended for those who preach them as well as for others, he will doubtless feel the duties of repentance." He was in general too greatly interested in the compilation of a Cherokee dictionary to bother much about the Presidential election.

The election was decided perhaps less by the popularity of Republican principles than by a last-minute quarrel between Hamilton and Adams because of which Hamilton tried to maneuver the voting so that Pinckney should be brought out ahead of Adams. A divided party never prospers with an electorate. When the votes were counted it was found that Jefferson and Burr had each received seventy-three, Adams sixty-five, and Pinckney sixty-four.

When the Republican electors cast their votes, their intention had been to make Jefferson President and Burr Vice-President. But as there was at that time no legal way of distinguishing a vote for President from one for Vice-President, clearly it should have been arranged that one of the electors should give a vote to Jefferson and not to Burr. This had not been done. The votes for the two were equal. According to the Constitution, it therefore fell to Congress to choose the President.

Thomas Jefferson

Among the Federalists were some who wished to take advantage of their opponents' carelessness and force Congress to prefer Burr to Jefferson. The Federalists in Congress were in a position to dictate terms. For six days there was a deadlock. Jefferson was approached and tempted to bargain. He would make none, for he was quite indifferent to the issue.

At last some of the Federalists, seeing that they could not force Burr on the House, determined no longer to thwart the clear will of the majority. "It was a criminal scheme and an unconstitutional plot to steal the election." Hamilton, at first, after the elections, had suggested that Governor Jay should call an extra session of the Legislature in order that that body might deprive itself of the power of choosing electors. "In times like these," he wrote, "it will not do to be too scrupulous." Yet he himself advised his friends to prefer Jefferson to Burr. "If there is a man in the world I ought to hate, it is," he said, "Jefferson. With Burr I have always personally been well. But the public good must be paramount to every personal consideration."

On 17th February, therefore, Jefferson was elected over Burr by ten States to four. Hamilton's motive in giving his advice has been much disputed. Some would have it that it was not that he loved Jefferson more, but that he loved Burr less. For Burr had outwitted him in the electoral games of New York politics. Yet it is more charitable to give this strange figure the benefit of almost the only doubt which a candid man can have in judging the motives of his career. Though unscrupulous, he was not petty. He had a certain sense that the game, even of politics, is more than the player of the game. The man who had won must, in sportsmanship, be allowed the fruits of victory. Besides, Burr, like St. Peter, Napoleon Bonaparte and several other historical characters, was "not even a gentleman." Yet the *Centinel* of Boston thought that "Mr. Burr . . . will eventually turn out good, as he is the grandson of the dignified Edwards, the great American luminary of divinity."

After the election of Jefferson, Adams had about three weeks of office to run. He used them to fill every position of public patronage which he could with Federalist nominees. His Presidency was to expire at midnight of March 3–4, and that night he sat up with John Marshall, signing the commissions of new judges.

Marshall was still filling in these commissions when midnight struck. In walked Levi Lincoln, Attorney-General in the new government.

"I have been ordered by Mr. Jefferson to take possession of this office and its papers," he said.

"Why, Mr. Jefferson is not yet qualified," answered Marshall.

"Mr. Jefferson considers himself in the light of an executor, bound to take charge of the papers of the Government, until he is duly qualified," said Lincoln.

"But it is not yet twelve o'clock," said Marshall, taking out his watch.

"This is the President's watch and rules the hour," answered Lincoln, taking out his and showing the hands pointing to midnight.

Lincoln would not allow a paper to be moved from the room and Marshall afterwards used to say that he had been permitted to pick up nothing but his hat. Yet he took in his pocket one or two commissions.

XIII

The new capital of Washington had been built in the previous year of 1800 and in the desolate and barbaric spot, as it then was, it was the duty of the President to live. Bareness possesses at least the merit of simplicity and Jefferson, determined to free the Government from these imitations of the ceremonial fopperies of a European Court, which had grown up under the rule of Washington and Adams and which so easily become the window-dressing behind which the rich can hide their baseness.

Professor McMaster[1] rejects the well-known story of how he rode from his lodgings, unattended, to take the oath of office, hitched his horse's bridle to the palisade, entered, did what he had to do and then, coming out, mounted and rode off again. It seems that the story was invented by certain humorists of Washington in order to deceive a poor English traveler, a Mr. John Davis—a design in which they were very successful, deceiving also a generation or two of Professors into the bargain. He was really inaugurated in most proper pomp. Yet certainly he received the Danish Minister in bedroom slippers and, in answer to the diplomat's complaint, quoted the repartee of Caraccioli to the King of Naples, who had complained of the tediousness of ceremony and to whom Caraccioli replied: "Your Majesty must remember that you yourself are but a ceremony." Jefferson was determined always to be more than that or nothing. He offended also the British Minister by his disregard of the etiquette of going in to dinner, and indeed discovered, as it is easy for the courageous Great to discover, that simplicity of manners is an infallible way of dividing interesting from uninteresting people.

Yet he did not rush into any opposite fad of the Simple Life. For that he was too good an Epicurean. He was the center of Washington society, a host at whose table good wine, good food, good talk were always to be found. He shut his door on none. "The wine was the best I ever drank, particularly the champagne, which was delicious," wrote Senator Plumer, of New Hampshire. "There was, as usual, a dissertation upon wines, not very edifying," adds John Quincy Adams, of serious Massachusetts. Jefferson's wine-bill for his two Presidential terms was $10,855.

---

[1] *History of the People of the United States from the Revolution to the Civil War*, 5 vols., by J. B. McMaster.

Of all the pictures of him of which history allows us to get a glimpse, this of the leader of Washington society is perhaps the most attractive. It is delightful to read of this truly good man going about and giving pain to impossible people. He was not at all rude by nature but he had the hatred of all healthy persons for ritual without dogma. His policy was deliberate, and its purpose to break those traditions of almost royal etiquette, with which the attempt had been made to surround the office of President. The only fear is that, through a defective sense of humor, he never entirely saw how funny he was.

He was, at first, though indifferent to the political chance which had brought him to Washington, yet jubilant at the victory of Republican principles. He thought that it was a "proof of the falsehood of Montesquieu's doctrine that a Republic can be preserved only in a small territory." It is today evident that, although Montesquieu underrated the capacity of the human race for calling things by their wrong names, yet he here made an observation of genius. An equal Government, which is what both he and Jefferson meant by a Republic, can only be preserved in a small territory.

Jefferson at once began his policy of financial reform. He was above the error of the modern politician, who imagines that a progressive reform means making the people pay to have something done by a Government which they had previously done very well for themselves. By reform he meant not that the State should do more, but that it should do less. With a magnificent gesture he abolished all internal taxation and—what is hardly less important—all internal tax-gatherers. Amazed Pro Bono Publico rubbed his eyes in incredulous surprise.

He came into office with peace upon his lips. Peace had been the grand purpose of his politics. Yet by the first of August the country found herself at war, though at a war of a sort at which the pale gibbering preëxistences of Gilbert and Sullivan must have mouthed in fury for not thinking of it first. It had been the custom of the previous American Governments to pay tribute to Tripoli for the safety of American commerce in the Mediterranean. Jefferson disapproved of this and, when the Bashaw sent some insolent demands, Jefferson replied with a squadron to hunt the pirates down. Against whom the war was fought was never clearly known, but the Americans won.

The main achievement of Jefferson's first administration was the Louisiana purchase. Louisiana was the name given not only to the area of the present State of Louisiana, but to the whole Middle-Western district of North America. From 1762 to 1800 this territory belonged to Spain. In 1800, by the Treaty of San Ildefonso, Spain ceded it back to France, who agreed not to resell it to any third power.

There were at that date no roads from the Mississippi to the eastern coast. All the commerce of the west had to travel down the river. In the policy of the possessor of New Orleans the United States were then bound to be interested. Jefferson determined to make an attempt to acquire it for his country. At first Talleyrand was unwilling to negotiate. But, in 1803, on the failure to subdue the revolt of Toussaint l'Ouverture in Haiti, Napoleon suddenly tired of this toy, the New World. War with Great Britain seemed certain to break out again. He therefore instructed Barbé-Marbois, his Minister of Finance, to sell. Monroe was sent over to negotiate and the price of sixty million livres was agreed upon. It was ten million more than Napoleon had expected to get. With this aid he was able to carry on his new war longer than would otherwise have been possible. All were satisfied, except the inhabitants of New Orleans.

Jefferson's only difficulty was that the Constitution made no provision for the incorporation of foreign territory into the Union. How, in strict propriety, should he act? He wished "to set an example against broad construction by appealing for new powers to the people." But Monroe argued that there was no time to be lost, since Napoleon might at any moment change his mind. Jefferson therefore contented himself with the ratification of the Treaty by the Senate and the voting of authority by Congress for raising of the purchase-money by loan. By an Act of 1804 he, as was said, "stepped into the shoes of the King of Spain," assuming as perquisite of the President the whole government and patronage of the territory. A small knot of Federalists, with a humorous malice that was surely justified, denounced the whole business as "unconstitutional."

It is the fashion to praise Jefferson for his bold preference for national interest over a pedantic interpretation of the law. Such praise is apt to miss the point of the accusation against him. The Constitution of the United States was a contract from which there was a dangerous probability that the central government would acquire more power than it was intended to acquire. Constantly matters were certain to arise which it would appear convenient, reasonable and without danger to the autonomy of the States to leave to the central government. One by one, a good case could no doubt be made out for each of these. Yet to a man who valued the liberty of the State, their cumulative effect must be disastrous. Jefferson, who more clearly than any other had pointed out this danger, more certainly than any other involved his country in it.

It is often assumed that only by some oversight did the Constitution neglect to make any provision for the acquisition of territory. If that be true, Jefferson's conduct is, of course, far more easily defended. But the assumption appears unjustified. The United States were intended to be static. An agricultural people were to live in freedom on the land, suffering as little as possible from the interference of Government and preserving a simple and ancient way of life rather than continually learning, by invention, new customs. For such a people no method of expansion was provided, because it was not intended that they should expand. The country, in its original area, was, if anything, not too small but too large. There was ample land for all. And, if it was true that New Orleans might always prove a menace to American commerce and shipping, the answer is clear that America was only intended to be most incidentally a commercial nation and that, as Jefferson himself powerfully pointed out, one of the greatest dangers to American republicanism was the growth of a strong vested interest of shipping. The purchase of Louisiana gave to the American character an invitation to instability which it has not been slow to accept.

Jefferson foresaw that, in the development of the West, a time might come when East and West would split into two confederacies. To this he was indifferent. "I believe it," he wrote to Dr. Priestley, "not very important to the happiness of either part. Did I now foresee a separation at some future day I should feel the duty and desire to promote the Western interests as zealously as the Eastern." Such a separation will, it may be, eventually take place. Yet Jefferson failed to foresee the disastrous influence which the West would have on the East before that separation. Rightly he insisted that the happiness of America depended upon the strong preservation of State loyalty. In the East the State was a real and historical unit. The Western State was an arbitrary bit that happened to fall between two lines of latitude or longitude. To it no man could be very loyal. And, as the West grew, the westerner came more and more to bring to politics a natural contempt for State Rights. By the man from the West the State has been destroyed. Andrew Jackson came from the West to kill Jefferson's doctrine of nullification. Douglas and Lincoln came from the West to trample in antagonism on the State's last freedom of secession. The Middle-West has become today, the enemy of all freedom, of all right living, of all things which Jefferson most loved.

The American Heresy

Only one man, I fancy, at that time saw the true character of the West—the great Talleyrand, who wrote an essay *On the Advantages of Withdrawing from New Colonies in Present Circumstances*. In a passage of wonderful wisdom he spoke of American civilization as "exhibited in space as well as in time—as the traveler moves westward, he appears to go backward from age to age." Having written, he withdrew.

By the Louisiana purchase the homogeneity of the United States was destroyed. It is essential for a happy society that its members should have the same philosophy. For all then recognize as reasonable the same restrictions upon their liberty. Lord Acton said that liberty was freedom to do what is right. The definition is partial but important. Where a man's liberty must be restricted, as, in a society, it in some ways must, it is tolerable that it be restricted according to his philosophy, tyrannical if it be restricted contrary to it—that is, if he be prevented from doing what he believes to be right. Now, if the society is not homogeneous, one group must necessarily be dominant over others. The State must be organized and liberty restricted on the assumption of some philosophy, which a certain number of the subjects do not hold. They then will suffer tyranny and be unhappy.

By the purchase the United States obtained a territory of a preposterous size. This territory it was quite impossible to fill with their own citizens, or even with emigrants from countries, supposing there to be such, whose citizens have more or less the same way of life as theirs. It has been necessary therefore to fill up the country with men of a culture entirely alien to their own. These men, possessing one culture, have been ruled by the laws and customs of another.

There are a thousand instances of this. One will be sufficient to show what is meant. A Prohibition law is perhaps no great hardship to a Puritan Middle-Western farmer, for his religion teaches him that it is wrong to touch alcohol, as the phrase is, anyway. Such a law is clearly intolerable to an Italian, to whom the drinking of wine is a part of everyday life and normal manhood, no more wrong than breathing. It would have been far better for the happiness of both groups had there been the two Governments in North America during the nineteenth century. The United States would have been the normal destination of the English-speaking emigrant, French Louisiana of the Latin.

It is, I suppose, true that the United States gained enormously in material prosperity by the purchase. I will not even trouble to look at the statistics which prove it. I speak of happiness, not money. A starving man is, I know, not happy. But I am ignorant of any evidence which proves a man of small sufficiency less happy than one better off, while, beyond that, the very rich are patently more unhappy than those of reasonable fortunes. Even without the purchase the agricultural, property-owning United States could have been rich enough to possess all the happiness which material comfort can give. As it is, they are too rich and therefore less happy than the people of other countries.

The purchase was the first of the three blows in the murder of Jeffersonian America. It would have been better if he could have been content to confine his interest in the West to the romantic. In this he excelled. He sent out an expedition of exploration under Lewis and Clark. It was brilliantly successful. They were the first Americans to cross the Continent from Atlantic to Pacific Ocean.

XIV

Whatever may be the reflections of posterity upon Jefferson's policy, it is but fair to admit that from his contemporaries it received little but applause. Their anxiety—a sensible enough anxiety—was that France would revive her old ambitions of before the Seven Years' War, and they were grateful to be peaceably rid of such a neighbor. Jefferson's popularity could be judged when, after four years, the time came for his reëlection. Previously he had gained only a bare victory. This time but two States of the Union declared against him and he received in the Electoral College one hundred and sixty-two votes to fourteen.

The history of Jefferson's second administration falls into three stories; those of the relations with England, of Aaron Burr, and of the abolition of the slave-trade. Of these the first and last are important. The second is interesting.

The wider dreams of Louisiana seem partly to have tempted Jefferson from his impeccable principles of foreign policy. It had never been clearly settled at San Ildefonso where the frontiers of Louisiana ran. And Napoleon, in the Treaty of Purchase, purposely left this problem as vague as he found it. From contention between Spain and the United States he could not but gain. Jefferson was surprisingly Chauvinistic in pressing for a solution. The Spaniards were amusingly indifferent. And Jefferson, in the high feathers of a patriot, began to talk, like an Adams, of natural friendship with England. "An English ascendancy on the ocean is safer than that of France," he wrote to Monroe. "The first wish of every Englishman's heart," he confided in Madison, "is to see us once more fighting by their sides against France." He would make a treaty with that George Guelph, who, thirty years before, "endeavoured to pervert the same into a detestable and insupportable tyranny," and it should come into force "in the event of our being engaged in war with either France or Spain during the present war in Europe"—and all because of the rude Spanish diplomats who would not be serious about a strip of land in Florida.

Yet these sweet dreams of English-speaking union were rudely shattered. The British Parliament passed a series of laws in 1805 against trade with French and Spanish colonies, and by the Essex judgment in July of that year American ships were barred entirely from those territories. "The first wish" of the Englishman's heart seemed to have been relegated to, at least, a second place. Those who attempted such a trade would be seized without warning and declared lawful prizes. It was a blow. What does a pacifist President do? Undaunted, he writes that the Government ought to take strong measures against England, France and Spain. Fortunately there is an Atlantic ocean in the way and no inconvenient Mrs. Partington to sweep it aside.

"Oh, the brave music of a distant drum."

Here was game bigger than a Bashaw. So there was a Confidential Message to Congress on Spanish spoliations, and then Fox joined the British Government, and Napoleon said that he would negotiate and afterwards said that he would not negotiate, and in fact did not, and Fox, who never was very dependable, died. So, to please everybody, Jefferson put his Vice-President on trial for high treason, which was generally agreed to have been the wisest way out of a very difficult situation.

The Vice-President was Aaron Burr, whom Hamilton had robbed of the Presidency. For this reason he hated Hamilton. And, hearing that Hamilton had spoken of his private character as "despicable"—as indeed it was—he forced him to issue a challenge to a duel and shot him dead at Weehawken, just across the river from New York but in the State of New Jersey, very early in the morning on 11th July, 1804. Now whether that was a good thing to have done or a bad thing, it is not for an impartial historian to say. It is sufficient and certain that he did it and that Alexander Hamilton—poor Don Quixote with a dash of Anti-Christ—ceased any more from troubling America by tilting at the windmills of a Virginian farmer.

Vice-Presidents, I suppose, will be Vice-Presidents. Yet Burr had no business meddling with an affair of murder. For a time he had therefore to flee from the high places, and in his exile he did most curious things. He plotted and plotted, but for what purpose has not to this day been exactly established. Jefferson thought that he "meant to place himself upon the throne of Montezuma and extend his Empire to the Alleghany, seizing on New Orleans as the instrument of compulsion for our Western States." And it seems that his plan was to use the discontent of the western farmers at the failure of the negotiations for the Florida Purchase, in order to detach Louisiana from the United States, and of the growing Mexican nationalism in order to detach Mexico from Spain. Having done this, he would unite the two amorphous territories into one higgledy-piggledy empire of jail-birds, fugitives from justice, French traders, explorers, farmers, financial speculators, untamed Indians, Spanish missionaries, "tinker, tailor, soldier, sailor," which Emperor Aaron I, of the dynasty of Burr, would bestride at least like a Colossus. Such stories passed from fashionable fiction when Cervantes laughed Spanish art into realism. In May, 1807, Jefferson had to have Burr arrested, and he was put on his trial before Chief Justice Marshall at Richmond.

Burr had a rare double claim to the good wishes of all ambitious Federalists. For not only had he defied the leading politician of the opposite party, but he had also shot a very dangerous rival in their own. With commendable generosity they took up his cause. A dinner was given in his honor on the eve of the trial. This dinner Chief Justice Marshall, with questionable propriety, attended.

The defense based itself upon an attack on the President. And Marshall, smarting under the memory of a hat but barely saved and judges' commissions irretrievably lost, summoned Jefferson to appear in Court. Jefferson refused, and in the end the Jury brought in a verdict that "Aaron Burr is not proved to be guilty under this indictment by any evidence submitted to us." He was later again committed for trial in Ohio. But, after giving bail for three thousand dollars, he forfeited his recognizances and fled to England. He lived to the year 1836, and that he was a man of some physical vigor is proved by his appearance, at the age of eighty, as an active party in a prominent divorce suit.

The trial of Burr had been immediately preceded by the abolition of the slave-trade. It was followed by the naval duel between the *Chesapeake* and the *Leopard*. The *Leopard*, a British frigate, had demanded of the captain of the *Chesapeake*, an American frigate, that he allow his ship to be searched on the suspicion that he was harboring British naval deserters. The commander of the *Chesapeake* refused, whereupon the *Leopard* fired upon her. America hummed and there were demands for explanation.

Before the explanation could come, a larger and more permanent cause of quarrel with Great Britain had arisen. Napoleon, unable to conquer England by direct invasion, attempted instead to ruin her trade by the enforcement of his Continental System and by the Berlin Decrees. The British Government replied by a third Order in Council, and Napoleon, in his turn, supplemented the Berlin by the Milan Decrees. The effect upon American commerce of the two policies was that the British, who held command of the sea, would not allow any American trade with the Continent of Europe which did not touch at a British port, and the French, who held command of the land, would treat as hostile and seize any vessel which did touch at one. Between the two, American commerce was destroyed and the United States were only saved from going to war with either of the two powers by the horrid thought that they would thus make themselves the allies of the other. Such double repulsiveness was a merciful dispensation of Providence. And Jefferson was able to satisfy American feeling by making a virtue of necessity and putting an embargo upon foreign trade. It was a dignified method of notifying foreign nations that he accepted their refusal to have anything to do with the United States.

This policy, certainly, caused considerable distress—though, doubtless, far less than a war would have caused. Jefferson was able to persevere in it until almost the end of his Presidency in 1809. But by that date a group of New England politicians, known as the Essex Junto, from Essex County in Massachusetts where was their main strength, began to threaten secession from the Union unless the Government were capable of finding a way of reopening trade. Northern politicians, who sixty years later were for a reason of commerce ready to preserve the Union by force, were at that date for a similar reason ready to destroy it. John Quincy Adams, son of old John Adams, called on Jefferson with confidential information that citizens of New England were in secret negotiation with the British Government and intended to arrange, not indeed a definite disruption of the Union, but an agreement by which, in return for concessions, they would see to it that their State neglected the Government's policy of embargo.

Now even of those laws, which are Federal laws, the responsibility for enforcement is upon the State authorities. And if, therefore, a law is so unpopular in some part of the country that the State authorities are not willing to take that responsibility, there is little that the Federal Government can do. If John Quincy Adams' information was correct, and if the Essex Junto could gain support for their plans in Massachusetts, the outlook was serious. The object of Jefferson's policy was to avoid foreign war. It looked as if he might only be able to avoid it at the price of civil war. And the veteran, on the threshold of retirement, was not willing to take the risk. He repealed the Tweedledum of embargo, substituted for it the Tweedledee of Non-Intercourse and drove home to Monticello.

XV

With this retirement that little side of Jefferson's life, the life of Jefferson the statesman, is finished. He gladly threw off the hole-and-corner drudgery of public life and the rest of his days were given to these thousand intellectual interests with which his ample mind was always stocked. He was like a schoolboy home for the holidays.

He had collected materials for a *magnum opus* upon Indian philology. These were placed in a large chest, which, on the journey home from Washington to Monticello, was entrusted to two negro boatmen. The negroes, excusably presuming that the chest of a politician returning from office would certainly be filled with silver and gold, pried it open and the data of the Presidential philology were, amid peals of happy African laughter, whirled by the wind to every scattered corner of the Southern States. Yet Jefferson was not discouraged. Architecture, mathematics, farming, mechanics, even Red Indian philology again—in these fields he walked like a man at home. The Presidency had passed to his disciples, first to Madison and afterwards to Monroe, and he was content to leave public affairs in such hands. Yet even in retirement he was often consulted, nor ever left very long without cause of complaint.

Before his first term was finished, the new President had allowed himself to drift into war with Great Britain. The Orders in Council, which were the cause of war, had, as it happened, been repealed before the declaration. The two items of news crossed one another on the Atlantic Ocean, but Madison, somewhat like a hostess who has arranged a garden-party for a doubtful day, seems to have thought that, since so much trouble had been taken to get the war ready, it would be a great pity not to have it after all.

The American hope was to capture Canada, and this, Jefferson foretold, would be "a mere matter of marching." As it happened,

General Hull, the American general, was defeated and had to surrender. The "mere matter of marching" was without arms and under escort. Jefferson found comfort in a study of mathematics.

The most important action of the war was Andrew Jackson's repulse of a British attack on New Orleans—some time after peace was signed. And indeed it is an unfair—but not a very unfair—summary of the history of this war to say that the cause of it was removed before it began, and that the fighting began when it was finished. The peace, which was signed at Ghent in 1814, left everything exactly as it had been before the outbreak—except for such "altered circumstances of the case" as the graves of a few poor men who had been killed.

Jefferson, burning with the jingo zeal of a retired pacifist, had been in favor of taking Canada as an indemnity for English outrage and then making peace, in order that the hands of the administration might be left free for a war with France—an occupation which has always seemed to possess a singular attraction for those who believe in peace at any price. However, as he admitted, "peace is better for us all."

The main interest of these later years is in his correspondence with John Adams. Their political quarrels had driven, and for many years kept, them apart. But now that neither cared much any longer for these causes of difference, a reconciliation was effected. And the two old men amused themselves by a long and interesting correspondence concerning their various philosophical opinions.

It is often said that, as men approach the grave, they grow kinder towards the doctrines of the Christian religion, whatever their feelings may have been in their stronger days. Of Jefferson the opposite was true. At one time he had been willing to call himself "a sort of Christian"—though he meant by that only some Early Victorian modernism about admitting the morality and rejecting the miracles—but in his old age he vigorously takes up the cudgels against the opinion of Mansfield that Christianity is a part of the common law of England. He preferred, it seemed, the mythical legal system of Connecticut, in which it was supposed to have been laid down that "the laws of God should be the laws of their land, except where their own contradict them"—as they frequently did.

These arguments led him to a line of preposterous reflection of patriotic anti-clericalism. "We are destined to be a barrier against the returns of ignorance and barbarism. Old Europe will have to lean on our shoulders and to hobble along by our side under the monkish trammels of priests and kings as she can." And to a lady he wrote, "My opinion is that there would never have been an infidel if there had never been a priest." That, if there had never been anything to disbelieve, there would never have been any one who disbelieved it, is a proposition, doubtless irrefutable in logic but hardly, one feels, very valuable for practical life. He was failing fast.

He had found in France the home of ideas. Through his long life he had seen in that country every opinion canvassed with blood. All solutions of the world had been freely placed before this people, whom he had admired. And now, the news from France was of a great writer, one de Maistre,[1] who had discovered, in that odd way that people have, a thing more modern even than modern thought—who had discovered the Catholic Church. Discovering, he had discovered also curious things about the Americans which the Americans themselves had least suspected. "The American revolt was made necessary by England's apostasy." "She lost the authority which was owed to her, because she repudiated the authority which she owed." The Spanish Inquisition and the United States of America were, among human

---

[1] Joseph Maire, Comte de Maistre (1753–1821), author of *Du Pape*, *Soirées de St. Pétersbourg*, etc.; leader of the Catholic reaction in political philosophy against the Voltairean and Encyclopædist Schools.

institutions, selected for special approval. It was a little inconvenient for a most respectable rationalist to find himself praised by a Papist, more bigoted even than the majority, for adherence to those principles of a church, the last relics of whose superstition he had imagined himself to have spent a lifetime in destroying.

Jefferson could not and would not understand it. Like many old men, he preferred to repeat violently the outworn catchwords of his youth. De Maistre was abroad with the rising generation. De Maistre had spoken those great truths, which we, that live, dare never again forget. Eighteenth-century rationalism was the outworn catchword of the dying, as wholly dead then as is nineteenth-century rationalism today. "I have little doubt," Jefferson wrote to Pickering, "that the whole of our country will soon be rallied to the Unity of the Creator"—by which he meant Unitarianism. "The day will come," he said again, "when the mystical generation of Jesus, by the Supreme Being as His Father, in the womb of a Virgin, will be classed with the fable of the generation of Minerva in the brain of Jupiter." To be able to distinguish what is from what you wish to be is a rare capacity. Jefferson had it until old age.

Yet on the whole the picture, which various of his guests have left to us of these closing years at Monticello, is a most pleasant one. He was the kindest both of hosts and of grandfathers, and these are indeed high virtues.

In 1817, his pupil, Madison, was succeeded as President by his pupil, Monroe. There began what was known as the Era of Good Feeling. Union at home and peace abroad was to be the policy. But Monroe had only been in office for a year, when there arose the most serious cause of disruption that the United States had had to face. Old Jefferson wrote that it filled him with terror "like a fire-bell in the night."

Independence had been mainly the achievement of the Southern States. In every way they were the leaders of America.

Yet the population, which, in 1790, had been about equally distributed between North and South, had by 1820 grown in such a proportion that the North had a preponderance in Congress of thirty votes over the South. There were on the other hand an equal number of Northern and Southern States, and, therefore, in the Senate their numbers were equal. That equality the South was convinced that it was essential for her to maintain, if her institutions were not to be under continual menace. The whole record of the Federalists could be quoted in justification of this feeling.

When, therefore, in this year of 1818, the question of the admission of a new State of Missouri, carved out of a part of the Louisiana territory, came up, the South was at once on her guard. The Southerner was apt to be slave-owning. A very large proportion of Southerners, at that date, would have been willing to condemn the institution of slavery. Yet they demanded that Missouri should be admitted to the Union as a slave State. Their reason was that it was essential to Southern safety that she should become a Southern State, and it was impossible to induce the Southerner to make up his proportion of the emigrants into that State if he could only do so at the sacrifice of what, rightly or wrongly, was a large part of his worldly wealth—his slaves.

Many men have been unable to make head or tail of this story of Southern agitation. Why it should be that people, who, a few years before, had been most open-minded concerning the abolition of slavery in their own territory, should suddenly demand a thing, as it appears, almost lunatic—that slavery be forced upon populations who do not wish to have it—they have been unable to explain. Until it is understood that the controversy about slavery was not primarily a controversy about slavery, the story is unintelligible. The fear of the South was that the North would use superior voting-power to vote to itself economic advantages at Southern expense. In order that such a thing should be prevented, equality in the Senate must be maintained.

For two years the Missouri question was in debate. In 1820 it was settled by the compromise that Missouri should be admitted as a slave State, that in the North-East there should, at the same time, be carved out the new free State of Maine and that for the future no slavery should be admitted north of the line 36° 30′.

Congress passed the required legislation. As was later to appear, it was very doubtful if it had the power to do so. But those, like Jefferson, who, though they disapproved of slavery, hated this sectional division of the country in which they saw the knell of the Union, were thankful even for such doubtful peace. As long ago as 1784 Jefferson had proposed that "after the year 1800 of the Christian era there shall be neither slavery nor involuntary servitude in any of the new States to be carved out of the western territory of Virginia." He had been defeated by only one vote. And now the old man accepted this compromise as a reprieve only, not as a final acquittal. He had perhaps seen enough of the North to know that there were two nations, not one, and that, in order that each should understand this, they only needed to see a little more of each other. As long as there were no roads the United States survived. Macadam made the Civil War inevitable.

There was one other great achievement of Monroe's Presidency, to which Jefferson contributed by advice—the enunciation of the Doctrine by which the President is today mainly remembered. Canning, the British Foreign Secretary, determined to checkmate the designs of Chateaubriand and the Czar, who were planning to interfere in Spanish America, in order to put down the revolting colonies. He therefore recognized their independence. He "called a new world in, to redress the balance of the old," and, by a diplomatic triumph, persuaded Monroe to announce that the price of a European interference would be the hostility of the United States. The effect of the Monroe Doctrine was to complete the isolation of the United States from Europe by the natural complement of forcing Europe to keep her hands off America. Owing to it the United States throughout the nineteenth century did not need to keep pace with the armaments of the other Great Powers—which, of course, saved a great deal of money. To it also are undoubtedly due such tattered remnants of independence as Mexico and Central America today possess. If there had been danger that other powers would seize those countries, the United States would certainly in self-defense have been forced to seize them themselves.

XVI

During the last years the interest which Jefferson could spare from his own affairs was given in the main, not to national or international politics, but to that great work, for which, together with the Declaration of Independence and the Statute of Religious Liberty, he desired to be remembered—the building of the University of Virginia. The old royal foundation of William and Mary slumbered and Jefferson's idea was to build a new, representative, republican State University of Virginia to which the talent of all the civilized world could be attracted. For the University a site was selected at Charlottesville within view of Monticello.

In no two things are a man's soul more clearly shown than in his taste in architecture and his opinions on education. Of the University of Virginia Jefferson was both architect and first rector. And even today a visit to Charlottesville will teach the traveler much of this great man. Order in architecture reigns there and a spaciousness and unhurried peace. Its style is classical. Jefferson thought gothic to be as barbaric as did his beloved Pope. "Gothic architecture," Coleridge says, "is infinity made imaginable." And Jefferson, that soul from the eighteenth century, thought that it would be very bad for the students to have infinity made imaginable. Infinity, he vaguely felt, was a very vulgar quantity. It sounded too much like theology.

It is intensely interesting to study this strange man's views upon education. The rates shall not pay a cent to the propagation of dogma, but they shall maintain a public library of carefully selected secular volumes. The students are to be more dogmatically warned away from dogma than they have ever, in any seminary, been doctored with it. There shall be no Professor of Divinity; on the other hand, there shall be "courses of ethical lectures, developing those moral obligations, in which all sects agree"— one hopes, in order to supplement the somewhat scanty hours allowed for sleep. For what place is more boring, as those who have suffered from it know, than that strange and last Nirvana of the non-sectarian, where progressive "guides, philosophers and friends" teach impeccable Nothing to pubescent agnostics? The Presbyterians who objected to the appointment of a Unitarian professor are denounced for wishing to revive the Holy Inquisition.

Jefferson did indeed extend to all "theological sects an invitation to establish schools near the University and to attend its lectures." But what ethical lectures meant, one may deduce from the course of reading which he drew up in 1814 for his grandson, George Wythe Randolph. "Under ethics come Locke, Stewart, Condorcet, Cicero, Seneca, Hutcheson, etc.; under religion sectarian, the Bible, Sterne's Sermons and Priestley's Corruptions of Christianity; under natural law, Vattel." In fact, people holding religious opinions were invited to come and be told why they were not true—and Jefferson was pained that the invitation was not accepted. All the Professors but one, he pleaded, were Episcopalians. But Episcopalian covers a multitude of opinions and one of them admitted that "there was not one, except Mr. Lomax, the Professor of Law, who was a communicant." Poor Mr. Lomax! The theological sects were, I fancy, wiser than he.

Once religion was forgotten and curriculum taken up, no man could be more dogmatic than Jefferson. "In appointing a Professor of Law," he says, "we must be rigorously attentive to his political principles." "No diploma," he writes, "shall be given to any one who has not passed such an examination of the Latin language as shall have proved him able to read the highest classics in that language with ease, thorough understanding and just quantity." But few of the present alumni of the University of Virginia would graduate, one fancies, under Jeffersonian examination.

No hope of the last century has been more patently falsified than that of a speedy millennium through universal education. We have turned out a generation able to read and write. But we have taught no one a just standard of values nor a capacity for judgment. Yet Jefferson, when he set hope in education, did not mean this modern half-education. And to his peculiar dreams a just posterity may accord a melancholy interest.

XVII

The end was at hand. In 1824 Lafayette came on a visit and stayed with Jefferson at Monticello. In the next year he returned to France, leaving his old friend very ill upon a sofa. He rode off, the last of those with whom Jefferson had hoped to see the golden years return and the earth, like a snake, renew her winter weeds.

The year 1826 was the fiftieth anniversary of the signing of the Declaration of Independence. As was but natural, an invitation was sent to Jefferson to attend the celebrations at Washington on 4th July. He had to write and refuse because of his health.

When that day came he lay in his last illness. "This is the Fourth?" he asked Nicholas Trist. Trist nodded. "Just as I wished," Jefferson answered, and at ten minutes to one the great pagan died.

"Man goeth to his long home and the mourners go about the streets." "Of making many books there is no end and much study is a weariness of the flesh." He died in personal debt and in the day of the destruction of his labors. Four years before he had said, "I regret that I am now to die in the belief that the useless sacrifice of themselves by the generation of 1776 to acquire self-government and happiness to their country is to be thrown away by the unwise and unworthy passions of their sons, and that my only consolation is that I shall not live to weep over it." He was, then, without illusion. With some dignity he, who had refused the comforts of a religion in his strength, refused them also in his last weakness. They asked him if he would see the clergyman. "I have no objection to see him as a kind and good neighbor," he answered.

Of his dead sister he had written:

> "Aevi virentis flore prærepta,
> Sit tibi terra levis;
> Longe longeque valeto."

["Carried off in the flower of thriving youth,
May the earth be light upon you;
A long, a very long farewell."]

And on his wife's tomb had inscribed:

> "Εἰ δὲ θανόντων περ καταλήθοντ᾽ εἰν Ἀΐδαο,
> αὐτὰρ ἐγὼ καὶ κεῖθι φίλου μεμνήσομ᾽ ἑταίρου." [1]

To those whom he had most loved he would bring no offering but the cold and beautiful despair of old paganism. For himself he asked no more.

> "ὀλίγη δε κεισόμεθα
> κόνις ὀστέων λυθέντων,"

---

[1] *Iliad*, xxii. 389-390. Even though they forget the dead in Hades, yet will I there remember my dear companion.

he quoted from Anacreon. "When my bones have rotted, there will be in the tomb a little dust." This was, he thought, the end of so much life and liberty, of so much pursuit of happiness.

On this same day died also John Adams. "It was a damned Yankee trick," said a patriotic Virginian. Adams was a little fellow, with the soul of a self-important town-councillor. After a hundred years the world cares little what he said or did. With Jefferson it is not so. Four or five times God, in His mercy, has raised up against His Truth an enemy, almost worthy of the combat. Here was one. His philosophy was a sentimental philosophy. His rationalism lacked the basis of reason. Of this, as of all great heresies, the end is nothing. Yet it was a great heresy and Thomas Jefferson a great heresiarch. And today, as the darkness gathers in and rich men bind down the poor with their mean reforms and puny slaveries, no man can be the worse if he remember Monticello and the great prophet, who, with all his failings and inconsistencies, yet dedicated a giant's strength to the service of Freedom.

It is a pity that he was such a prig.

John Caldwell Calhoun

I

To many it may seem surprising that, in a select quartet of American statesmen, the fourth place should be given to Calhoun. Americans are not wont to waste their time upon failures, nor Englishmen upon people of whom they have never heard. Yet the selection is, I think, just. Calhoun was, more than any other, the personification of an idea. Although that idea was defeated and destroyed, yet, if only that we may understand the history of the victors, it is necessary to understand the philosophy of the vanquished and to study the life of their leaders.

For all that, it must be admitted that it is impossible to write of Calhoun as one can write of Jefferson or Lincoln or Wilson. Jefferson left behind him his *Ana*, a monument of malice. No sooner was the breath from the body than the journalists got to work on sketch and anecdote about Lincoln and Wilson. But the friends of Calhoun had little leisure for such a recreation and he little desire for such an immortality. "All the South," once said a bitter Northern soldier, "is the grave of Calhoun." And all the South turned out to fight for the defense of that grave, as the warriors of a Greek city used to fight around the bones of their hero. The men who would have recorded their bright and creditable little Memories of Calhoun had other work to do and lie instead beside the Mississippi at Vicksburg or before Richmond or at Chancellorsville, by the side of Stonewall Jackson. It is for Calhoun a happy chance. He would not, we may be sure, have

John Caldwell Calhoun
From a daguerreotype

wished that even his words should outlive the thing which he loved. To the verdict of posterity he was utterly indifferent. He saw no reason why it should be wiser than its ancestors.

In 1781, General Cornwallis, marching up from Charleston through South Carolina, made it certain by his surrender at Yorktown that the little baby, who was to be born at Abbeville, in the West, in the March of the next year, should be born a citizen of a sovereign State.

In this rough western corner of the State young Calhoun grew up. For the first eighteen years of his life he, like Lincoln, had no regular schooling. His family was one more firmly established than was Lincoln's, the social position into which he was born a far better one. Yet between the boyhoods of these two there is some similarity. Both, free from the monstrous menace of a well-stocked library, learned to reason before they could learn to read. They suffered little from the benefits of education. At an age when young Woodrow Wilson was tricking himself into the delusion that he had a first-class mind by sitting up till after midnight and absorbing the thoughts of others, these boys were trying for themselves to follow out from their first principles the problems of the universe. They had not information at hand as a short cut to knowledge. On both of them their early upbringing left afterwards its mark. Their failing was to be that of a too objective intelligence. They saw too clearly to govern muddle-headed men successfully and were unable to dupe themselves with the glib prophecies and baseless comforts, without which none but the strongest dare face the horror of the world. They hated too much the bad logic which half-education produces readily to compromise with it. They lived too largely in the intellect because they had never been able to afford to live in a library. "I desire never to meet him again," a diner-out was afterwards to report on Calhoun. "I hate a man who makes me think so much." And his social reputation was to be that of the most brilliant monologist in America but of a bad listener. Novels he could never abide. In his youth he had read Locke's *"Essay on the Human Understanding"* as far as the chapter on Infinity—which is about half-way through the second book—but there, apparently, he stuck, and in the recreation of his later years his reading was of little else save the histories of Poland and of Rome. The only advice upon life which he was to find it possible to give to an aspiring young disciple was to "study less." It is a large contrast to the example of Jefferson.

From his twentieth to his twenty-second year Calhoun was, it is true, a student at Yale, where he had an opportunity of learning from the Hartford Convention his first lessons in secession and whence he graduated with high honors. That he had not till then received anything which a government authority would have consented to card-index as education, makes this feat all the more remarkable.

On one of his journeys from South Carolina to the North, as he was passing through Virginia, he was taken out of his way, in order to pay a visit to Jefferson near Charlottesville. "They talked on until after midnight, which was contrary to Jefferson's custom." And afterwards Richard Rush[1] recorded the secret that "Jefferson loved him." If so, it was one of those rare cases of love at first sight and both the older and the younger man, careful not to shatter illusion by repetition, showed, as far as we know, no desire whatsoever for a second meeting.

Calhoun returned to Abbeville to practice law, but for a lawyer's life he, like most good men, had a natural loathing. In 1811, after a couple of years in the State Legislature, he was elected Member of Congress for his district, and his political career had begun. He had no thought as he set out for Washington that he was leaving for ever that country life which he most loved.

---
[1] Richard Rush (1780–1859), politician and writer; son of Dr. Benjamin Rush.

"After two years," he said, "I will be back near my brother Patrick's." But success came too quickly, and with it ambition, and forestalled retirement.

II

The main problem of politics at that date was that of the relations of the United States with the "whale and the elephant," as Jefferson called them, with Great Britain, arrogant on sea with her Orders in Council, and France, arrogant on land with her Berlin decrees. By weak policy Madison, it will be remembered from the last essay, had allowed himself to be led to the brink of a precipice, over which he was very unwilling to go but whence there was no longer any possible return. A vocal and patriotic party of young men—not unlike the Boys, who, eighty years earlier, shouted at Walpole in the British Parliament—demanded that Madison carry his policy to its logical conclusion and declare war on the Government of George III. This party had won large success in the elections of 1811. To it the young Congressman from South Carolina attached himself. South Carolina was at that date the political leader of the United States. To be Congressman from one of her constituencies was to be certain of prominence. And success came to him from the first. The Speaker, Henry Clay, fresh with the blood of a Kentucky duel, appointed him to the second place on Congress' Committee on Foreign Relations, and, at the first meeting of the Committee, he was unanimously chosen its Chairman.

His part in the war was honorable but not creditable. He took from the first an extremely bellicose stand. He made himself responsible for presenting to the President a report demanding war. He was not even sobered into wisdom by the very hesitating support of the Senate and the opposition of many Republican

Senators. When the war came, he demanded the repeal of the Non-Importation Act, as smacking too much of the old Jeffersonian pacifism for which Jefferson was so busy apologizing, and angrily cried out, "We have had a peace like a war. In the name of Heaven, let us not have the only thing that is worse, a war like a peace." For the futility of the War of 1812 he must then bear a full share of responsibility. His excuse is his youth.

Four questions seem at that time to have mainly occupied his attention. On all of them his conclusions were those of an Imperialist. He demanded, first, an adequate policy of defence—especially the building of a large navy, the weapon, as he argued, best suited for the United States. Second, he demanded the covering of the country with a network of military roads, thirdly, the protection of American manufactures—at least, the cotton and woollen manufactures—by a tariff, and, fourthly, "to incorporate the subscribers to the bank of the United States."

It is interesting to note that in his support of none of his projects does he seem to have had much in mind the limits of power which the Constitution allowed to the Federal Government. On the contrary he took pains to pride himself on his superiority to the pedantry of the constitutionalist. "The instrument was not intended as a thesis for the logician to exercise his ingenuity on," he argued. "If the framers had intended to limit the use of the money to the powers afterwards enumerated and defined, nothing could have been more easy than to have expressed it plainly." The necessity of first obtaining the consent of the States, through whose territory the proposed roads were to pass, he waved airily away as not "worth the discussion, because the good sense of the States may be relied on. They will, in all cases, readily yield their assent."

The only danger which he saw in the encouragement of industry was—and it is a point of some interest and importance—"that capital employed in manufacturing produced a greater dependence on the part of the employed than in commerce, navigation or agriculture." On the other hand, industry shared with agriculture the advantage over commerce and navigation that "it produced an interest strictly American." Such observation in 1916, when the whole world could see these two evils, the one peculiar to the commercial, the other to the industrial state, would have been no especial argument of wisdom. In 1816 it was more remarkable. The individual has a natural right to property and needs it for his moral development. Yet it is the unsolved problem of industrialism that the efficient management of a factory forbids that individual freedom and absence of discipline which human nature demands. Thus the great defender of black slavery in the field began his political career by warning his country against the danger of white slavery in the workshop. There is, as we shall see, less in this that is surprising and paradoxical than might at first sight appear.

Some of Calhoun's admirers—and to some extent he himself—were afterwards to try to show by deft straining of words, that the speeches of the young Congressman were in every iota consistent with the later thunders of the great Nullifier. It is a wasted labor. The inconsistencies are patent, the explanation of them not discreditable. It may well be that, if the young Calhoun had been asked to define the relations of the State to the Federal Government, he would have used language not very different from that with which he was afterwards to defy Webster or Jackson. Yet clearly at this date he was not thinking about the problem which was afterwards utterly to dominate his mind. From the first his loyalty was to South Carolina and the South. In 1816, no interest, alien to South Carolina, threatened to dominate the Union and to stretch the Constitution in order to destroy that special Southern life which he so greatly loved. It was, therefore, but natural that he should be careless about State Rights and push forward projects which he believed to be to the benefit both of his own and other States, not pedantically careful to inquire the exact limit of strict constitutional right.

It is surely not inconsistent that a man should allow much freedom to a partner whom he still trusts which he would be reluctant to allow to one of whom he has come to be suspicious. Before his old age the South was to lose its dominance of 1816. And Calhoun—with how much justice will later be considered—was to believe that it was the intention of the North to use her superior voting strength and every advantage which she could twist out of the Constitution, in order to destroy the freedom and life of South Carolina. Not from pedantry but from common sense did Calhoun demand that South Carolina, if she was to be made to suffer all the disadvantages of the Constitution, should at least reap every advantage which interpretation could make it bear. The battle, if it must be fought, was better fought over the jots and tittles of the Constitution than over the blood-soaked plains of Georgia and the Carolinas. Sentence against sentence, speech against speech, there is then a real inconsistency between the young man who had not learnt the dangers of Union and the old statesman in whom hope was almost dead. Yet the inconsistency is to the discredit neither of the old man nor of the young.

III

Madison was in 1817 succeeded as President by Monroe, who inaugurated the Era of Good Feeling. The new President offered to Calhoun the Secretaryship of War and a seat in the Cabinet. This Calhoun accepted and had to resign his place in Congress.

He remained at the head of the War Office until his election as Vice-President in 1824 and the unbiased evidence seems to leave little question of the extreme efficiency with which he performed his duties. "General Bernard, who had been a favorite aide-de-camp of the Emperor Napoleon and saw and knew much of him, and who was chief of the Board of Engineers while Mr. Calhoun was secretary and had an equal opportunity of observing him, not infrequently, it is said, compared his (Mr. Calhoun's) administrative talents to those of that extraordinary man." Calhoun found his office in chaos and reorganized it on a system, of which it was the ironical glory that, as von Holst[1] says, it stood "even the test of the Civil War." He took the opportunity of office to forward his favorite project of military roads, one of the advantages of which would be, he said, the consolidation of the Union.

The War Office had the responsibility for Indian Affairs. Because he was to be the great champion of slavery, Calhoun, in the imagination of many, appears as an ogre of inhumanity, utterly careless of any cruelty that might be suffered by man or woman, if only they were not of European blood. Yet he took a far larger interest in the welfare of the Indians than did any other statesman of his day. Not until sixty years afterwards, when his memory had been stamped to the dust, and a generation, well-drilled in education, had been taught thoroughly from their textbooks that no intelligence ever came out of the Southern States, was it safe for a Northern politician, Carl Schurz, to disinter his schemes and claim the credit for their originality.

Calhoun argued that the Government's policy of ceding to the Indian tribes by treaty certain reserved areas and allowing them to live there in autonomy was the worst possible for the Indians. It deprived them of the virtues of the savage without giving them those of the civilized man, and, if continued, would prove a method of extermination, as certain as, if less pleasingly complete than, that of the humane Lord Amherst who favored the sale to them of smallpox-infected blankets. Indeed it is curious to notice

---

[1] *John C. Calhoun*, by H. von Holst. Houghton, Mifflin & Company. Boston, 1895.

John Caldwell Calhoun

that, if Calhoun erred in his suggested Indian policy, it was in too great a subservience to conventional Liberal catchwords. His desire was that the Indian should, as quickly as possible, cease to be an Indian and take an ordinary place in the citizen's life of the State. He believed only too easily that he could be fitted for this place by education and made certain investigations, as a result of which he claimed that the Indian had proved himself as apt a pupil as the white boy—which well may be.

"The degree of perfection," wrote his employees on taking leave of him, "to which you have carried the several branches of this department is believed to be without parallel." And such is the general verdict on his eight years' work. Yet that verdict is not unanimous. He gave a contract for the delivery of stones at Old Point Comfort to a certain Elijah Mix, without having offered the public advertisement which the law required. This Mix was a pleasant scoundrel, who not only failed to perform his contract, but, when in consequence, during Calhoun's Vice-Presidency, a second contract was refused him, in anger accused the Vice-President of having fraudulently obtained a share of the profits of the first.

Calhoun demanded an investigation of the charge by a Committee of the Senate, which reported that "They are unanimously of the opinion that there are no facts which will authorize the belief that the Vice-President was ever interested or that he participated, directly or indirectly, in the profits of any contract formed with the Government through the Department of War." Yet the story remained to color certain judgments upon his Secretaryship.

Most of the charges and gossip against him may be traced back to the *Diary* of John Quincy Adams, son of the friend and enemy of Jefferson, Secretary of State in Monroe's Cabinet and therefore Calhoun's colleague and rival. Between a gentleman of South Carolina and this very proper Puritan of New England there was little in common and little love lost. "Precedent and popularity," Adams recorded, "were the two motives of Calhoun's every action." And in 1831 he was to write—though, before 1831 came, each was to have given the other many a further cause of complaint—"His personal relations with me have been marked, on his part, with selfishness and cold-blooded heartlessness." In truth Adams saw in Calhoun a dangerous rival for the succession to Monroe. And he possessed a nose well-trained to smell out the moral deficiencies of his political competitors.

By the extinction of the Federalists party politics in the United States had come almost to an end. There was only one party—the Republican—and Monroe would have been elected President unanimously had not one elector purposely cast a vote against him, lest he should share a compliment which had been paid to Washington alone. The absence of an opposition, and consequently of the need for party unity, allowed, as was only to be expected, a division of the politicians into a variety of personal cliques, whose leaders intrigued against one another for the highest post. In the old days of fierce warfare party unity had been imposed by an organization, or caucus. This organization survived into tranquillity. Crawford of Georgia, the Secretary of the Treasury, was its nominee as Monroe's successor. But in all parts of the land the revolt against "King Caucus" was popular. Each of the three main divisions of the country had its own favorite to oppose to the party's official candidate. Jackson, the hero of New Orleans, was from the West, Calhoun from the South, and Adams of New England. Henry Clay, of Kentucky, the Speaker of Congress, was also a candidate.

Calhoun soon found that owing to his youth his chances of election were small and was persuaded to stand instead for the Vice-Presidency, for which his rivals allowed him a virtually unopposed election. He received, when the electoral college met, one hundred and eighty-two votes out of two hundred and sixty-one.

IV

The Presidential election was less easily settled. The largest vote in the electoral college went to Jackson. But, as he did not receive a clear majority, it fell, according to the Constitution, to Congress to select for President one out of the three first candidates in their voting. Their choice lay between Jackson, Adams and Crawford. Friends of democracy maintained that, as Jackson had received the largest vote, Congress was under moral obligation to select him. But, if such a doctrine were admitted, the transference of the election to Congress would be clearly turned into no more than a formal farce. If it was improper that Congress should have this power of selection whenever the electoral college failed to give any candidate a clear majority, then the Constitution should be amended and the power taken from it. But, as long as it was allowed to have the power, it clearly did right to exercise it. It therefore selected Adams, preferring him to the uncouth and irascible Jackson.

Yet there was reason for some suspicion concerning the impeccable propriety of the arrangement. For Henry Clay, of Kentucky, transferred the votes of his supporters to Adams, and owing to that transfer Adams was selected. When Adams, in his turn, appointed Clay as Secretary of State, the eyebrows even of the least cynical could hardly refrain from rising.

The quarrel between Jackson and Adams threw Calhoun into a great difficulty. The supporters of both had united in order to make him Vice-President. Which of the two should he now desert?

He had never had great reverence for what Benton, with Attic felicity, called "the demos krateo principle." His keen logic must have been well aware of the constitutional propriety of Congress' action. Nevertheless he threw his influence upon the side of Jackson. His motive is not clear. It is the custom to ascribe his conduct to vast and grasping Presidential ambitions. That he still had such ambitions is certainly true. But it is difficult to see what he stood to gain or lose by the advancement of one or other of his successful rivals. He may have thought that in the Vice-Presidency he could establish a claim to the succession to the leadership of the Jackson party. But within that party were dangerous rivals. Would not his chances of establishing such a claim in the Adams party have been as good, if only he had seen fit to join it?

The only reason, easy to discover, why he preferred Jackson was that, having sat with Adams in a Cabinet, he knew him the better of the two. In a few years, when he was to come to know Jackson, he was to prefer Adams. For the moment he presided in the Senate and allowed to its members, and especially to the alcoholic John Randolph, who had established by years of prescription and intoxication a certain not dishonorable license of abuse, a freedom of language concerning the Chief Magistrate which brought large question of his impartiality. A newspaper controversy arose, in which, in a manner reminiscent of the days of Jefferson and Alexander Hamilton, President and Vice-President attacked one another under the pseudonyms of Onslow and Patrick Henry.

V

During the last years protection, to which Calhoun had in his youth been favorable, had been becoming more and more clearly the first political issue of the day, and the protection demanded was that of the Northern manufacturer at the expense of the Southern exported cotton. As soon as he had grasped this, Calhoun had changed entirely his opinion upon the tariff and, re-examining the Constitution to see whether it justified these

Northern attacks, as he thought them, upon Southern life, had come to the conclusion that they were utterly unconstitutional.

In 1824 a new Tariff Bill was passed. Earlier tariffs, even that of 1816, had been, professedly at least, for revenue. This for the first time was admittedly for protection. The elections of that year returned a small protectionist majority and the policy was therefore continued. But while the United States were placing a tariff upon manufactured woollen goods, Great Britain was reducing her duty upon imported wool from a shilling to a penny in the pound. As a result, the British manufacturer, even in spite of the tariff, was able to flood the American market with his cheaper wares. And, by the year 1826, American woollen factories, which were chiefly in Massachusetts, were almost at a standstill. A demand came therefore from Boston for a new Tariff Act and a still higher tariff. And in January, 1827, such an Act was introduced into Congress. Van Buren, of New York, already foreseeing himself as Calhoun's rival for the succession to Jackson so maneuvered the voting in the Senate upon this Bill as to make the Ayes and the Noes equal. Calhoun, as Chairman, was thus forced to give a casting vote and to commit himself.

This was highly inconvenient, as his strongest support came from protectionist Pennsylvania, but he had by now been convinced of the determination of Northern industry to live at the subsidy of the South and therefore voted against the Bill.

Under the leadership of Senator Hayne, of South Carolina, the Charleston Chamber of Commerce prepared a remonstrance, denouncing the Bill as unjust and unconstitutional. From Georgia, North Carolina and Alabama similar remonstrances poured in, from Rhode Island, Pennsylvania, New York, Ohio and New Jersey demands for revision. The whole country was divided clearly into its two sections.

In January, 1828, a new Tariff Bill was introduced into and passed through both houses. It received the Presidential assent.

Until now the line between Protectionists and Free Traders had not been absolutely geographical, since there were in the South manufacturers of sugar and indigo, who stood to gain from the protective system. But the Tariff of Abominations, as the tariff of 1828 was called, seems to have persuaded all Southerners that the North was determined on their ruin for her own benefit and that to this general menace a general opposition must be shown.

Eight years before, at the time of the Missouri Compromise, Adams had written in his Diary for 24th February, 1820: "I had some conversation with Calhoun on the slave question pending in Congress. He said he did not think it would produce a dissolution of the Union, but, if it should, the South would be from necessity compelled to form an alliance, offensive and defensive, with Great Britain," which led poor Adams "into a most momentous train of reflection." Loyal to the Union, its friend, Calhoun had from his earliest youth never looked upon it as more than an alliance of the sovereign State of South Carolina with other sovereign States and been willing to contemplate the possibility that circumstances might arise which would make it necessary to dissolve that alliance and to form others elsewhere.

The right to secession was, at this date, taken everywhere for granted. Judge Rawle, of Pennsylvania, in his *Commentaries on the Constitution*, written in 1825, demands no more than that an act of secession should be a clear expression of the will of the people of the State, before the other States be required to accept it. "In such case the previous ligament with the Union would be legitimately and fairly destroyed." At the time of the making of the Constitution, he says, "It was also known, though it was not avowed, that a State might withdraw itself," while in three of the States—Virginia, Rhode Island and New York—the ratification of the Constitution was only agreed to upon this express condition.

The rights of South Carolina were then, to Calhoun's mind, not at all doubtful. The only question was, what was the most expedient policy with which to meet the Northern menace. To him, as her leading statesman, South Carolina looked for guidance. And, in answer to her demand, Calhoun, in 1828, issued his first great political manifesto, the *South Carolina Exposition.* The argument of the Exposition is that there is a permanent economic conflict between the North, ambitious to become industrialized, and the South, agricultural and determined to remain so. For the South needed Free Trade and a large export market in which her cotton could be exchanged against the imported British manufactures. The North needed the exclusion of those manufactures by a high tariff, in order that, freed from their competition, she might be able to build up her own.

Since the North had made up her mind to use a superior voting power in order to force upon the South an economic policy to Northern advantage and Southern disadvantage, it was necessary for the South, before she resorted to the ultimate remedy of secession, to ask what loopholes of self-defense the Constitution left to her. His answer to that inquiry was the doctrine of nullification. He appealed back to the Virginia and Kentucky Resolutions of 1798, in order to prove that the State had the right "to interpose" when the Federal Government attempted to exercise over her citizens any power which the Constitution had not delegated to it. In other words, he advised the people of South Carolina simply to ignore the new Tariff Law.

The first comment which every critic is inclined to make upon such a doctrine is that it is an invitation to disruptive anarchy. If every State is to take upon herself the interpretation of the concessions which she has made to the Federal Government, it is more than likely that one State will be found rejecting, and her neighbor enforcing, a law and there will appear the ridiculous picture of a Federal law, which is law in one part of the Federation and not law in another. To such an argument Calhoun answered that nullification did not mean, as is often popularly supposed, that a State was to obey or disobey each Federal Law at her own pleasure. He was too practical and too logical a man to imagine it tolerable that a State should remain a member of the Union, at the same time disregarding the Union's laws. Nullification was, he said, a method of appeal. If one State thus challenged a Federal law, it would give an opportunity to the other States to consider whether it was or was not desired to confer this power upon the Federal Government. If it was desired, an amendment conferring it might be added to the Constitution by the consent of three-fourths of the States.

To this answer there is an obvious objection. In theory, it is true, a State might nullify a law which she considered unconstitutional—not one which she considered unjust or unwise. But in the heat of party feeling the consciences of politicians might not be strong enough to preserve this distinction. If a fraction of a quarter of the States were to nullify a law, even though it were clearly constitutional, saving their faces perhaps by some lawyers' sophistry, the other three-quarters would be impotent. For they would be unable to reconfer the power upon the Federal Government by a new constitutional amendment. The doctrine of nullification thus made it possible for a quarter of the States in effect to nullify the whole Constitution, provided only that they were unscrupulous enough to do so.

On the other hand, if the States were not the judges, who was to be the judge of the legality of the actions of the Federal Government? Calhoun rejected the popular answer of the Supreme Court, because the Supreme Court was, he said, but the creature of the Federal Government. It was therefore unfit to judge between the State and the Federal Government. Yet the time was to come when the South was to look to the Supreme Court as the most certain defender of her threatened liberties. The obvious temptation, from which the member of a nullifying Convention would suffer, would be that of confusing expediency

John Caldwell Calhoun

and legal interpretation. It may be said that the Supreme Court would be under the same temptation. All human tribunals are, it is true, fallible and may interpret wrongly. Yet at least the Judges of the Supreme Court would be arbitrators, independent to the extent that, though appointed by the Federal Government, they could not be removed by it, and not, as a nullifying State, one of the parties to the dispute. Judges, too, are trained interpreters of law, answerable for nothing but their interpretation of law, whereas politicians, with whom presumably such a Convention would be filled, are on the one hand not trained interpreters, on the other dependent for the achievement of their ambitions upon the favor of a constituency, which, in a moment of passion, could hardly be trusted to keep clear the distinction between their representatives' interpretation of what the law is, and their policy concerning what the law ought to be.

Whether Calhoun was a statesman or a maddening pedant, ready to disrupt a Continent in order that he might have the luxury of an exercise of logic-chopping, depends upon whether we grant or not the original premise, which, in his opinion, made such an exact inquiry into the nature of State Rights necessary—the premise that the North was now determined to use her powers to destroy the economic life of the South—a premise of which the Tariff of Abominations was the proof. Similarly, whether Webster was more than merely a bad historian, inebriated, on the rare occasions when he was reduced to such an unalcoholic *pis-aller*, by the exuberance of his own verbosity, depends upon whether he was right in his conviction that "the plan of a Southern Confederacy had been received with favor by many of the political men of the South."

The fears of either of the two can be easily made to appear ridiculous if they are described too much in the language of conspiracy. Neither in the North nor in the South did a secret band of men meet together and swear an oath that they would not rest until they had accomplished a dastardly purpose. Yet it is true that there had been growing for some years subconsciously in the minds both of the men of the South and of the North feelings which, at about this time, began to be consciously acknowledged and allowed to shape policy. The psychological conflict was very similar to that which divided England, a few years later, over the Repeal of the Corn Laws. The North, the Cobdenites, had soaked themselves in the modern utilitarian philosophy, had come to believe that to prefer industry to agriculture was to be "progressive," that those who clung obstinately to agriculture were unprogressive and that the spirit of the times demanded that they should go to the wall. The South, on the other hand, had only accepted the bargain of the Union on the assumption that the power of government would remain in the hands of the landed classes, who alone have that understanding of tradition without which no society can be healthy, and, finding that power was passing into the hands not only of the North but of the industrial North, she became more and more doubtful of the advantages of the bargain. Webster, himself, was no especial advocate of Protection. Indeed his greatest speech was a masterly vindication of Free Trade. Nevertheless the spirit of Protection had captured the North. It was a spirit which the South could not afford to tolerate. And it was that spirit, and neither the virtues nor the wickedness of slavery, which at this date was the cause of conflict.

Calhoun, as he admitted, was "giving publicity to doctrines which a large portion of the community will probably consider new and dangerous." It was characteristic of him fearlessly to make clear the logical extremity, to which, in his opinion, the State had the right to go. But he by no means advised her as yet to go to that extremity, even though there may have been some force in Webster's gibe that his conduct was "as if one were to take the plunge of Niagara and cry out that he would stop half-way down." In 1828 Jackson had been elected President and

Calhoun, for the second time, Vice-President, receiving one hundred and seventy-one of the votes of the electoral college—eleven less than he had received four years previously. At first all was cordiality. And although, in spite of Calhoun's opposition, Van Buren, of New York, was appointed Secretary of State, yet three out of Jackson's Cabinet of six were generally considered friends of the Vice-President. Calhoun's counsel to South Carolina was then to wait for the accession of Jackson to the Presidency and see whether he would find a remedy for their grievances. Yet he was under no illusions. Jackson's electoral attitude towards the tariff had been a straddle. He had received the votes of the South as a Free Trader, and of New York, Pennsylvania and the West as a Protectionist. In him it was possible to have hope but not confidence.

VI

Jackson's first annual message was as noncommittal as his electoral promises. And soon Calhoun made up his mind that little was to be hoped for from the new Government. Though outwardly the relations between President and Vice-President were still friendly and Calhoun was frequently spoken of as Jackson's likely successor, in truth the two soon began to drift apart.

Of the character of Andrew Jackson many opinions are held. Some see the great hero of democracy who broke the power of the moneyed interest; others speak of him as little better than a savage, who, like a savage, hated all those old things which he had not the culture to understand. Both views, it is probable, are partly right. In his manners, as in his mind, he was rough and uncouth. And he hated alike the city and the stink of cosmopolitan finance, and also the strong local patriotism of the South-Eastern States, based upon a perception of differences whose subtlety barbarism was unable to grasp. These two hatreds dominated his politics.

The quarrel between him and Calhoun began as a personal quarrel. Eaton, Jackson's Secretary of War, used at one time to live with his lodging-house-keeper, whom he afterwards married. Jackson himself had married a divorcée and his temperament was such as very fiercely to resent any unjust persecution of a public man for the supposed irregularity of his private life, but Calhoun, who had through all his life extremely strict opinions upon sex, refused to receive Mrs. Eaton in his house. It might be thought that, whatever the former sin, since they had rectified it by marriage, it was no longer the business of others to judge. But such, rightly or wrongly, was not the opinion of Calhoun. He thus greatly offended Jackson, who took the refusal as a personal insult. Van Buren, a widower and "living," as von Holst says with quaint astonishment, "as a bachelor," seized the opportunity to supplant his rival in the President's favor by ostentatious civility to Mrs. Eaton.

Politics carried a step further what personality had begun. In February of 1830, on a motion brought forward by Foote, of Mississippi, concerning the sale of public lands, the doctrine of nullification was for the first time stated in the Senate by Hayne, of South Carolina. Webster replied to him. Hayne, it was generally agreed, proved himself the better historian. But Webster, with a purple appeal to the great destiny of united America, gave to the Northern cause that comfort of rhetoric which, to an English-speaking statesman, is often more valuable than accurate history.

It was not at first certain upon which side Jackson stood. The Nullifiers had hopes of committing him to theirs, and for this purpose, two months later—in April—invited him to a banquet to celebrate Jefferson's birthday. He saw the trap and was not to be caught. A series of toasts had been arranged, the

John Caldwell Calhoun

object of which was to commit those who drank them to nullification. Jackson attended the dinner. Throughout the toasts he sat stern and impassive. Then, when the volunteer toasts were called for, rose and gave "Our Federal Union. It must and shall be preserved." Calhoun, Vice-President of the United States, could hardly refuse to drink such a toast. He rose with the rest, though "his glass trembled in his hand and a little of the amber fluid trickled down the side." And later in the evening, when he gave to a now uninterested audience his toast of "The Union, next to our Liberty, the most dear," men felt that, though the Vice-President was perhaps the abler philosopher, the President was certainly the better strategist.

The utter discrediting of Calhoun in Jackson's eyes came eventually from a trick for which Calhoun always put the responsibility on Van Buren while John Quincy Adams put it on Crawford, Calhoun's old Cabinet colleague and Presidential rival, but which was probably really perpetrated in collusion between the two. In 1818, while Calhoun was Secretary of War, Jackson had been employed as a General in operations against the Seminole Indians, in the course of which he had, without orders, crossed the Spanish frontier into Florida and captured the forts of St. Mark's and Pensacola. During the election campaign of 1824, in which, as has been said, Jackson was defeated, this irregularity had been brought up against him by his opponents and it had been asserted that the Cabinet had considered the propriety of his arrest. Foreseeing that similar attacks would be made in 1828, Jackson, before the campaign commenced, had caused Calhoun to be asked for the true story. Calhoun had answered that Jackson's arrest had not been considered. Calhoun's conduct at this interview was certainly not entirely upright, for he made it his business to leave Jackson with the impression that he had been his defender in the Cabinet's debates. The truth was that, though there had not actually been any question of Jackson's arrest, there had been a question of reprimanding him and Calhoun, quite properly, had been in favor of a reprimand. Crawford, a bitter and disappointed man, now a semi-paralytic, who lived in retirement in Georgia, always imagined that he owed his defeat in the Presidential election of 1824 to some articles, called the "A. B. Papers," which appeared in Calhoun's journals and which were written by a certain Illinois Congressman, Ninian Edwards, a friend of Calhoun. These letters, of which Crawford always believed Calhoun to have been the instigator, accused Crawford of peculation while Secretary of the Treasury. They were afterwards found to be a pack of malicious lies. Hearing of the interview which had taken place with Calhoun before the election, Crawford saw an opportunity to ruin the man who had, as he thought, ruined him. He played his cards with a not very honorable skill. James A. Hamilton, the son of the great Alexander, the Washington agent of Van Buren before the latter became Secretary of State, was the manager of the intrigue from Van Buren's side. Crawford wrote a letter in which he asserted that Calhoun had demanded that Jackson be arrested. This letter was given to Hamilton, and by him to Major Lewis, Jackson's confidential adviser, the master of what was called the President's Kitchen Cabinet. Lewis informed Jackson.

Jackson was naturally furious. Calhoun, as it seemed to him, had used deliberate falsehood to obtain the succession and, as was to have been foreseen by one who knew the President's character, Jackson in his fury so lost all sense of reason as hardly to notice the amendment which Crawford then introduced into his charge—an amendment which altered falsehood to truth and which admitted that Calhoun had demanded not "arrest" but "a reprimand of some sort."

In spite of Mr. Bowers'[1] able defence it is impossible not to feel that Crawford's conduct was monstrous. In the first place, no

---

[1] *The Party Battles of the Jackson Period*, by Claude G. Bowers. Houghton Mifflin Company. Boston, 1922.

man of honor would have revealed a Cabinet secret; and, in the second, Crawford had himself been far more vigorous in hostility to Jackson than had Calhoun, whose behavior had been, as he wrote with dignity, "an affair of mere official duty, involving no question of private enmity or friendship." Yet Jackson, who judged men's characters by their support of or opposition to the seething projects which happened to be whirling through his tempestuous brain, was quite incapable of understanding such an objective view of obligation. Calhoun's chances of receiving Jackson's support in the achievement of his ambitions were entirely destroyed.

If the world owes any gratitude to Calhoun for his leadership and organization of the Southern cause, his quarrel with Jackson was perhaps providential. He was an ambitious man, and, as long as the achievement of ambition remained possible, he would always have been under the temptation to compromise with his principles in order to help its achievement. Intrigue and competitiveness had up to now played as large a part in his life and dominated his mind as much as those of any of his rivals. But he was also a man too clear-sighted to dupe himself with hopes and expectations which were impossible of fulfilment. After the quarrel with Jackson he knew, even if in brief moments he forgot it, that he could never be President of the United States, and was content for the rest of his life to be the first citizen of South Carolina, giving to her his undivided service.

On 26th July, 1831, he issued his *Address to the People of South Carolina*. Previously he had been content to appeal to history to show that the States were in fact sovereign. In the Address he argued from the dissimilarity of life, interests, climate, problems and population between State and State, that State sovereignty was the only tolerable political system for the United States. And on 28th August, 1832, in an open letter to Governor Hamilton of South Carolina, he rejected the Government's offered compromise of a reduced tariff. To accept would be, he said, to abandon their position. For the action of the Government, far from being a concession, showed protection to be "the settled policy of the country." He went on to restate his theory of State sovereignty and to argue that, if the appeal of nullification should fail and three-quarters of the States should decide against the nullifying State, there would be "present a case where secession would apply."

The Senate and President having ranged themselves in clear opposition, the statesmen of South Carolina made up their minds that their only hope lay in their own constituents. To them was submitted the question whether the moment for the appeal of nullification had now arrived, and the State was divided into the "States Rights and Free Trade" party, or nullifiers, and the "States Rights and Union" party, who maintained the right to secession but denounced nullification as a ridiculous compromise, lacking at once the dignity of secession and the benefits of Union.

Nullification failed to secure a two-thirds majority from the electorate of South Carolina. Yet Congress, frightened at its strength, repealed the Tariff of Abominations and offered South Carolina the compromise of a reduced tariff. The State rejected it as a bribe and, at fresh elections held in the autumn of 1832, nullification triumphantly carried the day. The Convention of the State met in November and solemnly declared the tariffs of 1828 and 1832 null and void, fixing 1st February, 1833, as the date after which they should no longer be "binding on the State, its officers or citizens."

Senator Hayne had just been elected Governor of South Carolina. Calhoun therefore at once resigned the Vice-Presidency and instead entered the Senate as Hayne's successor. The air was full of rumors of the fate with which he was to meet at the hands of Jackson. And, as he journeyed up from Charleston to Washington, crowds all along the route turned out to see him. The erudite compared his journey to that of Luther to the Diet of

John Caldwell Calhoun

Worms, the less lettered to that of a cow to the slaughter-house. In the Senate he had hardly a supporter, as he and Webster argued it out in a debate of giants. But old, alcoholic John Randolph, of Roanoke, almost ready for the grave, armed with five swear-words and the knowledge that he was the friend of freedom, made them bring him down to the House and, finding his view blocked by an offending hat, bade them "Take away that hat. I want to see Webster die muscle by muscle."

There is a popular tale, which admirers of Andrew Jackson have allowed themselves to believe, that Jackson, in a fine bravado of military bluster, threatened to hang Calhoun "as high as Haman"; that, partly owing to Calhoun's fear for his own skin, partly owing to Jackson's unflinching strength and readiness to use force to subdue rebellion, the movement completely collapsed and victory rested entirely with the Federal Government. Victory did rest with the Federal Government, but not as completely as Jackson pretended. It appeared otherwise only because Jackson, a master of bluster, had the talent, like most strong, silent men, of covering up his deficiencies beneath an avalanche of words, while Calhoun, unable to dupe himself and unwilling to dupe others with the hollow appearances of victory which satisfy most politicians for the absence of its reality, with an unflinching realism pointed out far more clearly than did his opponents the defeat which he had been forced to suffer.

Jackson, it is true, did answer South Carolina's challenge by asking Congress for the passage of the Revenue Collection Bill, which gave him the right to collect the revenue by force. This Bill was denounced in the South as the Bloody Bill and Jackson as the "driveling old dotard." Yet the bill was eventually passed, Tyler, of Virginia, the future President, alone opposing it. But it was not passed until Clay had first introduced another Bill to reduce the tariff. And, if to postpone Civil War be to save the State, then it is clear that the State owed its salvation at this time

The American Heresy

neither to Jackson nor to Calhoun but to Henry Clay, who in November, 1832, had returned to the Senate.

If, as Disraeli said, "Sir Robert Peel was Britain's greatest Member of Parliament," then Clay was surely America's greatest Senator. His was an extraordinary character. He was Tadpole and Taper and Rupert of Hentzau rolled into one. In private life a dueller who did not hesitate to kill his man, an enormous gambler, a heavy drinker in an age of heavy drinking, in public life an opportunist, an unscrupulous intriguer, he yet won the love of more men and women than any statesman of his time and on his deathbed could make the boast, which many nobler people might justly envy, that three times—in 1820,[1] in 1832 and in 1850[2]—he saved his country from Civil War. John Quincy Adams, who owed to him the Presidency, found him only "half-educated"—a judgment true, if not very important. More generous is the petulance of Calhoun, "I don't like Clay. He is a bad man, an impostor, a creature of wicked schemes. I won't speak to him, but, by God, I love him."

Clay arrived in the Senate and insisted that both sides accept a compromise, which he would introduce. Jackson was angry. Like the lady in the *Man of Destiny*, Clay had spoiled Napoleon's attitude. But the President did not feel strong enough to refuse. Whether Clay's reduced tariff was one for revenue or protection, he seems himself to have been uncertain. His language varied with the audience which he was addressing. And both sides, anxious to escape from a difficulty, were content that the word "protection" should not be too exactly defined. Because of this Bill a mass-meeting of nullifiers, held at Charleston, suspended their ordinance a little time before it was due to come into force. Yet the tariff remained, to be thirty years later one of the larger causes of the war. Nor, of course, could Clay's Bill bind future

---
[1] Missouri Compromise.
[2] Mexican Territory Compromise.

John Caldwell Calhoun

Congresses, who soon gaily forgot it and returned to a policy of naked protection.

Before the Revenue Collection Bill became law the cause for nullification was removed. The Bill was therefore no more than an abstract assertion of a right and, as it only conferred this special power upon the President for one term of office, was most unlikely ever to become more. Many people in South Carolina, content with what seemed to be a great practical victory, were for leaving the Government this child's game of claiming empty and impracticable rights. It was the argument of those who do not see beyond the evil of the single day and Calhoun was not of them. One of the bases of his political philosophy had been, as he had written in his letter to Governor Hamilton, that "Not a provision can be found in the Constitution authorizing the general government to exercise any control whatever over a State by force, by veto, by judicial process or in any other form—a most important omission, designed and not accidental." Once let this right of coercion be conceded to the Federal Government whatever its limitations and however exceptional the circumstances, and, as Calhoun saw, the days of State sovereignty were numbered. For "the precedent, unless the act be expunged from the Statute book, will live forever, ready on any pretext of future danger to be quoted as an authority to confer on the chief magistrate, or even more dangerous powers, if more dangerous can be devised." [1] It was, therefore essential that the act be repealed before it expired. And when he failed to secure its repeal he was under no illusions. "The struggle," he wrote, "so far from being over is not more than fairly commenced." He was clear-sighted and brave enough not to conceal from himself that there was very little doubt how it would end.

To protect his chest he took to wearing "under his clothing a large sheet of paper."

---

[1] [*Sic.*] "Such powers" between "magistrate" and "or" seems to have been omitted by mistake.

VII

One of the results of the contest for the Presidency in 1824 between Adams and Jackson had been the resurrection of party politics. Jackson had annexed the old Democratic party; Adams in secession created a new party—the Whig. By his quarrels, first with Adams and afterwards with Jackson, by his very clear and distinct policy, Calhoun had cut himself off from both of these. No longer ambitious, he was very well content that it should be so. Though fundamentally he differed from the Whigs even more than from the Democrats, his hatred of Jackson forced him usually to vote with the former in the divisions of the Senate.

Yet during these years there was growing up in New England a movement which was to be more important in the life of Calhoun than any of the questions upon which he himself was voting in the Senate. Up to this time the quarrel between North and South, it is important to notice, had had little to do with slavery. In his *South Carolina Exposition* Calhoun had mentioned "our peculiar labor" as one in a list of those things which made the civilization of the South different from that of the North and the preservation of State sovereignty essential. But he merely recorded its existence, giving it neither praise nor blame. Most writers, it is true, have maintained that slavery, though unmentioned, was the real cause of the cleavage between North and South. They have yet to prove their case. The tariff was an oppression to the South before the issue of slavery arose and it has remained an oppression long after slavery has been abolished.

In January, 1831, William Lloyd Garrison, of Boston, founded a paper, called *The Liberator*, to demand "immediate and unconditional emancipation" of all slaves. In 1833 was formed the American Anti-Slavery Society. Broad-minded slave-owners throughout the South had always been ready to recognize the theoretical evil of slavery and to admit the obligation to try to

John Caldwell Calhoun

work out some solution of the difficult negro problem if they were left free to do so. Slave-owners, for instance, had been prominent supporters of the scheme for repatriating negroes in Africa. As late as 1830 a Congress of Anti-Slavery Societies, to which came delegates from every Southern State, had met at Baltimore.

There may have been a certain half-justice in Garrison's gibe that the slave-owning abolitionist was willing "to assign the guilt of slavery to a past generation and the duty of emancipation to a future." Yet it is clear that his demand for "immediate" abolition—which meant, as he explained, abolition to be brought about as soon as possible and by all possible means—forced such people, whether they wished it or not, to abandon their philanthropic schemes. If slavery was to be abolished without fatal destruction of the prestige of the white race and consequently of all Southern civilization it is clear that it would have to be abolished by the slave-owners, voluntarily and without external coercion. In 1822 there had been a negro insurrection in South Carolina under a certain Vesey. As lately as 1830 there had been another in Virginia, under one Nat Turner, which was accompanied with horrible barbarities. Such, on the principles of Garrison, were the methods, thought the South, by which "immediate abolition" was to be brought about. The abolitionists therefore, accomplishing nothing else, at once drove abolition out of practical politics.

Nor is it right to think of Garrison and his supporters as a band of mild and amiable Quakers, like Benjamin Lundy who had toured the South in 1815 in order to ask slave-owners to set free their slaves and whose tour had met, if with very little success, at least with very little hostility. They opposed slavery through love not of equality but of anarchy. It was but one part of a general program, of which the other planks were teetotalism, communism and extreme feminism. It was a challenge to all ordered society—not least to the Union, which it denounced as "a league with death and a covenant with hell."

At first the North was as alive to the dangers of this brainless and subversive movement as was the South. Towards it she felt the hatred which reason should always feel for unreason. But she hated it also because the manufacturing classes saw, as the only possible result of its strength, the disruption of the Union, the economic unit within which they could sell their protected goods. The idea that the Union would be preserved, and abolition imposed, by force of arms, had at this date hardly occurred to any one. Most of the statesmen of the South were satisfied that the North treated the abolitionist movement with ridicule. Calhoun, almost alone, saw in it a challenge. Himself, he formed his opinions upon reason and cared less than nothing whether he was for or against the spirit of the age—that dignified phrase in which those capable only of parrot-like repetitions are wont to cloak their deficiencies. But he was wise enough to know that the electorate contained few like him. The American, he knew, was by nature repetitive and the philosophy of progress, which was dribbling over into the country from England, consecrated this custom of repetition.

The present abolitionist movement, run by lunatics and in league with anarchy, would fail. But abolition—abolition of other people's slaves—abolition without these handicaps—was a movement exactly "in accord with the spirit of the age." The idea, once suggested, was sure to grow. The New England conscience, easily forgetting that the slaves were brought to the South in Boston's ships and amply paid for, would soon be reveling in the luxuries of moral superiority. While others then were laughing at the abolitionist cranks, Calhoun, with a prescience grown by now almost uncanny, was bidding the South look to her defenses.

He did, it is true, see nothing morally wrong in slavery. Yet not through any love of slavery did he now throw himself passionately into this—his greatest—fight. What he objected to, was

John Caldwell Calhoun

not the abolition of slavery, but abolition, brought about in such a way, imposed by the North upon the South. Such an abolition, he saw, must mean the ruin of white prestige and consequently of all Southern life. Nor did he throw himself into the defense of slavery because it was the easiest to defend of the Southern institutions, but, like a good strategist, because it was the hardest. The South, he had now come to see, was faced with a hostile population, unable to understand the virtue of her civilization. She could therefore only hope to preserve her civilization by preserving complete autonomy. Once she allowed any institution to be subverted by external pressure, all her institutions were doomed.

In January, 1836, two petitions were presented for the abolition of slavery in the District of Columbia. There was no question that, if received, they would be overwhelmingly defeated. Yet Calhoun passionately demanded that they be not even received. Senators from the North assured him that there was no intention of touching the institution of slavery. Senators from the South assured him that, if ever slavery were touched, they would rally to his side in its defense. Neither the one class nor the other could see that there was here any justification for the refusal to receive a citizen's petition, a refusal the legality of which was very doubtful. How much better, they argued, that the petition be received and overwhelmingly defeated in order to teach abolitionists not thus foolishly to waste their time.

Calhoun would not admit such reasoning. He rounded on his Southern colleagues, who had said that "whenever the attempt shall be made to abolish slavery they will join with me to repel it. ... The attempt is now being made," he cried. The petition called the existence of slavery in the District of Columbia "a national disgrace and a national sin." If it was a national disgrace and a national sin in Washington, why was it not also such throughout all the Southern States? "The most unquestionable right," he said, at another time, "may be rendered doubtful, if once it be admitted to be a subject of controversy."

If we admit his purpose, Calhoun was right to go out and meet every attack upon slavery. To allow it to be spoken of as a thing only to be tolerated was the first step to its being spoken of as a thing not to be tolerated. Yet here he probably blundered. The only hope for the preservation of slavery and of Southern life lay in a rigid adherence to every letter of the Constitution. Calhoun could only expect this strictest interpretation when it suited him, if he also gave the same strictest interpretation when it did not suit him. He was from the opening of this battle under very little doubt concerning its end. Wealth and the spirit of the age, going, as they usually do go, hand in hand, may be despised but they cannot be resisted. Yet he saw that slavery would stand no chance if the moral case against it was allowed to go by default and the South to appear as a land of heartless ogres, taking advantage of legal quibbles in order to stand upon intolerable rights. The constitutional guarantees of slavery could only be maintained if a case for it was shown to exist apart from constitutional guarantees.

Calhoun was willing to undertake such a task. Slavery even "in the abstract," he said, was not an evil. It was "a good—a positive good." "Many in the South," he was afterwards to admit, used to think slavery "a moral and political evil," but "that folly and delusion are gone." He based his defense of it upon two principles—one historical, one biological. On the one hand "the relation which now exists between the two races in the slave-holding States has existed for two centuries. It has grown with our growth and strengthened with our strength. It has entered into and modified all our institutions, civil and political. None other can be substituted." On the other hand, "to destroy the existing relations would be to destroy this prosperity" (of the Southern States) "and to place the two races in a state of conflict, which must end in the expulsion or extirpation of one or the other. No other can be substituted compatible with their peace and security. The difficulty is in the diversity of the races. So strongly drawn is the line between the two in consequence and so strengthened by the force of habit and education, that it is impossible for them to exist in the community, where their numbers are so nearly equal as in the slave-holding States, under any other relation than that which now exists. Social and political equality between them is impossible. No power on earth can overcome the difficulty. The causes lie too deep in the principles of our nature to be surmounted. But, without such equality, to alter the present condition of the African race, were it possible, would be but to change the form of slavery."

Only prejudice can deny that there is much force in both these arguments. It is an easy and terrible thing to destroy a society. And therefore there is always much to be said for the maintenance of any institution which happens to exist, even though it be not theoretically the best. If it must be changed, it must be changed carefully. Conservatism is never ridiculous, even if Conservatives frequently are. On the other hand, real as is the equality of man, yet when a country is inhabited by two races, approximately equal in numbers and so different as to make intermarriage between them repugnant, the society must either live in chaos or the one race must be the ruler of the other. And it is very arguable that, the more definite the arrangement of superiority and inferiority, the happier the condition of both races. Slavery is the most definite of all such arrangements.

There is very little reason to think that the negro race has at all benefited by the abolition of slavery. The negroes, in the time of slavery, used, it is true, to look forward to a great day of freedom from captivity and found their main spiritual comfort in the Book of Exodus. It was much as the schoolboy vaguely looks forward to a fine, free life, which awaits him as soon as he is rid of the tyranny of school-rules and able to push out into the world. The reality has been found to have probably about as much, and as little, of the dream in the former case as in the latter.

I have heard negroes spontaneously appealing back to "seventy years ago"—the end of the slavery-time—as to one "when de niggers all was good," and contrasting it with the evil present "when de devil, he go up and down in Montgomery County." There is probably about as much truth in this as in the reverse picture. Certainly there were cruel slave-owners—in the West, mostly, on the Mississippi, in the country brought newly under slavery—though a witness as little favorable to the South as Mrs. Beecher Stowe admits that the worst slave-owners were often Northerners and Lowell's grotesque, "Birdofreedum Sawin,"[1] was, for what he was worth, of New England origin. But in the old slave States of the East, where the slave-owners were a special class, trained up to their responsibility, the descendants of five generations of slave-owners, where "slavery has grown with our growth and strengthened with our strength," there was too high a sense of honor among owners for much cruelty to be tolerated. As a lady once said to Calhoun, "Your plantation is a more eloquent argument for slavery than all your orations." At law the slave had no rights, but public opinion made the master not only master but also protector of his slave. To change the legal, without changing the psychological, relation between the two races would be, as Calhoun said with penetrating truth, but to "change the form of slavery." You have not today abolished slavery in the United States. You have merely abolished slave-owners. You have robbed the negro of his protector. Booker Washington, himself, spoke of "the immense amount of help rendered the negro during the period he was a slave." While it would be unfair to pretend that no such help is rendered to him today, yet it is

---

[1] A character in the *Biglow Papers*, who settles in the South after the Mexican War and becomes a slave-owner.

John Caldwell Calhoun

doubtful if he receives as much from the modern philanthropist as he did from the old slave-owner.

When Calhoun said that slavery was "the most solid foundation of liberty," he did not speak merely in the tedious and sophistical paradox of rhetoric. The negro, unable to recognize the equality of man or to think in terms other than those of master or of servant, is, if free, a menace to the general liberty and equality of society. As Lowell said, with large truth:—

> "Libbaty's a kind o' thing
> Thet don't agree with niggers."[1]

The laws, if they must cater for the negro as a free man, must be choked up with a catalogue of interferences, which would be quite unnecessary if they had only to deal with white men and the white men in their turn had personal responsibility for the black. The question was not whether one race should be free or two, but whether one race should be free or neither. One result of emancipation has been the destruction of the old freedom of intercourse of the two races. No longer, as of old, may white and black babies play freely together.

Calhoun, it must be remembered, defended not the slave-trade but slavery. In one passage, it is true, he does speak of the benefit to the African in being thus transported from his own country to the civilization of America. Yet this argument clearly defeats itself by proving too much. For it justifies not only the slave-trade but all modern philanthropic schemes for educating and improving the native or developing his country. Finer and more logical was his earlier condemnation of "this odious traffic." In general he held no brief for the slave-trade, for which the first responsibility lay not with the South but with England and the North. His concern was with the problem of the mixed populations which, from whatever cause, were found living side

---

[1] *The Pious Editor's Creed.*

by side—a problem for which a solution had to be found. One is apt perhaps to sympathize too much with him because of the cowardly futility of the answers that were given to his arguments in his day by such men as Lowell and are still given by many of those who write about him. He was told that he was opposing Progress—by which was meant industrial development. In the *Biglow Papers*, Lowell wrote of him: "Mr. Calhoun has somehow acquired the name of a great statesman and, if it be great statesmanship to put lance in rest and run a tilt at the Spirit of the Age, with the certainty of being next moment hurled neck and heels into the dust amid universal laughter, he deserves the title." As if he did not know that he was running "a tilt at the Spirit of the Age"! As if he was an opportunist party politician, anxious only to find a cry which would bring him back to office, or a publicist avid to discover what public opinion was and to repeat it in a loud voice! Not until Lincoln was there to be found one who would answer from first principles an argument from first principles. It was the only answer to which Calhoun would have listened.

Yet, at the end of all, one cannot but feel that Calhoun's arguments prove everything but what they profess to prove. They show admirably that Southern civilization would be ruined if abolition were forced on the South at Northern bidding; that, therefore, if Southern civilization were to be preserved, it was essential that for the moment negro slavery be preserved; that Southern civilization must be preserved in order that America should be saved from the industrial slavery which Northern capitalism would in time impose upon it; that, whenever it came to be abolished, slavery, that ancient institution, would have to be abolished slowly and without panic; but they do not show that slavery is good "in the abstract." That it cannot be. It was right to tolerate slavery then as it is right to tolerate capitalism today, but it was not right to praise it. No institution can "in the abstract" be good which is contrary to reality. Slavery is contrary to reality,

John Caldwell Calhoun

because it sets up a social relationship of inequality contrary to the religious relationship of equality and because, denying to the slave-class the possibility of property, it bars it from the full responsibility of marriage. It was an unnatural relationship, depriving the slave of his natural right to property and the master of his natural obligation to work.

Calhoun said—and, if one reflects on the condition of industrial England at that date, one must admit that it may well be true—that no manual laborer in the world received as large a return for his work as did the American slave in food and clothing. But, when the great Nullifier thought that that was a justification of slavery, he showed himself no more intelligent than a twentieth-century Socialist, who with exactly such a bait would by his schemes of compulsory insurance tempt the working man back into slavery. If one reads Calhoun's arguments concerning the benefits of slavery to the negro, one cannot but be struck by their amazing similarity to those of the Labor Party concerning the benefits of slavery to the working man. Of both the fallacy is the same—that of putting all their eggs into one basket. The Socialist would trust everything to the benevolence of the State—that is, of the politician. Calhoun trusted everything to the benevolence of the slave-owner. Now it is not logically impossible to own a slave and yet remember the equality of man. Yet very few souls are strong enough to do it. And the slave-owner, forgetting that equality, becomes wrong in his theology and by consequence wrong in everything else—his economics, his politics, his dietetics—since these are all only branches of theology.

One of the methods which the abolitionists chose for bringing about "immediate" abolition was that of distributing propaganda through the mails to the slaves themselves. It is doubtful whether it would not have been wiser to ignore the propaganda, but, rightly or wrongly, a cry arose throughout the South that this was intolerable. And Jackson, willing to pander to this cry, invited Congress to bring in a bill, making illegal "the circulation of incendiary publications intended to instigate slaves to insurrection." Calhoun would not have the concession. He warned the South not to be deceived. Congress, in this instance, might be deciding in her favor. But it was an intolerable arrogation that Congress should take upon itself to decide at all what publications should pass through the mails of the Southern States. Instead, he demanded that the Federal postmasters employed within a State be not allowed to circulate publications "forbidden by the laws of the said State." Thus would the purpose be attained and at the same time the right of the State safeguarded. Von Holst professes to find Calhoun's proposal ridiculous, because by it a postmaster in South Carolina might not do things which a postmaster in Connecticut might do. It is hard to see what is ridiculous in that. It is not legal to sell a Bible in the streets of Khartoum. Is that a reason why it should be made illegal to sell one in the streets of Boston? What may be printed or sold, clearly depends upon the social circumstances of a community. Where the circumstances differ, the regulations differ.

Calhoun next threw himself into the project for giving to the South an adequate service of railways. The enemy of compromise was here forced into compromise. The civilization of the South was, to his mind, worth preserving only because it was stable, static, agricultural and based upon the judgments of tradition. An expanding civilization, he thought, not thus based upon tradition, certainly perished. Yet his objection to industrialism was a hard and statistical devotion to freedom, not a romantic worship of imaginary "good old times." Machinery was good so long as men could use it, only bad when it began to use men. The Southern civilization, he saw must preserve itself, because it is not industrial. At the same time it could only preserve itself by becoming industrial. It must, to some extent, adopt mechanical improvements in order to protect itself against the menace of a mechanical civilization. Calhoun saw the necessity for such a compromise and eagerly pressed forwards his scheme for improvement of Southern railways.

VIII

In 1837 Jackson retired from the White House to enjoy the leisure of The Hermitage, Nashville. On laying down power he expressed but two regrets—that he had not had the chance "either to hang Calhoun or to shoot Clay."

That succession, for which Calhoun had at one time hoped, fell instead to Van Buren. Calhoun preferred Van Buren to his predecessor, shamefully though Van Buren had treated him in the Seminole affair and little though he approved of the principle, almost a principle of adoptive monarchy, which had enabled Jackson practically to nominate his successor. He usually voted in the Senate with the President's party rather than with the Whigs. Yet he was careful to keep himself as independent of the one as he had been of the other. During this session his main achievement was the introduction into the Senate of six remarkable resolutions. By these his plan was to secure official approval of the Southern interpretation of the Constitution and to establish a precedent to which the South might ever afterwards appeal back. The first resolution declared that every State "entered into the Union by its own voluntary act." The second denied that the "intermeddling" of citizens of one State with the affairs of another "under any pretext whatever, political, moral or religious," was "warranted by the Constitution." The third, advancing a step further, demanded that the Federal Government should "give increased stability and security to the domestic institutions of the States that compose the Union." The fourth especially mentioned attacks on slavery as "a manifest breach of faith and a violation of the most solemn obligations, moral and religious." The fifth declared that an attack on slavery anywhere was an attack on slavery everywhere. The sixth denounced as contrary to the Constitution any discrimination against Southern and Western States in the future because of their countenance of slavery.

These resolutions were all easily passed by the votes of Northern Senators, anxious only for peace and fearful of offending the slave power. But their very strength is the measure of their desperation. Calhoun argued that so strongly was the opinion of the age setting against slavery that only by such means could it be preserved. The retort to such an argument was obvious, and it came from many Northerners who had no desire to interfere with the institutions of the South. "If slavery can only be preserved by such means, if you can only mind your own business by interfering in ours, then it is an intolerable institution."

What did "intermeddling" mean? Most Northerners were willing to agree that, if any of their citizens behaved as John Brown was afterwards to behave and went into the South to raise a negro insurrection, it would be just that the law should punish him. Many even would agree that the sending of abolitionist propaganda to slaves should be prevented or that an adequate Fugitive Slave Law should be passed and enforced, for it was "so nominated in the bond." Further than that they would not go. Did Calhoun demand that they go further? Were the citizens of Massachusetts or New York, free to write or speak in criticism of their own laws, not to be free to write or speak in criticism of those of South Carolina? Again, what did he mean by the third resolution? What by the fifth? In what way shall the Federal Government "give increased stability and security to the domestic institutions of the State"? How shall they at the same time give increased stability to South Carolina's institution of slavery and to Rhode Island's institution of freedom? Where is the great logician who saw at once the danger in Jackson's proposal not to

John Caldwell Calhoun

allow the mails of the United States to be used for propaganda against slavery, arguing that, if the Federal Government were allowed to take sides for slavery today, it might take sides against it tomorrow?

Calhoun, as his wiser critics saw, was approaching perilously near to a contradiction of his own theory of State sovereignty. No doubt it was, in a sense, true that an attack on slavery anywhere was an attack everywhere. Political frontiers are not wholly the frontiers of ideas. People are always influenced by what their neighbors are doing. An attack on Conservativism anywhere is, no doubt, an attack on Conservativism everywhere. The defeat of Mr. Baldwin's Government in England in the election of 1924 greatly weakened M. Poincaré's Government in France. But what would Englishmen have thought of M. Poincaré if he had demanded of England for that reason that she did not dismiss her Conservative Government? Yet it was Calhoun's own argument that South Carolina was as different from Pennsylvania as was England from France. A Federalist might have denied the analogy; a Nullifier could hardly do so.

In a certain sense it is no doubt true that everything is everybody's business. A certain bloodless logical case could be made out, from that truth, for the desirability of a World State in which no eccentricity of conduct and no freedom of opinion would be permitted. But it is a case which we should expect from a Fabian Socialist rather than from Calhoun. The whole admirable argument for the division of the world into these water-tight compartments, called States, is that the application of such logic would be in practice intolerable. It is therefore necessary to hit upon some rough and ready arrangement of what is my business and what is yours and for each of us, as long as it is possible, to mind only our own. State sovereignty is only compatible with a wide tolerance for the opinions that are expressed and the things that are done in other States.

Nor was he content for long with merely committing the whole of the United States to the support of slavery. In 1835 the brig *Enterprise*, bearing on board some slaves, was forced by weather to put into Port Hamilton, in Bermuda. The British authorities claimed that the slaves became free men the moment that they touched British soil. On two similar occasions the British Government had previously yielded before American protest. This was the first of such incidents since the abolition of slavery throughout the British Empire, and because of that abolition they now refused to yield. Calhoun introduced a set of resolutions into the Senate, declaring that slavery was recognized by the law of nations and the British action consequently indefensible. These resolutions the Senate passed unanimously, although there were nineteen abstentions. His doctrine was adopted by American politicians of every party and, when in 1841 the authorities of Nassau repeated the offense of those of Port Hamilton under very aggravating circumstances, declaring free a shipload of slaves who had revolted against and murdered their masters on the high seas and then sailed their ship to British territory, Webster, who happened to be Secretary of State, made a protest to Great Britain based entirely on Calhoun's resolutions.

Yet what did Calhoun mean by declaring slavery to be according to the law of nations? What was this law? When was it passed? By whom? Or is the phrase not legal but theological? Is it one of the commandments of God that slavery should be supported, or at least tolerated? If this is what he meant, it was a foolish appeal for a man to make whose first purpose was the practical one of saving slavery. The decrees of the Almighty are doubtless immutable. Unfortunately the interpretations of them, given by Early Victorian cabinet ministers, were by no means so. And, bad theologian as it may have been, the Early Victorian world was more and more coming to the conclusion that in that sense slavery was not in accordance with the law of nations. On the one hand the only hope of saving slavery lay in a rigid adherence to the letter of the law. For to the unwritten law, the appeal in such a cause would in the nineteenth century be necessarily in vain. Yet, on the other hand, Calhoun was wise enough to see that a scrap of paper, unbacked by moral sentiment, could not avert a revolution. It was the dilemma from which he well knew there was no escape. He is called doctrinaire. If he had been merely doctrinaire he would never have seen the dilemma.

Feeling, it seems, that it was necessary to pander a little to the spirit of the age, he, in 1842, supported the Treaty of Washington between Great Britain and the United States for the suppression of the slave-trade on the African coast. To do so was wise, for it was not essential to his case to support the slave-trade. The only argument for slavery to which the nineteenth century would listen was the argument that it was the best solution of an existing situation. The less he took responsibility for that situation the better was his chance of a hearing.

IX

In the election of 1840 Van Buren and the Democrats were defeated by Harrison, a Whig, famous for his victory of Tippecanoe over the Indians, the log-cabin candidate, whose chief claim to political wisdom was, if one may judge from his supporters' electoral arguments, that he possessed no table manners. Only a month after his inauguration, before this claim could be properly tested upon the linen and crockery of the White House, Harrison died and was succeeded by Tyler, the Vice-President. His qualification for the post was a somewhat mythical descent from Wat Tyler. Wat Tyler, whatever he was, was not a Whig. And not many months had passed before his descendant had been drummed out of the Whig party because of his refusal to charter a bank, and for the rest of his term of office his Cabinet was composed of Democrats.

The chaos of party politics can therefore be easily seen. And it was thought that out of that chaos almost anybody might emerge as the Presidential candidate for 1844. The old days of nullification were now so far passed, Calhoun's predominance in the Senate so generally admitted, that the people of South Carolina began even to mention his name, and he so far forgot his dignity as to issue, under the name of another, a "puff" biography of himself. The ambition was impossible, for he had not even the support of the South. His only two assets were the loyalty of his own State and that of the Irish throughout the Union. In 1842 he had resigned his seat in the Senate in order, as was said, to become a Presidential candidate, but, eight months before the election, on 20th January, 1844, learning wisdom, he publicly withdrew his name and in March accepted instead from Tyler the Secretaryship of State. The previous Secretary, Upshur, had been killed by the explosion of a cannon on board the U.S.S. *Princeton*; and by an intrigue, of which a certain Henry A. Wise of Virginia was the leader, Calhoun was forced upon Tyler as Upshur's successor.

The first problem of that time was that of the relations of the United States to the newly independent Republic of Texas. Wise, ambitious "of planting the Lone Star of the Texan banner on the Mexican capital," and—a distressingly up-to-date politician—of robbing the Mexican Church, invited himself to breakfast with Tyler and forced Calhoun upon the weak President as the most uncompromising and able of annexationists. Tyler capitulated in a flood of tears. Thus did Calhoun become identified with an episode in some ways the most notable of his career.

Texas had been a part of the old Spanish Empire, and had become, by consequence, when that Empire fell, a part of the new Mexican State. Yet neither Spain nor Mexico had possessed the men to settle it and its European population consisted only of a handful of priests and soldiers living chiefly in the town of San Antonio. The Mexican Government had therefore allowed American citizens, nominally of the Catholic religion, to settle in the country. These Americans had, as might have been foreseen, but little sympathy with the Mexican Government under which they found themselves. They claimed that the promise of independent statehood, which they had been given, was violated. And, appealing to arms, by the battle of San Jacinto in 1836 gained their independence, which was recognized in the next year by France, Great Britain, Belgium and the United States. Texas, though its area was that of France, had a European population of only a few thousands, almost all of American origin. It was natural then that these Americans, free at last from Mexico, should wish for inclusion in their old motherland. In August, 1837, they made their first demand for annexation, but Van Buren would not hear of it—and so for the moment the matter dropped.

Calhoun saw the demand of Texas as an opportunity to be jumped at. He was convinced that the guarantees of the Constitution were not strong enough to allow the South to rest careless. Soon the increase in population would cause the North clearly to preponderate over her in Congress, the increase of States cause her to do so in the Senate. Her institutions would then be in danger. Yet how was this danger to be avoided? Either the South must herself expand and thus keep pace with the North, or she must secede.

Calhoun is sometimes accused of having grown, in his blind love of South Carolina, quite indifferent to the Union. The accusation is foolish. Had he been indifferent to the Union he would now have advised secession—for he had no manner of doubt of the State's right to secede. He did not advise it merely because he loved the Union and was determined not to leave it until every possibility of the other solution had been exhausted. For that reason he saw in Texas the salvation of the Union. For if only Texas could be added to the United States, a Southern and slave State, the South, he thought, would be able to hold her own against the North and would not need to resort to the remedy of secession. He was to go by tortuous ways in order to secure the annexation of Texas. But no man judges fairly his character if he cannot see that he chose those ways not because he hated the Union but because he loved it.

Calhoun's opinion, that by the annexation alone could the Union be saved, was known to his friends. It was not at first publicly declared, because it was, he thought, necessary for the success of his scheme to secure the still enormous influence of Jackson upon his side. And Jackson's influence would not be on Calhoun's side, such was his rancor, if he ever suspected that the side was Calhoun's. In 1843 Calhoun had caused to be sent to Jackson a letter out of a Baltimore paper, which, making no mention of slavery or the Southern interests, demanded the annexation of Texas for two reasons—that it would strengthen the Union and that it was necessary for American security, because, if the United States did not take it, Great Britain very soon would. The call of Imperialism aroused the old blusterer of the Abominations, the menace of Great Britain, the hero of New Orleans. Jackson was drawn and wrote an answer to the letter, as was desired. This letter was duly handed on to Calhoun.

The special purpose of this maneuver was to destroy Van Buren's chances of becoming Democratic candidate for the Presidency in 1844. Van Buren, the creature of Jackson, had refused Texan annexation in 1837. He had no influence save that which he got from Jackson's support. And Calhoun confidently calculated that at the publication of this letter, he would either have ignominiously to recant or to defy his master. Either would ruin him politically.

Upshur, Calhoun's predecessor, had been a vigorous annexationist but had found that the Texans, rebuffed in 1837, had used their six years of independence to grow wise in the ways of the world and were inclined now to play off Great Britain, France and the United States against one another, in order to see which of the three would give the best terms. They pointed out to the American Government that Mexico had never recognized their independence. It was more than likely that Mexico would consider their annexation as a hostile act. Were the United States willing to take the consequences of this and to defend Texas against hostile attack? Annexation without such a guarantee they would not accept. Upshur was unwilling to say either "Yes" or "No," and was only relieved from his embarrassment by that timely explosion of a cannon, referred to above. Such was the situation into responsibility for which Calhoun entered in March, 1844. Its difficulty was that the President, or his Secretary of State, had no right thus to commit the United States to war. To other men this difficulty might seem pedantic but to Calhoun it was clearly essential, if one remembers the ultimate purpose of his whole policy, that, if it could possibly be avoided, he set no precedent for an executive officer of the Federal Government acting beyond his powers. He tried therefore at first to soothe the Texan delegates with pleasant phrases. They were not to be thus deceived. They would not accept annexation until he promised that a squadron actually would be in the Gulf of Mexico and troops concentrated on the southwest frontier. The President, he had to declare, "would deem it his duty to use all the means placed in his power by the Constitution to protect Texas from all foreign invasion." There was a saving phrase to the last, for, unless Congress supported him, the Constitution placed no powers in the President's hands.

On this promise Texas signed a Treaty of Annexation. This treaty, ten days later, was laid before the Senate, together with a correspondence between Calhoun and Lord Aberdeen, the British Foreign Secretary, and Mr. Pakenham, the British Minister, which professed to justify it. The gist of Lord Aberdeen's letter was that the British Government would be glad to see the abolition of slavery in Texas made the condition of the recognition of that country's independence by Mexico but that it would use no "improper" means to bring that recognition about. Calhoun's reply was that this statement of British policy and her announced intention to exert influence, even if only indirectly, upon the politics of Texas, forced the United States "in self-defence" to annex Texas.

Von Holst is severe in his judgment upon the morality of this reply. He argues that it is untrue to pretend that British policy forced the hands of the United States, because, as far back as 1837, Calhoun had favored annexation and because Upshur had been in negotiation for it before Lord Aberdeen's letter was written. The first argument is unworthy of so eminent a historian. Calhoun did not say, "I was convinced by Lord Aberdeen's letter that Texas ought to be annexed." He had, it is true, been in favor of that annexation for a long time and for other reasons. But the American Government had not been in favor of it. Van Buren had refused it. And Calhoun, as Secretary of State, was not giving an exposition of his own political opinions but a history of the reasons, whether good or bad, which had led the American Government to adopt its present policy.

The second argument has slightly more weight. It is true that the American Government was certainly negotiating for Texan annexation before Lord Aberdeen's letter was written, and that therefore, when Calhoun said that "they remained passive so long as the policy on the part of Great Britain . . . had no immediate bearing on their peace and safety" and that this policy was "for the first time" avowed in Lord Aberdeen's letter, his statements were not strictly true. Yet it is true that the motive which led Upshur to open negotiations with the Texans was just such a fear of Great Britain—the information that Texan abolitionists had invited Great Britain to buy up Texan slaves and free them, promising in return cessions of Texan land, and that the proposal had been favorably entertained. This news had reached the Government unofficially from Ashbel Smith, Texan Minister in London. There was no reasonable doubt of its accuracy and it clearly made prompt action necessary if the Monroe Doctrine was to be saved. Yet diplomatic courtesy, not allowing it to be quoted in an official document, demanded that Calhoun, hitherto guileless and unsuspecting, "for the first time" received information of the policy which Lord Aberdeen had for some years been pursuing, when Lord Aberdeen publicly confessed to it.

That the British Government disliked slavery, was, as von Holst says, notorious. That it would interfere in order to abolish it, was not notorious. Lord Aberdeen, it is true, said in his letter "we shall not interfere unduly, or with an improper assumption of authority with either party, in order to assure the adoption of such a course." But this letter was, it must be remembered, the letter of a schoolboy who half-suspected that the master had seen him out of bounds and was trying desperately to excuse himself. What was "due" and "undue" interference? Was the acceptance of Texan land, or the granting to her of a loan, in return for abolition of her slavery, a due interference?

What then is the substance of this accusation of monstrous wickedness against Calhoun? The interference of Great Britain in Texan affairs did lead the United States to interfere there too. That Calhoun would have favored such interference anyway, is perfectly true. But it is likely that, but for fear of Great Britain, the Government would never have been able to adopt Calhoun's policy. And there is surely no large immorality in stating—more especially when it happened to be true—that the Government acted from the more popular rather than the less popular motive.

His other sin—that of pretending that Lord Aberdeen's letter "for the first time" informed him of his policy—must be laid to the account of general diplomatic custom rather than that of Calhoun's soul. Perhaps it is a great wickedness that statesmen are required to tell such lies. But it is by no means certain that the cause of the world's peace would be greatly served if, instead, they were expected to add as a postscript to their despatches, "It is true that the first occasion on which you found it convenient publicly to state that you would stab me in the back, if ever you got half a chance, was on 26th December, 1843, but, owing to the fact that I pay a man to report your private conversation, I was aware that that was your intention as early as the previous October." Important as is respect for the moral law, life is, one cannot but feel, too short to linger long over so very drab and uninteresting a peccadillo.

Fear of Great Britain was certainly one motive which caused Calhoun to hurry. Another was that, apart from any pressure that Lord Aberdeen might bring to bear, it was probable that before long the anti-slavery party would get the upper hand in Texas and abolish slavery there. All authorities seem agreed upon this. Calhoun himself admitted it and admitted that it was a reason why Texas must be included in the Union without delay. If he honestly believed that slavery was "a positive good," there is, I suppose, nothing very shocking in this. For those unable to go to that length with him, the only defense is that the South could not expand into Texas unless the Southerner could take his slave with him, and that therefore without slavery the whole purpose of the annexation would be defeated. Instead of righting the preponderance against the South, it would increase it.

Yet if the purpose of the annexation was to preserve slavery in the South, by what argument could a citizen of any of the free States be induced to indulge in a war or the risk of one for such a purpose? Such a man, a model of constitutional propriety, might agree that it was entirely the business of each State to decide for herself whether she should be slave or free. Yet it was unreasonable to expect that he should have a bias in favor of slavery. Indeed, on the principles of Calhoun, it was almost an impertinence, an "intermeddling," if he had any opinion at all on its merits outside his own State. Why then should he be eager to see accomplished an annexation which, he was told, brooked no delay, because, if it was not accomplished quickly, the citizens of an independent State would abolish their own slavery? Even Southern Democrats saw the unreason of such a demand. Calhoun delayed submission of the treaty until after the Baltimore Democratic Convention had met and, rejecting Van Buren, had chosen as their candidate Polk, of Tennessee, upon the platform of "the reannexation of Texas at the earliest practicable period"— reannexation, because of a somewhat flimsy legalism that Texas had been included in the Louisiana purchase. Even with such an advertisement of popular feeling, the Senate unceremoniously rejected the Treaty by thirty-five votes to sixteen.

The strict constitutionalist had here a curious pair of strings to his bow. It was the business of the Senate to ratify all treaties. On the other hand it was the business of Congress to admit new States to the Union. To which House then should the present arrangement be properly submitted? The answer should be, I suppose, "Both." The Senate should first have ratified the Treaty with Texas and Congress afterwards admitted her as a State. But Calhoun and Tyler chose to argue—the position is difficult to defend—that the support of either one House or the other was all that was required. On the second day after the rejection of the Treaty Tyler sent a message to Congress in which he stated that that House was "fully competent, in some other form of proceeding, to accomplish everything which a formal ratification of the Treaty could have accomplished." "The great question," said Tyler gaily, "is not as to the manner in which it shall be done, but whether it shall be accomplished or not." Congress did nothing, leaving the issue to be settled by the people in November.

The American Heresy

The rejection of the Treaty had created a new problem. Calhoun had given to Texas a conditional promise of support against Mexican invasion "during the pendency of the Treaty." The Treaty, rejected, was no longer pendent and Calhoun was therefore freed from his promise. Many in Mexico, well aware that annexation would soon come up again, thought this an opportunity—and perhaps the last—to invade and reconquer a Texas for the moment without an ally. The Texan Secretary of State inquired of Calhoun what would be his policy if such an invasion were to take place. Calhoun was in a difficulty. If he said that he could not support Texas, she would turn, as she openly threatened, to Great Britain. If he said that he would support her, the Democratic party would probably lose the November election, on success in which he utterly depended for the accomplishment of his policy. After six months of prevarication in September, he took advantage of some tales of Mexican tampering with the frontier Indians, perhaps conveniently invented for the occasion, and authorized the troops of the United States to enter Texas whenever Texas requested them to do so. Texas was thus saved from flying into the arms of Great Britain. But many prophesied that Calhoun had only saved her at the expense of the Democratic party's success in the election. Such prophecies he confounded by a bold and very original move. He told the truth.

He told—or, rather, since his position would not allow him to take an active part in the campaign, caused his supporters to tell—the North that the South demanded Texas, because without it she could not feel secure within the Union; that if she could not have Texas she could not allow herself to be still further weakened by paying the tariff of 1842; that if she could have neither Texas nor the removal of the tariff she must find refuge in secession. Before this threat Northern voters, afraid of the risks of Civil War or secession, came obediently to heel. The Liberty party, the party of the Abolitionists, ran a candidate of their own, who, splitting the vote, caused the Whigs to lose New York and Michigan, which they would otherwise have carried. The Democratic party's demand for a frontier along the line 54° 40' won some Northern support. As a result fifteen States went Democratic and eleven Whig, and Polk was elected.

Tyler accepted the election as a mandate. "A controlling majority of the people," he wrote, "and a large majority of the States, in terms the most emphatic," have demanded annexation. He determined to proceed by joint resolution of the two Houses, Congress passing a resolution in favor of annexation, the Senate one which should give the President the option of either submitting the resolution to Texas or of drawing up a new treaty. Calhoun's advice was "to act without delay." The Cabinet was at once called together and a despatch sent off "late in the evening of March 3," inviting Texas to accept the terms of the resolution. On March 4 Tyler's term of office expired.

It is not possible wholly to defend Calhoun's conduct in this. Whatever might be the doubts about the correct constitutional procedure, it is certain that that of joint resolution was unconstitutional. He preferred it to that of a ratified treaty because the resolution required only a majority, a treaty a two-thirds majority in the Senate. Such a majority he was afraid that he would not be able to secure. Yet to explain thus is not to excuse but to condemn. It is beyond denial that he used a high-handed method to evade a constitutional safeguard, because it happened to be inconvenient. The straightforward course would have been to use to the Senate the language which five months before he had used to the electorate, saying to them, "Gentlemen, we consider the annexation of Texas essential to our safety. Either then you must ratify this treaty for us or else we must use our right of secession."

Calhoun's hurry came from the certainty that Polk would not reappoint him as Secretary of State. Himself, he trusted Polk more than did many of his supporters. In order to secure the votes of Pennsylvania, Polk had straddled during the election, concerning the tariff. Throughout the South he was therefore denounced as a Protectionist and there was talk of a second essay of nullification. Calhoun, the grim and wise strategist, was quick to prevent such wasting of ammunition in repelling phantom attacks of nonexistent enemies. He had something better to fight against than election promises. Because of them it would be madness to throw away their great victory. The new Government was too far committed by the old to draw back from the annexation of Texas, even had it wished to do so. And, Texas added, Calhoun calculated that the balance between North and South in the Senate and Congress would be restored. The South could then abolish the tariff and remove her other grievances at leisure. And, as it happened, the tariff of 1846 proved to be far more favorable to the South than any of the previous twenty years. It was not the hour to talk about nullification.

Calhoun, seeing his opportunity, refused the Embassy at St. James', which Polk offered to him, and returned to his place in the Senate.

X

During Calhoun's Secretaryship another territorial problem besides that of Texas had been before the country—the problem of Oregon. The territory then known as Oregon, out of which have been formed the modern States of Oregon, Idaho and Washington and the Canadian province of British Columbia, was claimed by both Great Britain and the United States, and had, as a compromise, been held by those powers in joint dominion. Ambitious Imperialists were anxious that it be brought under unaccompanied American rule and pressure was put upon Calhoun to repudiate the agreement with the British Government and advance the American claim to the whole territory. But Calhoun saw that, if an appeal were now made to arms, the United States would certainly be defeated and therefore lose the whole territory, while, if the present compromise were continued for a little longer, their expansion westward would every year strengthen the American position, until eventually the British would in all probability cede their entire claims. His policy was therefore one of "wise and masterly inactivity." But Polk in his inaugural address threw over Calhoun's caution, declaring the right of the United States to be "clear and unquestionable"—which it certainly was not. And, after an insincere attempt at agreement, he announced in his Message to Congress "that no compromise which the United States ought to accept can be effected." General Cass, of Michigan, an Imperialistic Northern Democrat, angrily asserted that "war is almost upon us." The Jingo press and people caught up the catch-phrase of "Fifty-four-forty or fight." Calhoun was aghast at such blundering. Yet, honest though he was in his hatred of war and his contempt of a statesman who committed his country to a war in which she must certainly be unsuccessful, Calhoun was suspect in his criticism. The Western Democrats accused him of "Punic faith" in having accepted their support in the fight for Texas and refused to give support to them in return in their fight for Oregon. Imperialists jeered that he would have been willing enough for war and annexation, had Oregon been another Texas and lain to the south of the Mason-Dixon line. The jeer was natural and partly just.

Yet the parallel between Cass' conduct over Oregon and Calhoun's over Texas was only partial. Neither was the desire of the one nor of the other to see the territory included in the United States immoral. The population of Texas was mainly American and the American claim to Oregon perhaps slightly better than the British. Cass' folly was in thinking Oregon worth a war to the United States—more particularly a war which would be very unlikely to bring them the territory. Had Calhoun been guilty of the same folly concerning Texas? It is true that he had given to Texas a promise of defense against Mexican aggression. But, in the first place, such aggression, if it took place, would be unjust aggression, for, though the Mexicans obstinately refused to give recognition to plain facts, Texas was an independent State and it was no longer the business of Mexico what arrangements she might make. In the second, to challenge Mexico and to challenge Great Britain were two very different things.

It must be admitted that Calhoun had once said that the annexation of Texas should be carried through without delay, even at the cost of a war in which Great Britain was on Mexico's side. For this his rhetorical exuberance was to blame. But, in serious judgment, every one knew that Great Britain would not fight about Texas, whereas she very well might fight about Oregon. It would too be at least geographically possible for the United States to fight a war in Texas; a war in Oregon, with no road across the Continent, with the United States fleet—such as it was—all in the Atlantic, would be for them quite impossible. At the same time Calhoun recognized that Polk had destroyed that goodwill without which the continuance of joint occupation could only lead to friction. Settlement by compromise was therefore necessary. So, in answer to the bellicose resolutions, he introduced into the Senate a counter-resolution, that an agreement which put the frontier at the forty-ninth degree would not "abandon the honor, the character, or the best interests of the American people." Polk, grateful to Calhoun for saving him from his embarrassment, signed in June, 1846, a treaty with Great Britain upon the terms suggested.

That his motive in opposing war was not merely one of anxiety to prevent a growth in Northern strength, that he was not reckless in his demands for extension of territory even south of the Mason-Dixon line, Calhoun was soon to have an opportunity

John Caldwell Calhoun

of proving. The boundary between Texas and Mexico had never been agreed upon, but Calhoun, when still Secretary of State, had written to the Mexican Government "that it is his"—the President's—"desire to settle all questions between the two Governments . . . on the most liberal and satisfactory terms, including that of boundary. Willing to guarantee Texas against Mexican aggression, he had yet no wish for war if it could possibly be avoided.

Polk, while paying verbal homage to Calhoun's policy, soon made it clear that Mexico would be forced to accept the Rio Grande frontier, which Texas claimed but which Calhoun had never intended to demand, and, in order to avoid any future frontier disputes, to sell to the United States California and New Mexico as well. He sent orders to General Taylor to take possession of the disputed strip of territory between the River Nueces and the Rio Grande. Calhoun was anxious to prevent war and urged that a resolution of restraint upon the President be moved in the Senate. Yet he would not move it himself because he was afraid that if he appeared in opposition to the Presidential policy his influence in favor of a peaceful settlement of the Oregon question would be destroyed. The opportunity was therefore lost.

General Taylor advanced to Fort Brown—now Brownsville—on the eastern bank of the Rio Grande. General Ampudia, the Mexican General, lay opposite at Matamoras. Taylor sent to Ampudia a message that if he crossed the river it would be considered an act of war. As the title of Texas to the territory was disputed and quite uncertain, this message was monstrously provocative. On 23rd April a reconnoitering squadron of American troops was captured by the Mexicans. Polk, in delight, declared that "war exists, and, notwithstanding all our efforts to avoid it, exists by the act of Mexico herself." And on the excuse of a dispute about a scrubby strip of dust and cactus men from Yucatan to Maine marched off to kill.

Calhoun declared with vehement earnestness that he would sooner stab himself to the heart than vote for that lying clause. He "flung the back of his skeleton-like hand upon the desk before him with such energy that men looked from all parts of the hall as if to see whether it had not been shattered to atoms by the blow." The more shallow-minded of Southern politicians hailed the war with joy, thinking that it would bring an increase of Southern strength. Calhoun was too wise for such easy confidence. Texas had established an equality between South and North under which the Southerner could again feel confidence in the Federal Government. For a desperate moment Calhoun had hoped that by the happy accident of its annexation the Union might be saved. But he knew well that a war with Mexico could but result in further vast accession of territory to the United States, that the North would never abandon that territory to slavery nor the South to freedom, that there would be inevitable and bitter conflict for it between the two sections the end of which no man could foretell. The war, he said, "has dropped a curtain between the present and the future, which is to me impenetrable; and for the first time since I have been in public life I am unable to see the future."

How just were his fears, how foolish the confidence of the other Southern politicians, was early shown, when in August of 1846 Congress, on the motion of Wilmot, a Democrat from Pennsylvania, resolved that "slavery and involuntary servitude should be forever prohibited in any territory" which might be acquired from Mexico, having previously rejected by sixty-nine votes to fifty-four a motion to divide the new territory by continuing the line of the Missouri Compromise to the Pacific.

The proviso was defeated in the Senate, but only by Southern votes. All knew that it was the end of the truce—that gentlemen's agreement of the Compromise, to which twenty-six years before the young Calhoun, a member of Monroe's Cabinet, had agreed and which he had since honorably kept. He had loathed the war; he had condemned the reckless and foolish challenge which the politicians of the South had thrown down. But, when the North answered that challenge by the avowal of determination to destroy the balance of the Constitution upon which Southern freedom depended, Calhoun took his place among his own people. Men, filled indeed with a certain crude moral enthusiasm but with no understanding of the motives of human conduct deep enough to enable them to rebuild where they would destroy, were coming out to kill a lovely thing. He who had not asked for the combat, which had been caused by Northern aggression and hastened by Southern arrogance, determined to make one last stand against these forces, knowing well what would be the end of it all and very glad that he was an old and broken man. A Senator accused him of acting from personal ambition. At one time the charge might have been true but now it was too false even to make him angry. "The Presidency," he said quietly—one wonders if Polk was told of it—"is nothing." He went, like a bridegroom whose wife lies dying upstairs. "The day that the balance between the two sections is destroyed," he said, "is a day that will not be far removed from political revolution, anarchy, civil war and widespread disaster." That day, he could see only too well, had come.

It was necessary for Calhoun to make quite clear what was, in his opinion, the nature of the Missouri Compromise. By the Missouri Compromise Congress had agreed that slavery should not exist north of the parallel 36° 30'. Calhoun claimed that this compromise was not a law, since the Constitution gave Congress no power to exclude slavery from a Territory in which it guaranteed equal rights to the citizens of all States, but a treaty. The Southerner, still having the constitutional right to take his slave into any territory of the United States, had agreed for the sake of peace not to exercise that right in certain territories. He had not forfeited that right. And now that by the Wilmot Proviso the North had shown its desire to break the spirit of the treaty, the South too was free from obligation. Desperately attacked, she must desperately defend herself by claiming her every right. When the proper time came the Supreme Court should be invited to judge whether her interpretation of the Constitution was correct. If other methods failed, she would force recognition by closing her ports to all Northern ships.

When therefore, in 1848, a bill for the organization of Oregon territory came before the Senate Committee, Calhoun demanded that the clause prohibiting slavery be struck out. Oregon was, of course, far north of the Mason-Dixon line and it was freely admitted that slavery would never get a footing there. Yet Calhoun was determined, in answer to the Wilmot Proviso, to force the admission that Congress had no power to prohibit slavery in a territory.

The Democratic party had split into two groups—Northern and Southern—but upon this question of slavery in the Territories they reunited upon the catchword of "non-interference." By non-interference the two wings meant two quite different things. The reunion was only nominal. The Southerner meant that he had the right to take his slave into any Territory of the United States and the Federal Government no right to stop him; the Northerner meant by it only his new doctrine of "squatter sovereignty," invention of Cass and Dickinson, by which the people of a Territory themselves should decide whether their Territory were to be slave or free—a thing which, upon Southern interpretation, they had no right at all to do.

The result of Calhoun's objection was that the Territory of Oregon remained for the moment unorganized. This was clearly intolerable and, to remedy it, on 18th July, 1848, Clayton, with Calhoun's consent, introduced a bill by which the provisional laws of Oregon should be recognized "till the Territorial

John Caldwell Calhoun

Legislature could enact some law on the subject of slavery." At the same time New Mexico and California should be organized as Territories and the question of their slavery placed outside the power of their Legislature and rested "on the Constitution, as the same should be expounded by the judges, with a right of appeal to the Supreme Court." Confident that the Southern interpretation was correct, Calhoun was anxious to obtain a ruling which would put those who advocated the exclusion of slavery from the Territory into the clear position of aggressors. His were the tactics which were afterwards to force from Chief Justice Taney the Dred Scott decision.

Yet it soon became evident that, constitutional right or no constitutional right, the people both of New Mexico and California had made up their minds that their countries should not be used as the battle-grounds for the contentions of North-Eastern and South-Eastern politicians. By the catch-phrase of "No niggers, slave or free," they asserted their determination to keep clear of the whole problem.

Calhoun thought it necessary to give to the North a demonstration of Southern solidarity. For no concession would ever be made to a South which was believed to be divided. He therefore summoned sixty-nine Southern Senators and Representatives to meet in the Senate Chamber on 23rd December, 1848, and submitted to them a draft of *An Address of the Southern Delegates in Congress to their Constituents*. It is perhaps the clearest statement that was ever penned of that cause for which the South was afterwards to fight—and the truest. It is not necessary to repeat in detail the reasons why, if slavery was to be preserved, the South must act as she was acting. Today, Northern statesmen, he argued, might sincerely repudiate any desire to interfere with Southern institutions. Yet, as he well knew, the spirit of abolition was soon to conquer the North. In victory it would be irresistible. And then, if she had the predominant position to enable her to do so, the North "would emancipate our slaves under color of an amendment of the Constitution." This emancipation would not establish a relation of equality between the two races where there had previously been one of slavery. Between white and black equality was impossible. All that was possible was that the two races should "change conditions."

To most Southerners his fears still seemed exaggerated. He failed to win that unanimous support which might just possibly have caused the North to hesitate and thus have prevented war. Only two Whigs would sign the Address, and several Democrats also refused. In sixteen years' time those who laughed at his fears were to see the negroes parading the streets of Charleston and singing:

> "De bottom rail's on top now,
> And we're going to keep it dar."

"Many of the most intelligent men," wrote Horace Mann,[1] "are convinced that Mr. Calhoun is resolved on a dissolution of the Union." How unintelligent of those most intelligent men not to see that through love of the Union he had tried every expedient, possible or impossible, rather than advise the South to resort to the plain remedy of secession! Yet it is true that he, who had made it a life's task to save "slavery and the Union," by now saw clearly that the two could not both be saved and that beside slavery the Union was "as nothing." If only he could have got unanimous Southern support he would now probably have advised secession. To advise a divided South to secede would be foolish.

Disappointed of unanimous support from the Washington politicians, he thought that the only hope now lay in the summoning of a Southern Convention. "In my opinion," he wrote, "there is but one thing that holds out the promise of saving both

---

[1] Horace Mann (1769–1859), miscellaneous writer of abolitionist opinions.

ourselves and the Union, and that is a Southern Convention." Unwilling that South Carolina should again assume the lead, he tried to induce Mississippi to issue invitations to the other States to such a Convention. Meanwhile, until Southern opinion was formed, little could be done. He seems to have occupied the next months mainly in the composition of his two posthumously published works—his *Disquisition on Government* and *Discourse on the Constitution and Government of the United States*. Both are masterly examples of lucid précis-writing. They are chiefly interesting today for the strange suggestion that the Constitution of the United States should be modeled upon that of Rome, that there should be two Presidents, one from the North, the other from the South, each with a veto upon all legislation. It is a plan, unworkably complicated, seeming to possess all the disadvantages and none of the advantages of disunion, nor can he have ever imagined that there would be the smallest chance that it would be tried. He left it among his papers, one suspects, so that even from his grave he might refute the libel of those who said that he did not love the Union, and might prove that even in the last hour of despair his quick brain was busy exploring every chance for its preservation.

XI

In 1849 Polk had been succeeded in the White House by Zachary Taylor. At the end of that year the Legislature of California demanded admission to the Union without slavery. The population, which had grown rapidly owing to the gold-rush, was sufficient for Statehood and it was clearly impossible to force upon them a slavery which they would not have. By this demand Calhoun and the South saw the balance of power definitely and finally upset. And, though it was impossible to refuse it, they were determined that it should not be granted until the North had made satisfactory concessions upon all other points. At last, now that it was too late, the South listened to the warnings of Calhoun. Now for the first time she was united.

Calhoun was suffering from an acute pulmonary affection, aggravated by heart-disease. He was not himself able to make that last protest against the murder of the South which he was to leave to the world as a memory. He could only be led, stumbling, into the Senate Chamber and helped into his seat. The shadow of death was, as all knew, on his face, as he, with his hollow and haggard eyes—"a ghost with burning eyes," a child had once called him—glanced proudly round upon that assembly where, as a master, he had now ruled, off and on, for a quarter of a century, and none could be sure that the shadow of death was not also on the face of the Senate and of the whole country.

A little wind perhaps blew in from a window. Amid an utter silence Mason of Virginia rose, a manuscript in hand, to read out this last warning of the great prophet. The scene was almost unreal. It had about it something of the appearance of a funeral, but of one more terrible than any funeral of life. For the corpse himself sat there, silently watching his own interment, and as he watched a clear and measured and mathematical voice read out his death-sentence upon his mourners.

In his moments of high passion Calhoun did not use that spread-eagle, purple oratory for which the South is famous. His speeches rather resemble the inhumanly dry, precise, inevitable reasoning of a schoolman. Now therefore was neither anger nor abuse. His argument ran coherently from proposition to proposition; that there was a special Southern civilization which a Southerner must love and wish to preserve; that the South had at first only joined the Union because her position in it was, she thought, strong enough to guarantee the safety of that civilization; that by the tariff she had been economically so weakened

John Caldwell Calhoun

that she could no more hope thus to defend herself; that the overthrow of the balance of the Constitution would rob her also of political defense. "The cry of 'Union, Union—the glorious Union' can no more prevent disunion than the cry of 'Health, health, glorious health' on the part of the physician can save a patient lying dangerously ill." Can, then, the Union be saved? "Yes, easily. . . . The North has only to will it to accomplish it." But he knew very well that the North did not will it and could not will it. For time would make her not less, but more, hostile to the institutions of the South. There was no remedy either along that path or along any other. He had looked back into the past and, like the old king in Xanadu, he

> ". . . heard from far
> Ancestral voices prophesying war."

"As things now stand, the Southern States cannot remain within the Union."

Two friends led him slowly out of the Chamber, and as he stumbled heavily towards the door neither from floor nor gallery came any sound save that of the heavy breathing of a sick man. "If any senator," he had remarked, "chooses to comment upon what I have said, I trust I shall have health to defend my position." But it was not to be. Three weeks later a message was brought to the Senate that the senior Senator from South Carolina was dead. And to his friends it was told that his last words were: "The South, the poor South, God knows what will become of her!"

XII

His two great rivals, Webster and Clay, survived him by some two years, till they, too, died, leaving to smaller men their ghastly heritage. To Clay, the agile discoverer of the happy, compromising formula, to Webster, the Imperialist, intoxicated by his own rhetoric, their country owes much. But a just posterity would not, I fancy, have given them a place in the company of Calhoun.

Many find it difficult to judge Calhoun fairly because of their prejudice against slavery. It is true that he did think slavery "a positive good" when the best that can be said of it in true morals is that under certain circumstances it is the least harmful of possible arrangements. For that he is to be blamed. Yet his political conduct was based, not on his opinion of slavery, but on the one clear premise that the North, incapable of understanding her traditions, would break the Southern life if she got the chance. The premise granted, all logically follows. His love was for liberty. He had no half-wit's ambition to extend slavery to distant lands for its own sake. He wished New Mexico to be slave only in order that South Carolina might remain independent.

Whatever be our judgment upon his wisdom, the fair historian will say that Calhoun—the later and purer Calhoun, at any rate—was not a man to "turn a coat to decorate a coat," that he never stooped either to flattery or to abuse, to deceive others or to deceive himself, and that these gifts are rare among politicians. Yet, if the premise of his life was false and ridiculous, we must add that here was a verbose alarmist for whose rhetoric the world has had to pay dearly. If, on the other hand, that premise was true, his place, though he was neither impeccable nor infallible, is yet in the first rank of American statesmen. And true it surely was. The new spirit of the age was against him. That spirit he saw as a whole and challenged as a whole. A people, he thought, must live upon its traditions or perish, and industrial capitalism, whose very advertisement was that it was daily changing man's material condition of life, was the enemy.

The old Southern slavery had been, at least, one of the institutions of a stable society. The new industrial slavery was to

John Caldwell Calhoun

be mere brute force acting upon chaos. It had been a dogma of the Jeffersonian political philosophy to be intensely suspicious of an industrialism which replaced thought by superficial culture, democracy by hypnosis, and did violence to reason in holding up wealth rather than happiness as the end of man. For the first seventy years of independent America the normal American thought of his country as erected in protest against this disorder of the will which made men in Europe clamor always for a higher material standard of living, and which must of its nature—since matter is limited and appetite unlimited—lead finally to disaster. Since the Civil War it has been thought normal in America, as in England, that man should desire and should be invited to desire as much material wealth as he can get. Calhoun, in his time, saw growing up that new spirit of the age which thought of appetite as a thing merely to be indulged, not merely as a thing to be feared, watched and controlled. He saw disaster in the growth of that spirit. Was he not enormously right in his foresight? How much understanding of that old Southern life would he have found in the new generations of Henry Fords and Carnegies and Rockefellers? And is the day so very far distant when the new slaves of the North, doomed to slavery, because a man, though he be called a voter and a citizen, who thinks material things more important than freedom, lacks a philosophy which will prevent him from selling his freedom for material things—when these new slaves will read again, perhaps with despair yet nevertheless with understanding, the works and speeches of a great gentleman who never feared to call a spade a spade and a slave a slave?

Webster said of him in a funeral epigram, more exactly true perhaps than its author guessed, that he was "a Senator of Rome, when Rome survived." The phrase is perfect. Jefferson fought against the Christian revelation. To Calhoun, the confident Unitarian, it never occurred to accept it. He, in this no more typical of the South than Jefferson, was a pre-Christian. His was the spirit of those great men, lords, who knew neither anger nor laughter nor injustice, who gave to the world all that mere man can give and who fell in the hour when the world came dimly to guess that what mere man could give was not enough; who, themselves possessing a passion for the Public Thing, were willing to confer on the Empire which they ruled, order, prosperity, administration, roads, everything which the subject could ask—save only the citizenship of Rome. Calhoun held these truths to be self-evident—that all men were born equal and that negroes were not men.

The people of South Carolina took the body of their great king and buried him. On his tomb it was enough to write "Calhoun." Nor would he have wished for more. But, if we must search out for him a longer epitaph, there is none of which he would have been more proud than that jeer of the Northern soldier at the moment of Confederate defeat, "The whole South is the grave of Calhoun."

Abraham Lincoln

I

A FRIEND TOLD ME that he once overheard in a theater in Victoria, British Columbia, the following conversation:
"'Im's one of the six greatest men that ever lived. H. G. Wells says he is."
"'Oo is?"
"'Im. Abe."
"What? Abe?"
"Yes, Abe."
"What? Abe Lincoln?"
"Yes, Abe Lincoln."
Thus is history made.

No appetite is more rare than that for truth. Most men of all nations are wholly indifferent to their origins, and, of those who study history at all, the greater part study it not from a desire to learn the truth but from a passion to hear themselves praised. Only by a recognition of this can the legend of Lincoln be explained. For Lincoln was the creator of the modern United States. For the praise of such a man the market is unlimited. But blame of him approaches perilously near to blame of his handiwork. There is no market for blame.

The Confederate Government, with foresight that has been proved most just, warned the Southern people during the war that "Failure will compel us to drink the cup of humiliation even to the bitter dregs of having the history of our struggle written by

New England historians." The North won the Civil War and the North today has money. Money controls journalism. Journalism controls literature. If you would write about Lincoln, either you may write for the Sunday School and tell the story of the noble leader, unstained by vice, struck down in his moment of noble victory; or else you may give to your narrative a neat spice of realism and artfully fail to conceal how the character of the great President had to it a regrettably Rabelaisian side, and that even in the days of highest moral endeavor he would often tell before the ladies stories which a man of nicer taste would have realized to be unfit for the ladies' ears. For by this more subtle flattery Babbitt is shown that heroism, saintliness, success, patriotism may easily be combined with Rabelaisianism—just such a Rabelaisianism as Babbitt would find it most inconvenient to banish from his own character. He sees himself reflected in Lincoln.

Of Lincoln's private life it will be sufficient to say that from a close scrutiny he emerges with credit and on the whole lovable. The only unattractive trait is that of excessive ambition. But certainly he does not emerge the Abraham Lincoln of the child's picture book, a loving son and husband. Of the nearer domestic relationships only in that of father was he at all successful. Between himself and his wife there was nothing in common, and what chance of intimacy would otherwise have existed was not improved by his constant comparison of her, greatly to her disadvantage, to his first and dead fiancée, Anne Rutledge. "My heart lies buried there," he said of Anne's grave. It was not intended as a compliment to Mrs. Lincoln.

To the memory of his dead mother he always professed great devotion. It emphasized the contrast of his sentiments to his living father, to whom, when summoned to his deathbed, he replied in refusal that an interview would probably be equally painful to both parties. He kept through life both the directness and roughness of the backwoods.

Abraham Lincoln
From an old engraving

The American Heresy

It is the custom to speak of him as the stern enemy of corruption and a pious Christian. He was neither the one nor the other. The most that can be fairly said is that in politics he was a little less lax, in religion a little less silly, than many of his contemporaries. He did not look on himself as the possessor of any special mandate either for honesty or for orthodoxy. His administration stands certainly in creditable contrast to the public auctioning of a nation which did duty for government in the years of reconstruction after his death. No one has ever suggested that the Presidential pockets were themselves lined—and that is much. Yet on political honesty his opinion was, it seems, both cynical and sensible—that he had on his hands a quarrel large enough to occupy his whole energy and that he would not wantonly add to it other quarrels by upsetting established customs of peculation. Therefore he perpetuated Andrew Jackson's spoils system by which every office from President to village postmaster was redistributed as a reward for political services when a new President came to power. And when Benjamin Butler politely threatened with rape any of the ladies in New Orleans who did not show respect to the United States flag—"she should be treated, and held liable to be regarded, as a woman of the town plying her avocation," was the exact wording—Lincoln, though he transferred him from his post, yet accepted the argument that the man's political influence and the power of blackmail which he possessed were too great to justify a prosecution.

In religion he was never a Christian. At the age of twenty-five he was an atheist and had written, under the influence of Tom Paine and Volney,[1] an essay "to abolish Christianity." A wise friend prevented him from the indiscretion of publication. Yet he remained what was then known as a free-thinker—that is to say, he rejected the possibility of miracles and maintained that

---

[1] Constantin François Chassebœuf, Comte de Volney (1757–1820), author of *Les Ruines*, etc.

Abraham Lincoln

"God was not a person." He is not to be largely blamed for finding that refuge of skepticism which is so much nobler than a false faith. His opinions after all were no sillier than those of many men with a hundred times his opportunities. Yet, when Lord Charnwood[1] writes that "it would be unprofitable to inquire what he meant by this expression," one can only ask, "What inquiry could be more profitable?" For a man's ideas are his religion, or the lack of it.

The first temptation is to interpret such a phrase as a confession of pantheism—a polite atheism—and to suggest that Lincoln thought that God was not a person in the sense in which Chief Justice Taney thought that a negro was not a person—that is, that He had not got a vote and might therefore be omitted from electoral calculations. This theory the Second Inaugural Address, and other evidence, does not allow us to sustain. Lincoln had certainly, at least towards the end of his life, a real faith in God. What part of the Christian conception of the Deity did he reject?

No doubt in rejecting the personality of God he imagined himself to be rejecting a bespectacled, middle-aged gentleman, sitting on the top of a cloud. To such a Jehovah the provincial pulpit of his day had introduced him, to a God Who placed some predestined beetles at a certain distance from His throne, bidding them crawl back to Him and knowing very well that they would be unable to do so. Yet his faith lacked more than an understanding of a few doctrinal definitions. And the more that we search his so-called religious utterances, the more do we find that he possessed a strong moral sense but no religious sense at all—that is, he had, it seems, no feeling or faith that this world was other than self-sufficient or that a living God would afterwards pass judgment for the acts of this life. A few experiments at table-turning were his only traffic with a Heaven or Hell. Who understands this understands much of modern

---

[1] *Abraham Lincoln*, by Lord Charnwood.

America, of which this man is so largely the pattern. For of that country the dominant note is the sufficiency of one world.

Nor is it possible to understand properly the Civil War unless we contrast this lack of faith with the strong presence of it in the chief leaders and patterns of the South. When Lee said, "In a mixed community of black and white, slavery, under Christianity, is the best system," the words "under Christianity" were not a mere vague affirmation of the reality of moral values. By the word "under" he meant that the religious relation of equality must transcend the social relation of inequality. The system of slavery, he felt, was only to be tolerated in a society where the slave-owner lived with the knowledge ever present before him that he would be called upon one day to give an account of his stewardship, receiving for it reward or punishment. Calhoun, it is true, was an exception. Yet such a faith had Lee; such a faith had Beauregard, that fine Roman soldier; such a faith, too, of a more fiery sort, had Stonewall Jackson, the seventeenth-century Covenanter, and Jefferson Davis, the vague High Churchman.

Lincoln had departed then, far from the Protestant tradition in theology. He had departed as far in ethics. And it is of the virtues—the real virtues—of his private life that his Puritan admirers cannot bear to hear. For they were not the Puritan virtues. Yet in this side of him a normal instinct will find most that is attractive. It is possible to forget his vulgar and violent itch for competitive success as we think of him in the early days, lounging over the bar of some western frontier saloon, swapping dirty stories into the small hours of the morning, or breaking his usual abstinence by hoisting a whisky-barrel on his knees and drinking from the bung-hole. He told the Presbyterians of New Salem that "if we take habitual drunkards as a class, their heads and their hearts will bear an advantageous comparison with those of any other class." It would have gone ill for the North at Appomattox had he held any other opinion.

Abraham Lincoln

It is often amusing to speculate concerning the great, if they had not happened to be historical, by what novelist they would have been created. Of Lincoln there can be no doubt. If God had not made him, Charles Dickens must certainly have done so. Lincoln with his preposterous hat, his uncouth form, his long, lanky, ill-fitting suit, his irrepressible conversation, looking, as was once said, "like a country farmer riding into town wearing his Sunday clothes"—he is of the flesh of Samuel Weller and Mr. Micawber, and at the last he will be found not at Gettysburg nor the White House nor even Springfield, but at the enormous inn at the world's end, where all the company of Pickwick for ever meets and tells unending stories till the death of time. It is a great company.

II

Of Lincoln's early life not much need be said. He followed the Western round of "tinker, tailor, soldier, sailor." For a time he served in the Indian Black Hawk War. His prospective captain was a certain Fitzpatrick, against whom he had a grudge because of a debt of two dollars which Fitzpatrick had failed to pay. When the company had to reëlect its captain, Lincoln therefore stood against Fitzpatrick and was to his surprise successful. The drill-book education of the future Commander-in-Chief was incomplete. Not knowing the command for putting a body of men on the march into single file in order that it might get through a gate, he once announced, "The company is dismissed for two minutes, when it will fall in again on the other side of the gate." His career was brief. He was soon afterwards cashiered because his whole company appeared on parade intoxicated—a rare military distinction.

From 1834 to 1842 he sat as a Whig in the State Legislature of Illinois. From 1842 to 1846 he took no active part in politics. In

1846, the year of the Mexican War, he was elected to Congress as one of the members from Illinois. In that war he, like most Whigs, played a dubious part. He opposed it, denounced it, but, since the country had got entangled in it, voted the supplies for its prosecution and, as a consequence, suffered the invariable fate of Asquithian Liberalism. At the next election the Whigs lost the seat.

In 1849 he tried, but failed, to get from Zachary Taylor, the new President, a Commissionership in the General Land Office. Thus, during the important years of 1848 and 1850 when the problems of the new Territories were bringing the slavery question up to fighting pitch, while the world thundered Lincoln practiced law at Springfield, Illinois, and in the evenings fled for refuge from his wife's conversation to the less repulsive study of the works of Euclid. "When Sundays came, instead of going home, as did his companions, he lingered to pursue his Socratic studies among the loungers of the tavern."[1]

1858 saw his return to public life. The occasion of this return was the election for a Senatorial vacancy in the representation of Illinois, for which he and Stephen Douglas, the Democratic leader, were candidates. Lincoln stood, not, as of old, as a Whig but as a Republican, a member of that new party which had been formed to oppose the extension of slavery and the repeal of the Missouri Compromise, for which Douglas had been responsible in his bill for the admission of Kansas and Nebraska into the Union. Of the circumstances and aims of that party some account must be given.

The famous Compromise by which, in 1820, Henry Clay attempted to preserve the Union by a removal of slavery from controversial politics has already been described. As Calhoun saw, the whole question was inevitably reopened by the immense acquisition of territory in 1848. Even if such a reopening had not

---

[1] *The True Abraham Lincoln*, by William Eleroy Curtis. J. B. Lippincott Company. Philadelphia, 1903.

been inevitable, the proposal of Wilmot, which Lincoln, among others, supported, and the demand of California to be admitted into the Union as a free State, would have made it certain. To quiet this conflict, Clay, in his old age, gave to his country the second Compromise by which the South, in return for the admission of free California, was granted an effective Fugitive Slave Act and the legalization of slavery in Utah and New Mexico.

The Compromise of 1820 had been a compromise in the sense that the leaders of both North and South accepted it. The Compromise of 1850 was not such a compromise. Webster supported it and the Northern States. It received some support in the South. By the combination of these votes it was forced through Congress and the Senate. But even in its passage it was hailed by the dying and awful mockery of old Calhoun. At his tomb it was to fall.

In 1850 Calhoun died. The leading figure was now Stephen Douglas, a Democrat from Illinois, the rival of Lincoln. Douglas' main interest was not in slavery upon the one side nor the other but in the great Imperialistic advance of the American nation to the Pacific Ocean. That dream had captured his mind, just as the minds of men in England were captured by the poetry of Imperialism at the end of the last century. To him therefore it was a great relief that this irrelevant cause of discord in one nation had, as he thought, been settled by the Compromise of 1850. How it had been settled it can hardly have been within his curiosity to inquire. He turned himself to the more proper task of organizing an Imperial continent.

For this purpose he produced in 1854 a bill for the establishment of territorial governments in Kansas and Nebraska. Both these Territories were to the north of the line 36° 30' and therefore, it would seem, should naturally be free. So in the first draft of the bill it was provided that they should be.

Yet afterwards he, as chairman of the committee, accepted an amendment of one Dixon, of Kentucky, by which the validity of the Missouri Compromise was denied and the question whether the Territories be slave or free was to be decided by the votes of the inhabitants of each Territory. This amendment was passed. The result was that the great problem of how to obtain sufficient settlers from the East to populate the new Territories at once solved itself. It became a point of honor to both North and South to carry the Territories for their interest. Migration was organized and subsidized by slavery and anti-slavery societies with an efficiency and lavishness with which Government could never compete. Douglas, with satisfaction, saw his Territories quickly filling up.

Mr. Rhodes,[1] it is true, explains Douglas' conduct as that merely of an unscrupulously ambitious man. He was anxious, he thinks, to make some bold bid which would establish him more firmly in Southern favor than any other Northern Democrat. Douglas was a politician and, no doubt, this motive was present to his mind. To pretend that it was the sole motive is ungenerous to the man who was brave enough to risk the enmity of the whole South at the time of the Lecompton incident. He supported the amendment because he honestly thought that it would make it easier to attract settlers to the Territories. Had he opposed it, the Bill would have been held up and the whole settlement of Nebraska indefinitely postponed.

Douglas himself had enormously the instinct of a European, the instinct that the European must, to preserve his superior form of society, rule the non-European, if both are found in numbers in the same State. He would, he said, be on the side of the white man in any controversy with the black and on the side of the black in any controversy with a crocodile. "If Americans were fit to rule themselves, surely they were fit to rule a few niggers." But whether the white man's superiority was or was not expressed in the institution of slavery, he was quite indifferent.

---

[1] *History of the United States*, by James Ford Rhodes. The Macmillan Company. New York, 1906.

He cared not, he said, "whether slavery was voted up or voted down." He cared only that the Territories should be populated. Douglas' blunder was to estimate the interest of others in slavery by his own. He did not think that they would care enough about it to fight about it. In that he was wrong and in the tale of murder and counter-murder which was the history of "bleeding Kansas" is written the awful commentary on squatter sovereignty.

III

Douglas was able to carry his amendment, but only in face of large opposition. In that controversy died the Whig party and the opposition to Douglas, a hotch-potch of seceding Democrats and old Whigs, emerged as a new political party, the Republican, which offered itself to the electorate as the supporter of a high tariff and the resolute opponent of any extension of slavery. One of the local leaders of this party was Abraham Lincoln. As such he returns to public life.

It is possible to understand very little of the subsequent history either of Lincoln or of America unless the two planks of the Republican party are clearly grasped. The man who writes that the Republican party was formed in order to advocate a certain policy towards slavery and mentions nothing of its policy towards the tariff, makes nonsense of his story. The connection between these two things and the reason for that connection can be clearly understood by one who has followed the story of Calhoun. The capitalist financier of the east coast who could not face free English competition to his manufactures wished to live at the subsidy of the cotton-growing, exporting, slave-owning States of the South.

The Republican party, as does every political party, contained men who belonged to it from a variety of motives. There were, no doubt, some who cared nothing for the tariff and perhaps did not understand the arguments for or against it, and cared only that the area of slavery should not be extended. But these were not the men who made the party. The party was made by people who feared that the policy of Douglas would wreck the Union and that, if the South broke out of the Union, she would throw down her tariff barrier against English goods which would thus compete within that area upon equal terms with those of the Eastern manufacturer. This the capitalist could not afford to allow her to do. To ensure the adequate defense of his interests he formed the Republican party, in the ranks of which Lincoln enrolled himself.

It was a purely Northern party which did not attempt to appeal to the Southern voter. Its economic program was nakedly "Make the Southerner pay." It was a challenge to the South. To that challenge the South made a reply. Her reply was given by Calhoun, as we have seen, at the first suggestion of the Wilmot Proviso. It was to question the validity of the Missouri Compromise. The Missouri Compromise was, as has been said, in the Southern view, not a law but a treaty. By that treaty the South, through her plenipotentiaries, had agreed for the sake of peace and as a part of a bargain not to exercise to the full her constitutional privileges. As Jefferson Davis said, this Compromise was accepted simply as a method of peace, "however it may be condemned as the assumption by Congress of a function not delegated to it." It had received such "a quasi-ratification by the people of the States as to give it a value which it did not originally possess." The Southern privileges in law remained.

In 1854 that treaty, of whose termination the Wilmot Proviso had given notice, came finally to an end for two reasons. It came to an end because Douglas and Congress virtually abrogated it by inviting slavery into Kansas and Nebraska, but also because the program of the Republican party announced that the period of treaty was at an end and that the North, or at least an important part of it, intended to exercise to the full every power that it could gather from the Constitution in order to win an economic victory over the South. In the Presidential platform for 1856 the Republicans had denounced "those twin relics of barbarism, polygamy and slavery." The conjunction was both provocative and stupid. For "a relic of barbarism"—an institution which, coming down from other times, "has grown with our growth and strengthened with our strength"—there is always much to be said. It must be handled tenderly. Slavery was such a relic. Polygamy, the theological experiment of Mormon Utah, had no right to such respectable abuse. It was no more than the latest fad of the latest religion, the last step in evolutionary progress. To dignify such a thing as "a relic of barbarism" was a misuse of language; to compare it to Southern slavery was an insult.

Soon after this a test case caused the Supreme Court to give its judgment upon the validity of the Southern interpretation of the Constitution. Before the repeal of the Missouri Compromise a doctor had taken his slave, Dred Scott, into the territory to the north of 36° 30′. Dred Scott was persuaded to sue his master in the Federal Court and to claim that, by virtue of the Missouri Compromise, he was now a free citizen.

The decision in the Supreme Court was given by Chief Justice Taney. Taney made it clear that, if he had been a private person expressing a political opinion about what ought to be, his answer would have been very different, but, as the interpreter of the Constitution, he could not but admit that the Missouri Compromise was from the first unconstitutional, that Congress was acting *ultra vires* in attempting to prohibit slavery in a Territory and that Dred Scott must therefore be returned to his master. With this judgment five judges agreed and two disagreed.

Mr. Rhodes argues that Taney's was a one-sided and sophistical interpretation of the Constitution and claims that, until 1840, no one even dreamed of thus interpreting it. But surely in his argument there is a misunderstanding. Before 1840 no Southerner, it is true, dreamed of claiming his extreme rights under the Constitution, nor was Taney, merely a legal interpreter, advising him to claim them in 1857. But the Southerners had only not claimed that right because they had not doubted that, if they thought themselves forced to it, their right of secession would be allowed and therefore they did not feel themselves at danger within the Union. The more it came to be doubtful whether they would be allowed peaceably to secede, the more was it necessary to insist upon every right which the Constitution granted to them.

For Dred Scott no tears need be shed. He had served his purpose and soon passed by inheritance into the hands of a Massachusetts Congressman by whom he was liberated. More important is it that the South had completely won. One main plank in the Republican platform had been kicked clean away. For the ultimate interpreter of the American Constitution is the majority vote of the Supreme Court. From it alone there is no appeal. By its interpretation Congress could not prohibit slavery in a Territory. In order that Congress should prohibit slavery in a Territory the Republican party had been formed. By the decision they had, it seemed, been driven into a naked defense of high tariffs and nothing else.

The reply of the Republican party was bold, unexpected and debatable. It was to defy the Supreme Court. They declared that they would accept the Dred Scott decision as a particular decision but not as an interpretation of the Constitution. In the most literal sense they took the law into their own hands. It is true that they pretended a justification in the appeal to the dealings of Andrew Jackson with the National Bank during his Presidency. It was claimed that Andrew Jackson had said that, though the Supreme Court had declared the Bank constitutional, he thought it unconstitutional. So he did. What of it? Though President of the United States, he was an ignorant man, and wrong. The weakness of this appeal was shown by the necessity under which both Seward, who was generally thought of as the leader of the party, and Lincoln felt themselves of trying to buttress up their refusal to accept the decision by unsubstantiated charges of collusion between Taney, Buchanan and Douglas.

Yet the Republican position could be held in good faith. All turned upon the legal question of the powers of the Supreme Court. And, if any one wanted proof that difference of opinion was possible concerning those powers, he had only to appeal back to the *South Carolina Exposition*. Taney and his colleagues, it was argued, in so far as they professed to decide more than the immediate question submitted to them, could only be speaking *obiter*. Yet to what conclusion did such an appeal lead? If the Supreme Court could not interpret the Constitution, nobody could interpret it. And where there is no interpreter there is no sovereign. "It returns to the sword." The Supreme Court had been, it must be remembered, the Northern refuge from nullification. Calhoun, from his grave, could now answer, "We tried to obtain our rights by nullification. You refused them to us and sent us to the Supreme Court. The Supreme Court gives verdict in our favor and you waive its verdict away as an *obiter dictum*."

If the Supreme Court is the interpreter of the Constitution, then what the Supreme Court thinks constitutional, is constitutional. The one phrase is shorthand for the other. And when Jackson came to break the bank, he broke it not by declaring it unconstitutional but by withdrawing from it all the national deposits, a right which the Constitution had assigned to the President.

Those who live according to our form of life, the South could now say, are in a minority. Our guarantee that within the United States the majority will not use its power to destroy that life lies only in the Constitution and its interpretation by the

Supreme Court. If the North will no longer accept general rulings of the Supreme Court as general rulings, we have no longer any guarantee. If, as is sometimes said but not, I think, proved, Jackson formed his opinion upon the advice of Taney, then his Attorney-General, this in no way alters the legal position but merely shows evidence of a certain ironic laughter among the Gods. The declaration was one, if not of war, at least of hostility. At its birth the Republican party had announced that it would use every constitutional means to force the South into economic vassalage. Now it was prepared to use every means, constitutional or unconstitutional, upon which it could lay its hands.

The position of the South and of the Republicans was now clear. But there was a third group of opinion—the Northern Democrats—whose support was obviously of great importance to either side. That party was the party of one man—Stephen Douglas.

Stephen Douglas, as we have seen, cared enormously for the Union and nothing at all for slavery. He had attempted to drive slavery out of politics by the doctrine of squatter sovereignty, and had failed. The only effect had been to destroy what President Pierce had called "the sense of repose and security restored to the public mind throughout the confederacy." Was not this a Heaven-sent deliverance to him? The Southern Democrats were now the constitutionalist party. Impetuously he declared for them, accepted the Dred Scott decision, proclaimed that by it the whole question of slavery had been taken out of party politics and denounced the disloyalty of all those who would still introduce it there.

The bold reply of the Republican party to the challenge of the South could conceal from no man of intelligence that, at the beginning of 1857, Stephen Douglas was the master of America. The rump of the old Whig party was insignificant. He was the one Northerner of the first rank who stood outside the Republican party, and stood therefore for obedience to the Constitution. With such a program and the support of the South it seemed certain that in 1860 he must be elected President.

Towards the end of 1857 there did indeed arise an issue upon which he felt himself forced to oppose a certain body of Southern opinion. A convention of slave-owners had met at Lecompton in Kansas, declared itself representative of the citizens of the Territory and demanded the recognition by the Union of a slave-owning Constitution. The President, Buchanan, was disposed to grant the demand. Douglas, informed of the bogus nature of the convention, for honesty and the credit of his principle of squatter sovereignty opposed it. Yet this was no disagreement on principle but merely on the *bona fides* of individuals. It was not in itself sufficient to lose Douglas the support of the South in three years' time. At the beginning of 1858 the Republicans still lacked salvation.

IV

It was the year of their last chance. For Stephen Douglas was one of the Senators for Illinois and it happened that in this year he had to seek reëlection. Clearly the Republicans must use the opportunity of the campaign either to embarrass their opponent or to make terms with their conqueror.

Many, among them Seward of New York, were in favor of the latter policy. They argued that, though Douglas supported the Union for a reason different from that of the Republicans— for he cared nothing about a tariff and was, if anything, a Free Trader—yet his Imperialism made the Union very safe in his keeping. By his protest at Lecompton he had shown that he would insist on an honest interpretation of squatter sovereignty. It was the most for which they could hope. Let them make terms while they could. This was probably the doubtful but dominant opinion of east-coast Republicans. In the West it was different. The West could gain nothing from the tariff. There, if a man had joined the Republican party, he had joined it because he believed slavery to be wrong and objected to the countenance of it by the Federal Government which an extension of its area would imply. To such a countenance Douglas was gaily indifferent. Therefore Douglas must be opposed.

The man who was chosen to oppose him was Abraham Lincoln of Springfield, and the election campaign consisted of a series of public debates between the two candidates. From a study of them much may be profitably learned. It has been the fashion to praise both the philosophic intelligence and the good manners of the two rivals. Certainly such praise is deserved. "I have known," said Douglas in his first speech—and it was the tone in which, with few exceptions, he debated throughout—"personally and intimately, throughout a quarter of a century, the worthy gentleman who has been nominated for my place and I will say that I regard him as a kind, amiable, intelligent citizen and an honorable opponent." Those who retain a comfortable belief in the world's inevitable progress may wisely contrast this picture of two self-made men discussing ultimate truths in terms of courtesy with that of millionaires loudly laying down the law, which is the modern substitute for democracy. Douglas and Lincoln both had something to say and said it like gentlemen.

The debates took place, one in each of seven out of the nine Congressional districts into which Illinois was then divided. The opener used to speak for an hour, his opponent reply for an hour and a half, and the opener then wind up the debate in another speech of half an hour. No hall was big enough to contain the audiences, of which that at Charleston was supposed to have been as large as twenty thousand. Therefore the debates took place in the afternoons and on the prairie.

Abraham Lincoln

It is important to see clearly what it was that they did have to say—what was the corner into which it was Lincoln's purpose to drive Douglas—a purpose in which eventually he succeeded.

Douglas had the enormous advantage, in the eyes of moderate men, that his program advocated no violation of the Constitution. It was also possible that his Presidential candidature might receive the support of the South. Of these two advantages the Republicans, if they were to have any hope of success, must in some way deprive him. The attempt to do so is the history of the Lincoln-Douglas debates. They are games of chess, and Douglas is checkmated if Lincoln can force him into a position where he must admit that there were circumstances in which he too would violate the letter of the Constitution.

The opportunity upon which Lincoln saw that he could damagingly challenge Douglas was that of the relation between squatter sovereignty and his acceptance of the Dred Scott decision. On the one hand Douglas declared that the inhabitants of a Territory had the power to decide whether that Territory should be slave or free. On the other hand the inhabitants of a Territory had no power at all unless it was delegated to them by Congress, and by the Dred Scott decision Congress itself had no power to prohibit slavery in a Territory nor to delegate to any one else the right to prohibit slavery. What was the use of a right to decide if they were only allowed to give one decision? What happened if the inhabitants did vote their Territory free?

Douglas tried hard to escape answering this question but, eventually cornered, he replied, "that slavery would, in that case, not be unlawful in the Territory, but would never actually exist there if the territorial legislature chose, as it could, to refrain from passing any of the laws which would, in practice, be necessary to protect slave property." This answer was immensely popular with the constituents of Illinois, who were shocked by the apparently insane injustice of forcing slavery upon a population which did not wish to have any of it. It ensured Douglas his election and to Lincoln's friends the raising of the question appeared a monstrous blunder. They foretold to him its immediate result. But Lincoln answered, "Gentlemen, I am killing larger game; if Douglas answers, he can never be President and the battle of 1860 is worth a hundred of this." He was right. Douglas became Senator. He could not possibly become President.

Let Douglas' dilemma be clearly understood. He hoped to be acceptable to the South as a Presidential candidate because on the one hand he alone would guarantee to the Southerner his full rights under the Constitution and on the other could command in the North sufficient following to carry that minority of States without which a Southerner's candidate could never be elected. If to Lincoln's question he answered that squatter sovereignty must be forgotten and the Dred Scott decision stand, he would then lose Northern support, and thus lose his usefulness to the South. If he answered, as he did answer, that squatter sovereignty must stand and a merely nominal adherence be given to Dred Scott, then the South would see that they could no more rely on Douglas than on the Republicans to grant them their full rights. Lincoln's object was to make it clear to the South that the only difference of opinion in the North was upon rival plans for breaking the law. In this he was entirely successful.

V

Two years had still to run before the next Presidential election, when, as was now evident to all, the issue of peace or war would be submitted to the judgment of the electorate. In those years little happened that could increase the probability that the issue chosen would be that of peace. They were filled with the quarrel in the Senate of Douglas and Jefferson Davis, the Southern leader. By that quarrel the sectional lines of division were yet more clearly drawn.

There was another quarrel, even more serious than that between Douglas and Davis. During the years of fighting in Kansas a prominent part had been played by one John Brown, a Puritan farmer. This man had at one time made a living by wine-growing and wine-marketing, but had afterwards abandoned that trade for the more original practices of a maniac with tastes in Biblical massacre. He imagined himself divinely commanded to hew all Amalekites in pieces before the Lord, for, as he said, "without the shedding of blood there is no remission of sins," and this command he interpreted to mean that he was to murder at sight all slave-owners and afterwards to mutilate their bodies. One victim was found with his fingers and arms cut off, his head cut open and a hole in his breast, another the same, but with a hole in his jaw, a third was stabbed in the breast after he had been shot dead." Of another "the skull was split open in two places and some of his brains washed out by the water. A large hole was cut in his breast, and his left hand was cut off, except a little piece of skin on one side." It is to no purpose to prolong the list. When charged with his conduct Brown explained that, "disguised as a surveyor," he had first interviewed all his victims and each of them "had committed murder in his heart."

Wearying of mere murder and mutilation, in October, 1859, he devised a new plan, that of invading Virginia and freeing the land "by the sword of the Lord and of Gideon." For this purpose he crossed the Potomac and seized Harper's Ferry. But, fortunately, the negroes refused to rise and Brown was captured and hanged. He met his end with much fortitude.

One does not wish to speak without charity of a poor and ignorant man who was clearly but a homicidal lunatic. Yet it is a sign of the moral havoc which is caused by an appeal to arms that, before the end of the coming war, decent men upon the Northern side were shouting his name in a rallying song to one another.

Lord Charnwood finds much to praise in Lincoln where praise is doubtfully due. It is strange therefore that here, where he was most indubitably right, he should be condemned as coldhearted. Lincoln was a Southerner from Kentucky and he had no sympathy with the use of such weapons for political ends. "That affair," he said, "in its philosophy corresponds with the many attempts related in history at the assassination of kings and emperors." Longfellow, Emerson and the New England poets talked in a very different strain and gave the South every reason to believe that it had no security that such a business, if repeated, might not find general backing in the North. Victor Hugo wrote from the safe distance of Guernsey, where the negro menace to his three mistresses was not large, the epitaph for Brown of "*Pro Christo sicut Christus.*" One may observe with restraint certain differences between the two characters. In better sense and better charity was the prayer of Stonewall Jackson, that "*if possible*, Brown might be saved." "With God all things are possible."

VI

In an atmosphere thus charged the Presidential election of 1860 came up to be fought. Douglas was the candidate of the Northern Democrats, Breckinridge of the South, and Bell of the old Whigs. These mattered nothing. For with the Democrats split, North from South, it was certain that whoever was the Republican candidate would be the President. The denunciation of slavery and polygamy had been dropped from their platform. "There is but one plank—that on the tariff," wrote the *New York Tribune*, "which will be likely to give rise to objections in any quarter." Whom, in this responsibility, was the party to select?

Abraham Lincoln

The selecting convention met at Chicago towards the end of the spring. There were before it several candidates. Of these by far the strongest in popular opinion was Seward of New York, the author, or at least the repeater, of the phrase that between North and South there was an "irrepressible conflict," the opponent of the repeal of the Missouri Compromise by which Douglas had sought to throw Kansas and Nebraska open to slavery, the master of the powerful political machine of his State, "a believer," as was said, "in the adage that it is money that makes the mare go," and generally looked upon as the established leader of the Republican party. After his the next best-known name was that of Chase, Governor of Ohio, reputed a Radical. Third, perhaps, came that of Abraham Lincoln, of Illinois, who had acquired some reputation from his debates with Douglas, more from his alleged power of bending a poker between his fingers. There was a host of other candidates, of whom one only requires mention—Cameron, of Pennsylvania, who offered himself as the candidate of the strictly capitalist wing of the party, to whom the increase of the tariff was a plank more important than any other.

It is certain that Lincoln threw himself with all eagerness into the task of forcing his nomination upon the Convention. There is a story of how he paid a hundred dollars to a gentleman from Kansas to come and support him with his vote. Brass bands, blazing the virtues of "Honest old Abe, the rail-splitter," paraded the streets of Chicago. The saloons rained whisky. Lincoln's supporters had engaged a man whose voice "could be heard above the howling of the most violent tempest on Lake Michigan to shout for him." In spite of this assistance, on the first two ballots Seward was found to be leading, but not by a margin large enough to give him that majority over all the other candidates combined which was necessary for selection. Lincoln was second.

A deadlock seemed to have been reached from which only the political maneuver of David Davis, Lincoln's manager, discovered an escape. Cameron was well down the list. He had no chance, nor probably intention, of being selected. The object of his candidature was to win for himself such a position that he might sell to one or the other of the candidates at a critical moment the support of some powerful Eastern States and receive, as his price, a guarantee that the new President would in no way compromise upon the high tariff which Cameron's capitalist interest was determined to demand in order to avert war or secession.

Tom Hyer, a noted bruiser and supporter of Seward, asked as unanswerable the crude question, "If you do not nominate Seward, where will you get your money?" But David Davis, a shrewd man, had a ready answer. He had in his pocket a letter from Lincoln telling him that he would consider no bargain made in his name at the Convention as binding. Of the value of this letter both Davis and Cameron seem to have taken an estimate. For between them a bargain was struck by which Cameron withdrew his candidature and handed his votes over to Lincoln in exchange for a promise of a seat in the Cabinet which Lincoln would probably form. A similar promise was made to one Caleb Smith. By this maneuver Lincoln was selected, Caleb Smith became Secretary of the Interior, Cameron Secretary for War, and David Davis, for his services, a Judge of the Supreme Court. Seward declared that very evening his support of the party's nominee. When Douglas heard of the selection he said, "You have nominated a very able and a very honest man."

It is not suggested that Lincoln allowed himself to be in any way sold by this maneuver. Indeed, it is certainly true that, in itself, he disliked it, for he afterwards fought hard against fulfilling his part of the bargain towards Cameron. That he fought hard against it and yet in the end, finding, to quote a very good phrase, that Cameron was "earnestly defended by some of the best people of Pennsylvania," was forced to fulfill it, admirably shows the position in which his managers had placed him.

Lincoln, rightly or wrongly, always believed in a high tariff. In a sense, therefore, he sacrificed no principle in a bargain with Cameron. But in politics the question is sometimes not what a man believes but how much he believes it. The two questions that ran continually in Lincoln's mind were slavery and the Union. He did not believe in a tariff very much. Cameron and the capitalists believed in it intensely.

It has already been shown why the South had a large interest in the destruction of the tariff. In that interest clearly lay one possible way for the salvation of the Union. Lincoln would not compromise about slavery. He might very well be tempted to compromise about the tariff, to repeal it to prevent secession. For a protectionist might very plausibly argue that free trade was a smaller evil than war or the disruption of the Union, and Pennsylvania had heard rumors that the West was inclined to interpret the tariff plank in some milder sense. The policy of Cameron and the capitalists was to destroy Lincoln's power of making such a compromise. They entirely succeeded. Later, by the end of 1861 when Cameron had been publicly shown to be running his department for the financial profit of some private friends, Lincoln felt strong enough to get rid of him. At the critical time when peace and war were in the balance he was not strong enough. He did not yet dare to defy the king-makers and for this reason the last words on his lips in the last debates before war were not some fine sentiment concerning slavery or the Union, but, "And open Charleston as a port of entry, with their ten per cent tariff! What then would become of my tariff?"

No appeal that could be made to the attention of the people was neglected. "Monster wigwams and long processions of 'wide-awakes' with torches, transparencies and music attracted listeners to the political speeches." Thus spoke *vox Dei*. And on the night of 6th November Lincoln sat alone with the operator in the telegraph-box at Springfield. Before the divisions of his opponents it was soon clear that he had been overwhelmingly elected. Yet how curious an instrument of democracy is the representative system. The votes recorded for Lincoln were far fewer than the votes recorded against him, 1,857,000 to 2,804,000.

Pennsylvania and New Jersey made little doubt upon what plank the victory had been won. "The Pennsylvania journals, without distinction of party," wrote the *National Intelligencer*, "admit that the result of the recent election held in that State was mainly determined by politico-economical considerations growing out of the tariff policy to be pursued by the Federal Government." "Our election on Tuesday," said the *Philadelphia American and Gazette*, "determined that the vital and absorbing question in this State is protection to American industry." "The tariff plank," chimed in the *Philadelphia North American*, "constitutes the essential plank in the platform of the Lincoln party."

The only hope of the South had been to throw the election into Congress. She had now as little illusion as the North-East. The news of Lincoln's election was greeted with a howl of execration. Breckinridge had fought upon one issue alone—that the South be allowed the full rights of citizenship to which the Constitution and the Dred Scott decision entitled her. On that issue he had been defeated. In his stead had been elected a man, of whom personally little was known but who was the representative of a party of which the declared aim was to deprive the Southern citizen of his full rights, and who was, it seemed, the servant of a powerful financial interest, whose intention was to bleed the South white for the subsidy of the North. It was taken to be a declaration of war.

VII

On 6th November Lincoln was elected President. On 10th November the Legislature of South Carolina summoned a specially elected Convention of the State to decide with what policy this challenge should be met. On 20th December this Convention passed "the Ordinance of Secession of South Carolina and its repudiation of the Treaty called the Constitution of the United States." The ghost of Calhoun had sent out its last tremendous challenge to the gathering darkness of the times. Lincoln thought that "the people of the South have too much sense to attempt the ruin of the Government." "The pulse of the Stock Exchange," wrote Lowell, "remains provokingly calm."

It is well here to examine more closely the arguments of the South in favor of their conduct and such answers to it as have been made—the case for secession, first, in constitutional law, secondly, in common sense.

Did then the Constitution allow secession? Nowhere does it answer the question in so many words and—for what it is worth—its sub-title is, it must be admitted, Articles of Confederation and Perpetual Union. To that there are three answers. First, the answer of history; it is unquestionable that if the people—those in the North even more than those in the South—had had the smallest suspicion at the time when the Constitution was presented to them for acceptance that they were forfeiting their right to secession if they accepted it, its rejection would have been certain. None of the parties to the contract imagined that by the contract they were forfeiting that right. To the contrary, even such a limited Union was only with difficulty achieved, and by the unsparing use in all parts of the country of the argument that no man need be afraid to come in, since his State would preserve the right to secede should she ever want to do so. Virginia, Rhode Island and New York, as has been said, all solemnly affirmed this right in their articles of accession to the Union.

Lincoln denied the right of secession by the claim that "that was fully discussed in Jackson's time and denied not only by him but by the vote of Congress." But whoever suggested that constitutional rights could be settled by the *obiter dicta* of a President or by a snap majority of a chance Congress? The Republican party was on the horns of an insoluble dilemma. For sovereignty must be in one of two places—in the States or in the Supreme Court. If it lay in the States then a State might secede. If it lay in the Supreme Court then slavery could not be excluded from a Territory.

Secondly, there is the answer of general common opinion before men's judgments were warped by the particular controversy—always an important thing to discover. The right of secession was always affirmed in any general and noncontroversial exposition of the Constitution. For instance, both Jefferson Davis and Lee learnt it first from the lectures delivered at the official military academy at West Point. Rawle, of Pennsylvania, as we have seen, only demanded that an act of secession be a clear expression of the will of the people of the State, before the "ligament" could be "legitimately and fairly destroyed." The horrified cry of those who opposed Jackson's policy towards nullification in 1832 had been that he was denying "even the right of secession"—that last and unquestionable right, as it was thought, of freedom.

Thirdly, there is the argument of common sense, or philosophy; if A makes a contract with B and B fails to perform his side of the bargain, A, if not entitled to compensation, is at least freed from the obligations of the contract. The view of the South was not, as one might gather from some arguments that she had kept the contract for a couple of generations and now, being bored, would whimsically abandon it, but that the North had broken the contract by the Republican refusal to accept the Dred Scott decision and the endorsement of that refusal by the people in their election of a Republican President. The United States were therefore at an end. It remained only to declare them so. The question to the South was not "Had the South the right to break the contract?" but "Had the North already broken it?"

On the larger ground of common sense where did the South then stand?

There were, she argued, two different civilizations—the Southern and the Northern. Of that difference the existence of slavery in the South, its absence in the North was one piece of evidence, but by no means the only one. The difference would survive the abolition of slavery, for it was a difference of philosophy of life. The westward extension of American territory threw these two forms of life into conflict. Had that extension taken place some years later it is very possible that slavery would by then have been abolished. Such abolition would not have prevented the conflict. For of these two forms of life—the one static, content to live on its inherited land and refusing to sacrifice its fundamental agricultural life for a temporary increase of wealth, intensely tenacious of property—the other dynamic, expanding, indifferent to the distribution or the manner of wealth—the one must conquer the other. "A house divided against itself cannot stand," said Lincoln. Seward spoke of "the irrepressible conflict." Garrison, the abolitionist, called the Union "a League with Death and a Covenant with Hell." Horace Greeley said, "Let our erring sisters go"; Wendell Phillips, "that you could never raise a regiment in Boston to coerce the Gulf States." There was ample recognition by intelligent men of all opinions that here were two quite distinct forms of living. If the South valued theirs and thought it worth preserving, what should be their policy?

There were five ways in which the South could preserve her civilization from being swamped from the North. First, there was the policy of extending the area of slavery westwards, thus preserving equality against the North by keeping pace with her.

Second, she could drive some bargain by which the North would abrogate the tariff in order to preserve the Union. Thirdly, there was the revival of nullification. Fourthly, there was the plan left by Calhoun in his last testament, by which the division of the country into North and South should be explicitly recognized and each part, on the old Roman model, should have a separate President, possessing a veto on the acts of his colleague. Fifthly, there was secession. In independence they could be content with their old restricted area because they would no longer be at the mercy of the high tariff of the Eastern financiers.

Of these plans the first had been tried. The election of Lincoln was the mark of its final failure. The Southerner could not expand unless the area of slavery expanded. For he could not be expected to expand at the expense of his property. In any event it was a policy which put the South at a large disadvantage. For the civilization of the South was by its very nature, as has been said, static and conservative, its virtue that it was stable and not restless.

The second plan might possibly have given, at any rate, temporary peace. But Lincoln, President by grace of a financial group and a minority vote, was not strong enough to make the concession. The third and fourth were too artificial for practical politics. They had all the disadvantages of secession, none of its advantages, and would more certainly be refused. The Southern leaders were, therefore, forced back upon the fifth policy.

This line of argument has been respectably challenged at two points. First, there is the challenge that was given most sanely and forcibly by Lincoln himself in his Cooper Union speech. This challenge started from the proposition that slavery was wrong. By that he meant what Jefferson had meant, not what Mrs. Beecher Stowe and *Uncle Tom's Cabin* meant. He did not condemn the slave-owner personally nor deny that the guilt of slavery must be shared between North and South nor support any wild plan for forcing abolition upon the South. The fathers of the Constitution had made a bargain and that bargain must be kept. Whatever was "nominated in the bond"—effective Fugitive Slave Laws and the rest—must be given. But to give one iota more than was nominated in the bond was to compromise with evil. "We must put back slavery where the fathers put it." If it be true that the Southern form of life is so bound up with slavery that it can only survive by an extension of the slave area, then it is bound up with vileness and it must perish. Why should right make way in order that wrong may survive? We will not attempt to force abolition on the slave States. More, with our faith, it is impossible to ask of us.

This argument is clearly strong and is often spoken of as unanswerable. Certainly the opinion of Jefferson upon slavery was very different from that of Calhoun. Certainly, also, slavery is an evil. Those Southern politicians, such as Alexander Stephens, or Calhoun himself, who argued otherwise, ranted. The best society is an equal society. Lincoln was right, as a logician, to "protest against the counterfeit logic which says that since I do not want a negro woman for my slave I must necessarily want her for my wife." Nor had the real answer to Lincoln anything to do with the merits of slavery. It might well have come, as it did often come, from a man who hated slavery. Lincoln claimed to be interpreting the mind of the founders of the Constitution. In defying the Dred Scott decision he was appealing to the spirit of the Constitution against the letter. Seward, his Secretary of State, had even said that there was "a law higher than the Constitution"—the law, apparently, a bitter Southerner might have gibed, of Supply and Demand. To the South it was sufficient that the letter was violated. Lincoln himself might be a reasonable man, prepared to break the law only where it and common sense were at patent variance. But the South had no peaceful protection against the North except that of the guarantees of the

Constitution. The North could now overwhelmingly outvote her. That preponderance was certain to increase. What guarantee had she that, in this tension, the next President and the next Congress would be as reasonable? Was it not Lincoln's theory that the word of a President or a vote of Congress could interpret the Constitution? Might not a chance majority be used to destroy every institution and object of affection in Southern life? One has only to think of the gang who got power after the war—Stevens, Sumner and the rest—in order to realize that such a fear was far from unreasonable and to condemn Lincoln for short-sightedness in having done his part in making it reasonable.

The other challenge to the case of the South is that which is put most forcibly by Cecil Chesterton.[1] It is that the Southerner was not truly of a separate nationality as is the Irishman or the Pole. Both Southerner and Northerner felt, in their bones, American. Even Jefferson Davis so loved the Stars and Stripes that he wished to retain them as the flag of the Confederacy. What could be more logical than that he should do so? The Stars and Stripes were the symbol of loyalty to the Constitution. This Constitution the South had kept, the North had broken. If there was an essentially American attitude towards life, that attitude was found not in the North but in the South. The North was a cosmopolitan appendage.

Mr. Johnston[2] tries to cover up the weakness of the historical and legal arguments of the North. He first maintains that the sovereignty of the State can only have been a paper sovereignty because no State was willing to act on it by seceding alone. But the Principality of Monaco is not likely to invade the French Republic, acting alone. Yet she is certainly sovereign. It is not

---

[1] *History of the United States*, by Cecil Chesterton. Chatto and Windus. London, 1919.

[2] *American Political History*, by Alexander Johnston. G. P. Putnam's Sons. New York, 1905.

necessary to behave like a lunatic in order to prove that you are a free man. Second—and it is a common line of argument—he uses the metaphor of growth. "Under unity the States, once perhaps sovereign, had grown together. It was pedantry to be blind to that growth." If the psychological relations between two parties have changed, that may be an argument for making a new contract. It cannot be an argument for breaking an old one. And surely Southern resistance proves that this psychological change had not taken place. In the North and the West, indeed, there had grown a feeling for consolidation and nationalism, which eighty years before did not exist. This Imperialism of Webster and of Douglas was a not ignoble dream. It was more respectable by far than the British *fin-de-siècle* Imperialism, in whose name a gang of Jews walked over South Africa, armed with sixpennyworth of clap-trap and a pot of paint, marking red on the map all places which seemed likely to contain valuable concessions. Nevertheless, when the North and West spoke of "closer union," they meant a union which made the whole country more like the North and West. It was their error to think of the industrial and "progressive" civilization, of which they were a type, as normal and enduring. It was abnormal and, whatever may come of it, it will certainly not endure.

It cannot be too often repeated that there were in America two geographical conflicts—one between North and South, the other between East and West. Wise statesmanship would have realized that the chief guarantee of freedom was a strong state-loyalty and that freedom is more important than power. It would therefore have guarded against a westward extension which would make necessary the creation of new States—arbitrary units, powerless to evoke true loyalty.

Thus the statesmen who come from the West, from Andrew Jackson to Lincoln and Douglas, have had the least sense of State rights. The East, as a whole, had kept the old feeling more vividly, but the North-East, although from it came all those Northerners who would have let the South secede, yet was to some extent corrupted by the economic advantages of Union and the cosmopolitan influx of population. The true spirit of the founders of the Constitution towards the State was preserved in the South-East alone. The war, in which those States went down, was thus not only a victory of North over South but also of West over East.

Cecil Chesterton, through his admiration for Andrew Jackson, overstates, I think, the artificial character of the Southerner's state-loyalty. Tennessee was not very much; Georgia or South Carolina was a man's all. Yet he certainly makes a true point when he says that there are few, if any at all, among Southerners, who today "would still wish to secede if they had the power." In Charleston, the Hellas of Hellas of secession, I have heard on a national festival the members of a public-luncheon club repeat a declaration of loyalty "the Union, One and Indivisible" which would have surprised even Alexander Hamilton in his grave. Why is this?

It is perfectly true that the Southern representative system before the war was anomalous. The slave, though of course he did not vote, yet counted as three-fifths of a white man. Therefore the large plantations, where black population was plentiful and white scanty, became almost the pocket-boroughs of the slave-owners who had an influence in their States wholly greater than that of the "poor, white trash" of the towns. Yet there is no reason to think that "the poor, white trash," had the decision been theirs, would have decided differently from the slave-owners. The war was to prove that they were, if anything, the more bitter of the two.

The reason lies elsewhere. The old South was not beaten and persuaded. She was beaten and murdered. The new South is merely the less developed part of the United States. The South under defeat lost her philosophy, whereas the Poles and the Irish have kept theirs. For that of the former, unlike that of the latter, was based upon mere taste and not upon the rock of religious truth, outside herself. But the fact that this life perished does not prove that it was a good thing that it perished.

The South has now allowed herself to be made a part of the industrial world of the North. The agricultural life of the States is today sacrificed to the building up of the nation's manufacturing predominance. A prosperity which is built upon manufacturing predominance may be brilliant but is necessarily unstable. Tastes change, and the consumer who bought at one market yesterday will buy at another tomorrow. The industrial United States have their troubles before them. In those troubles the South will now be involved. Had she won her independence she would not have been involved. It is a superficial judgment which says that the new United States, because they have survived the period of sixty years, have been a success and soundly built and that those who tried to escape from them were unwise.

VIII

For these reasons, on 10th December, 1860, South Carolina declared herself an independent Republic and hauled down the Stars and Stripes from her public buildings, substituting for them the Palmetto flag of freedom.

Lincoln had been elected President in November. He did not of course come into office until the following March. It fell therefore to Buchanan, the old President, to find a policy of remedy. Historians have not been kind to Buchanan nor can it be denied that the blame that they have showered upon him is mostly justified. Either South Carolina might secede or she might not. Either her independence should be recognized or she should be coerced. But Buchanan maintained that she might not secede but could not be coerced. By a policy of strict inaction he hoped that some automatic solution of the difficulty would appear.

The Union forces held several forts round about Charleston. Of these the most important was Fort Sumter. These forts South Carolina demanded in virtue of her independence. They were prepared to buy them from the Union Government. In the forts themselves, on the other hand, provisions had run short and Major Anderson, the Union commander, concentrated all his forces in the largest of them, Sumter, and sent a request to the Government for reinforcements. Which demand should Buchanan obey? Buchanan vacillated miserably. He sent a transport to Fort Sumter. It was fired on by the South Carolinians—the first shots of the war—and had to retreat. Buchanan accepted this check and did not make a second attempt. Thus did he leave the problem to his successor, Lincoln.

It would be strange if these four months had not been filled with a last attempt at compromise. Lincoln himself had tried in December to open a correspondence with his old friend, Alexander Stephens of Georgia, afterwards the Confederate Vice-President. The final attempt that was made stands to the name of Senator Crittenden of Kentucky, the chairman of a Committee of thirteen appointed by the Senate. He proposed that the line of the Missouri Compromise should be extended to the sea and that this prohibition and permission of slavery should be placed in the Constitution as an amendment.

Oklahoma was an Indian reservation. California governed herself by the blunt and sensible dictum of "No niggers, slave or free." The South would have gained by the compromise nothing but New Mexico and barren Arizona. In return she would have surrendered her large legal claims under the Dred Scott decision. Yet for the hope of peace she seemed ready to accept, as also did the Republican party. Lincoln rejected the scheme and wrecked the hope. His argument was that the founders of the

Constitution admitted slavery to be a necessary evil. In order to form the Union they had to allow it. But since it was an evil they purposely refrained from giving it explicit recognition. A constitutional amendment proclaims—or used to proclaim—general philosophical principles upon which American society was built, not police regulations imposed by the whim of a chance majority. It was vital that slavery should not be elevated into such a philosophical principle. The distinction, one feels, would be worth drawing in a lecture-room, but such a pedantry is dear at the price of a million lives.

Yet Lincoln, I think, had a further reason for rejecting the compromise. He knew that the South felt passionately that her way of life was threatened by the predominance of the North. The compromise did not in any way remove that predominance. Lincoln thought that sooner or later it would be bound to break down. He took the responsibility for breaking it sooner rather than later.

The next proposal was that Crittenden's scheme be submitted to a plebiscite. This was rejected because, as Seward said, it would be "unconstitutional and ineffectual." There was, as Seward might be reminded, at such times as it suited him, "a law higher than the Constitution." The scheme would certainly have been approved by the people.

The result of this rejection was in the North a panic for peace, led to some extent by that same moneyed interest which had refused compromise. The Stock Exchange was less provokingly calm than Lowell had found it five months earlier. In the South the example of South Carolina was followed by Mississippi, Florida, Alabama, Georgia and Louisiana. The seceding States met at Montgomery, in Alabama, adopted a provisional constitution and elected Jefferson Davis their President and Alexander Stephens Vice-President. Davis left his women-folk to the care of his negroes and came to take up his duties. General Beauregard was sent to Charleston to watch Fort Sumter. Poor Lowell must have been hardly able to recognize his staid, familiar Stock Exchange, so changed it was.

IX

To the Presidency of such a country, to a task, as he himself said, "greater than that which rested upon Washington," Lincoln set out from Springfield on 11th February, 1861. On the 4th March old Buchanan, as is the duty of the outgoing President, escorted his successor to his inauguration. Chief Justice Taney, the author of the Dred Scott decision, administered the oath of office. Douglas, that fine patriot, so soon to lay down his life for the country which he loved, so unfairly overblamed by the black-and-white journalists, stood by his victorious rival's side and held his hat and cane.

Lincoln delivered an address which he had been writing off and on for the last six months on the backs of old envelopes. He shocked the prudery of his audience by contrasting the Southern view of the Constitution as "a free-love arrangement" with his own preference for "a regular marriage." His last sentence alone is today much quoted. "The mystic chords of memory, stretching from every battlefield and patriot-grave to every living heart and hearth-stone, will yet swell the chorus of the Union, when touched again, as surely they will be, by the better angels of our nature." The exuberance of the rhetoric is held to excuse the absence of meaning.

The rest was a sober argument in favor of the Republican program and is only notable because in it Lincoln gives his support to the proposal which Congress had resolved to recommend, of placing in the Constitution an amendment forbidding the Federal Government to interfere with the domestic institutions of the States, "including that of persons held to service." Why then had he rejected the Crittenden Compromise?

The day after the delivery of this address word came from Major Anderson at Fort Sumter that, unless reinforced, he could only hold out for a few weeks more. The decision upon this policy was therefore the first duty of the new Cabinet. Granted their principles—that the Union must at all costs be maintained, that its maintenance implied the maintenance of the Federal forts—Lincoln had laid down both these propositions only the day before—it seems, as one looks back over fifty years, extraordinary how such a body of men should have hesitated over their decision. South Carolina claimed the fort as symbol of her independence and for no other reason. General Scott, the Government's military adviser, had indeed said that Fort Sumter, to be held, required a reinforcement of twenty thousand men and such a force was not available. But that was not the point. It was important—not that Fort Sumter should be held (for it was of no military value) but that South Carolina should be compelled, if she would have it, to declare her hand and take it by force. Yet in the debate of the Cabinet only two—Blair and Chase—were for sending reinforcements. The rest were opposed. Lincoln reserved judgment.

The logic of the case against the Cabinet is overwhelming. Yet it is easy to see how men would shrink from the responsibility of taking any step that would make the fearful business of war more nearly inevitable. Cecil Chesterton says that "to many thousands of lips sprang instinctively and simultaneously a single sentence: 'Oh, for one hour of Jackson!'" In the hearts of many thousands more was a profound thankfulness that the solution of this problem was not left to the hands of that great hero of melodrama.

There were also other reasons than those of timidity which seemed at this moment to justify inaction even at the cost of some sacrifice of principle. On 6th February had met at Washington, under the summons of Virginia, a Peace Conference consisting of delegates from twenty-one States. This was still in session and it was clearly most important to avoid, if it were possible, any offense which might add to the number of seceding States. The Peace Conference, "threshing again," as Lowell said, "the already twice threshed straw of debate," did little but show how clear-cut was the difference between South and North. In the South there was much dispute about the expediency of secession under particular circumstances. Jefferson Davis, Alexander Stephens, Lee—most of the leaders—were for a much more cautious policy than that which was pursued. But no one doubted that the State had the right to secede if she wished to do so. Virginia laid down the concession of this right as a basis of the Conference decision. By its refusal the Conference became futile. Yet it is easy to see how timid men would take its existence as an excuse for delay.

And to those who argued—it is a plausible argument—that the issue was not large enough to justify the horror of war every hour's delay was an advantage. In the North was a great volume of sentiment for peace which grew with every day of reflection. To the South, though her opinion was far more nearly united, yet the more that the Government abstained from provocation, the more open to ridicule seemed Jefferson Davis' complaint of "wanton aggression upon the part of others." Lincoln was therefore probably right to decide—though the decision came almost too late—that he would provision Fort Sumter, but not reinforce it. To refuse to allow soldiers to starve to death was no extravagant provocation. Seward, as we see from his strange paper, "Some Thoughts for the President's Consideration," would have solved the problem by vaguely embroiling the nation with whatever foreign countries were guilty of the accident of existing. Lincoln's was the wiser plan. A large responsibility rested on the side that first fired upon the other's flag. This responsibility—although the details of the story are still obscure—the South accepted.

Abraham Lincoln

It has been already told how, in Buchanan's time, a transport was fired upon while making its way to Fort Sumter. For some reason or other the incident passed almost unnoticed. A gentleman from Alabama, a liar, said to Jefferson Davis, "Unless you sprinkle blood in the face of the people of Alabama they will be back in the old Union in ten days." Whether for this reason or for another, instructions were sent to Beauregard to demand the surrender of Fort Sumter. Anderson had not yet received the provisions that were on the way to him and replied that if he did not previously receive either them or instructions he would surrender on 15th April.

On 12th April, by some unexplained accident or blunder, a shot rang out across the bay of Charleston. It carried away the Stars and Stripes which floated over Fort Sumter. The provision-ships were in the offing but they came too late. The war had begun.

The South and the North stood to one another very much in the relation of the British Government to the Trades Union Council at the time of the General Strike in 1926. There were doubtless bad slave-owners in 1861, as there were certainly bad coal-owners in 1926. Yet the South, like Mr. Baldwin, stood for a certain organization of society—not theoretically the best, perhaps not even practically the best, but at any rate one which gave that minimum of order without which even improvement is impossible. The North, on the other hand, was taking action which, whatever its intention, must inevitably result in the overthrow of that organized society. How utter that overthrow would be, the full horror of Reconstruction and the Black Terror, few at that time probably foresaw. Some such result they did foresee and knew that, in place of an ordered peace, the Northern politician had nothing to offer but a few phrases which did not correspond to any reality and would be utterly impotent to prevent the collapse of society into chaos. Society is according to the Divine plan, chaos contrary to it. The side which defends an organization of society against those who would merely destroy is therefore always in the right. For this reason, and not for any random romanticism with which her defeated cause may have afterwards been invested by the writers of best-sellers, it would have been well for the world if the South had won.

Yet this by no means says that she was right to take the offensive at that moment. What were the grievances from which an individual Southerner—say, Jefferson Davis—suffered at the time of secession? No doubt he had been impoverished by the tariff. He had perhaps reason to complain of the unfair working of the Fugitive Slave Laws. The propaganda of the abolitionists had possibly caused a certain insubordination among his slaves—though the very confidence with which he entrusted his womenfolk to the care of those slaves proves how small had been the effect of this propaganda. Clearly they were not nearly large enough to justify an appeal to arms. Why not wait until the North, by definite act, had shown her ill-will and driven them to resistance? "I acknowledge," Douglas had frankly told an audience at Norfolk, in Virginia, "the inherent and inalienable right to revolution when a grievance becomes too burdensome to be borne." But Lincoln's election "is not such a grievance."

Calhoun used to argue that the South must strike quickly, because every year she grew weaker and the North stronger. But on that argument her moment for resistance was already long passed. The North had over her a preponderance of four to one in white population and five hundred to one in manufactures. A direct military victory for her was a mathematical impossibility. Her chances lay only in Northern divisions or foreign intervention. For neither of these was the moment chosen especially favorable. For both it was essential that the North should be the patent aggressor.

Beauregard then did his cause but an ill service when he fired upon Fort Sumter. There was hardly a man in the Union who was easy in his conscience about the right of the Federal Government to coerce a State. Beauregard by firing upon the Stars and Stripes gave to those uneasy consciences just the excuse which they needed to rally to the Northern side. Until the shot rang out across the Bay of Charleston there was still a chance that Northern opinion would have demanded that the South be allowed peaceably to secede.

War, it has been said with patent truth, is the result of conflict of wills. Tragedy is the result of conflict within a single will. What could be more futile than to bring it forward as an argument against Lee, that there was much to be to be said for the North, or against Lincoln, that there was much to be said for the South? As if these great men did not know this! There was no man in America who loved his State who did not also love the Union, nor who loved the Union and did not also love his State. However clear it may have been to his academic mind which of the two loyalties in the last resort he would choose, he had never contemplated the making of the choice. But when the flag crumpled down over Sumter the choice had to be made. A State had fired upon the flag. Every man had to be prepared to kill something he loved in order to save something he loved more dearly. It was not black and white as when the Prussians went into Belgium.

If you would learn how an American felt this double loyalty you can find no better teacher than Walt Whitman. A piece of prose does not become verse by leaving all the commas out and ending the lines at the wrong places and such oddities as,

> "Raised in Virginia and Maryland and most of them known personally to the general,"

or

> "For who except myself has yet conceived what your children *en masse* really are?"

can only compete with one another for the prize of the worst poetry of the human race. Yet his poems are intensely interesting—not as poems—which they are not—nor as a philosophical record of good thinking, but as a historical record of thinking. For he set out, as he said to:

"Report all heroism from an American point of view"—

a profession that, under efficient organization, has since become both more profitable and more common—and it is possible therefore to find here the shifting record of the thoughts of the average man during these years.

Thus there appears this double loyalty in:

"I will make a song for these States that no one State may under
      any circumstances be subjected to another State,
And I will make a song that there shall be comity by day and by
      night between all the States and between any two of them,
And I will make a song for the ears of the President, full of
      weapons with menacing points,
And behind the weapons countless dissatisfied faces;
And a song make I of the One form'd out of all,
The fanged and glittering One whose head is over all,
Resolute and warlike One including and over all
(However high the head of any head that head is over all)."

Those who have tried it in some mild degree will admit that the great advantage of making songs is that one may make as many as one likes and that there is no reason why they should not all contradict one another. But General Beauregard had made a sterner "song for the ears of the President." It too was

"Full of weapons and behind the weapons countless dissatisfied
      faces."

"At news from the south"—the news that the song had been sung—Whitman "struck with clenched fist the pavement"—an unnecessarily painful piece of symbolism, one would have thought—and took firmly the Northern side. He would now reverse his song and sing first

> "The idea of all, the Western world one and inseparable,
> And then the song of each member of these States."

Still to the end both songs are to be sung.

The same record can be found in Artemus Ward's[1] imaginary interview with Jefferson Davis. "J. Davis," he says, "there's your grate mistaik. Many of us was your sincere frends, and thought certin parties amung us was fussin' about you and meddlin' with your consarns intirely too much. But, J. Davis, the minit you fire a gun at the piece of dry-goods called the Star-Spangled Banner, the North gits up and rises en massy in defence of that Banner."

The feeling of the North could hardly be better expressed.

X

With that "news from the South" the North seemed suddenly to spring into unanimity. Douglas, Buchanan, Everett—all speaking for those whom they led—pledged their support to Lincoln in the prosecution of the war. With the same news the first Lincoln, the mere politician, fades from history. Those who have studied the story of his rise to power will have missed much if they have found in this man's character nothing either lovable or noble. At the same time biographers, piously turning again the thumbed pages of his record, have, I think, quite failed to prove that there was in it anything outstanding. In his larger acts of judgment he had been much at fault. The charge cannot be quite refuted, that twice he had seriously helped the

---

[1] Artemus Ward, pen name of Charles Farrar Browne (1834–67), American humorous journalist.

cause of war—once from a motive of personal ambition and once of pedantry. He had the vices of competitive passion. He became President of the United States not through merit but as a political accident. None of those who selected him seem to have been at all conscious that they were bringing on to the stage of the world a great figure. Indeed, he was selected at Chicago in preference to Seward mainly because he was not a great figure. The more that one reads the more justifiable appears the error.

The character of Abraham Lincoln was, it seems, of the kind that is formed and fortified by the granting to it from outside of a clear purpose for its action. That purpose South Carolina had given him. In a moment the old shuffling politician was dead. A nation in arms had found a leader. Among the early papers of his boyhood there is one in which, at the bottom of some subtraction sums, appear the words,

> "Abraham Lincoln, his hand and pen,
> He will be good but God knows when."

God appointed His time. It was one stranger even than the dreams of Illinois.

The day after the news Lincoln called upon the militia of the States to furnish seventy-five thousand men to suppress an "unlawful combination." A few days later he issued an appeal for volunteers, to which by June three hundred thousand, it seems, responded.

The two immediate problems were to preserve Washington and to prevent the area of secession from growing. The two were clearly connected, as the moral effect of the fall of Washington on the doubtful States would certainly be immense. As important would be its effect on Europe. The danger was great, for across the Potomac the Confederate flag could be seen flying over Alexandria. Washington stands between the State of Virginia,

Abraham Lincoln

which seceded, and that of Maryland, which looked as if she was going to secede. The Sixth Massachusetts Regiment, on its way to garrison the capital, was mobbed in the streets of Baltimore and forced to fire upon the crowd. A regiment from Rhode Island and the New York Seventh Regiment were reported on the way as reinforcements but they did not arrive. Lincoln paced his room in the White House in an agony of doubt. "Why don't they come? Why don't they come?" he cried, and to the Massachusetts men, in impatience: "I begin to believe that there is no North. The Seventh Regiment is a myth. Rhode Island is another. You are the only real thing." Had the South known of her opportunity she could probably have marched into the capital. It is her tragedy that she did not do so.

Meanwhile, of the slave States which had not been represented at Montgomery, Virginia, North Carolina and Tennessee had by now followed the rest into secession. There remained Delaware, Maryland, Kentucky and Missouri. Over Delaware slavery had no hold. She was hardly more than technically a slave State. Kentucky declared herself neutral. That neutrality Lincoln of course could not admit in theory, but he scrupulously respected it in practice. In Maryland opinion was at first violently in favor of the South. Baltimore's treatment of a Massachusetts Regiment we have seen. The transport of troops across her territory had for the time to be forbidden, but later feeling unaccountably subsided and the State relapsed into neutrality. Missouri alone was forced into loyalty by military arms under General Lyon, who used the German population to coerce the English-speaking. Of this local war the negro population asked, with curiosity: "If de Dutch take Camp Jackson,[1] is we niggers gwine to be free?"

Lincoln's first essay at war-making did little to increase his reputation. The Confederate Congress was to meet at Richmond,

---

[1] A fort near St. Louis.

in Virginia, on 20th July. A newspaper cry was raised through the North that its meeting should be prevented. To this cry Lincoln and his Cabinet were so foolish as to pay attention. They overbore the first military advice and insisted that an army, under General McDowell, advance into Virginia. Twenty miles south of Washington this army was beaten and broken at Bull Run by the Southern generals, Beauregard and Johnston. It returned in rout to the capital. First blood was to the South.

The earliest news to reach Washington had been of Northern victory. Lincoln believing them to be true had gone out for an afternoon's drive. Only on his return did he receive a telegram which said: "General McDowell's army in full retreat through Centreville. The day is lost. Save Washington and the remnant of the army." He received the news without a word.

Yet the military consequences of Bull Run were not large, for the South was unable to follow her fugitives to Washington. She was, as Johnston said, "as much disorganized by victory as the North by defeat." Its moral consequences within the country were no doubt of some importance. But the main fear of the Cabinet was that any appearance of weakness would lead to the recognition of Confederate independence by Great Britain and France. Both powers had reason to wish for a Southern victory, partly from that general malevolence by which the foreign policies of all countries can be to some extent explained, but also from their own interests. In France the brain of Napoleon III was beginning to spin out those schemes of Mexican Empire which were afterwards to lead Maximilian to a firing-party at Queretaro. For their realization Northern defeat was necessary; for no Government of integral United States could ever tolerate such a violation of the Monroe Doctrine.

England's sympathy for the South was for two more concise reasons—cotton, and that sentiment which we have always felt towards those struggling to be free of any yoke other than our own. Yet it happened that the British Cabinet had definitely decided to take no action, and France to wait upon British initiative. Early in May Seward had brought to Lincoln the copy of a rude despatch which he intended to send to the British Cabinet, lecturing it upon its duties. It is Lincoln's main achievement in foreign policy that he so altered this despatch that, preserving the substance, he yet transformed it into one calculated to make future relations easier rather than more difficult.

Only once afterwards was there serious danger of a quarrel with England. Towards the end of this year two Southern envoys, Mason and Slidell, were taken off a British boat upon the high seas. Lincoln's Cabinet rightly saw that this was a breach of international law and that they must be handed back, and trouble was thus averted. Lincoln, himself, seemed to miscalculate the readiness with which American opinion would recognize its obligation. He suggested arbitration, which would certainly have been rejected. The more statesmanlike plan—that which was adopted—was Seward's, and Slidell and Mason went on to their envoyships in Paris and London.

English intervention was now hardly possible, though still strangely expected in the South. French intervention was still quite probable and indeed might well have taken place but for the blunders of Slidell's diplomacy. It was essential to Napoleon's policy that the South should win, and very desirable that she should win with her own troops and money. Slidell, by always exaggerating the Southern success, created exactly the wrong impression. Napoleon thought that the South would easily win unaided. Had he had a suspicion of her ultimate defeat he would have intervened at once instead of letting Bazaine potter about all Mexico. It is probable enough that such an intervention would have been immoral. Nor can any one be ambitious to keep the conscience of the Second Emperor. Yet to be willing to fight and unwilling to fight your enemies was not a blunder into which the peculiar lucidity of Corsican morals was very apt to fall. And the enemies of Napoleon's schemes were not a gang of half-naked savages at Oaxaca but the armies of the North before Richmond.

From the first months of its power the especial vice of the Republican party, the influence of money in its councils, began to make itself evident. The first scandal was that of Frémont. Frémont, to whose name a vague romance is usually added by the title of "the Explorer," had been a settler in California in the days before the Mexican War. He had played a part both prominent and profitable in the intrigues by which the American consul at Monterey used every diplomatic privilege in order to violate every diplomatic obligation, and eventually succeeded in procuring California from Mexico just before the discovery, or at any rate the publication, of its gold resources.

When the capitalists formed the Republican party, one of their difficulties was that on the whole the Mexican War had been a Southerner's war. This, though not all to the credit of the South, at least made it difficult for the Republicans to find an appropriate war-hero for their candidate. Frémont, if he had not actually fought in the war, had at the least been far enough away from everything else at the time to make a colorable pretense of having done so. He was therefore run as their candidate for the Presidency in 1856. He proved a reasonably successful candidate and in his ambitions foresaw himself as Lincoln's successor in 1864. Therefore, to aid this purpose, he had used his political influence to obtain from Lincoln the command of the Union forces in Missouri. The fighting side of war did not particularly appeal to him and his army was soon reduced to an open joke. It was a business of job-making and job-taking. As the report of Congress' Committee said, "The system of public plunder which pervaded that department was inaugurated at the very beginning and followed up with untiring zeal, the public welfare as entirely overlooked and as effectually ignored as if the war was gotten up to enable a mammoth scheme of peculation at the expense of the public to be carried out."

His purpose was not to win battles but to seize an opportunity of appearing to the world as the chivalrous soldier of freedom. He therefore proclaimed martial law in Missouri, liberated all the slaves, and confiscated the entire property of all those whom a court martial might declare to have taken any part with the enemy. His policy was supported by fine quotations from the New Testament, which it was hoped one day to exchange against the hard cash of electoral votes. Such language in such a mouth is, in the vigorous but not sufficiently offensive phrase of Blair, "like a painted woman quoting Scripture."

Lincoln wrote Frémont and asked him to withdraw the monstrous proclamation. Frémont refused, demanding that, if Lincoln disapproved, he must overrule him publicly. In this way he hoped to transfer from Lincoln to himself the abolitionist and humanitarian vote in the Republican party. Lincoln did overrule him and, a few months later, removed him from high command, but he was able to bring sufficient influence to bear to prevent his own disgrace.

The end of the year showed to Lincoln the chance of freeing himself from that influence by which he had climbed to power. The War Department, of which Cameron was the head, was run for the private profit of certain individuals. "Thad Stevens," said A. B. Ely, repeating the Washington gossip of the day, "said Cameron would add a million to his fortune. I guess he has done it." And, though personal corruption was not proved, it was amply proved by Congress' Committee of investigation that, as the *New York Tribune* put it, "he has been surrounded and pressed upon by troops of noisy well-wishers who would have scorned the idea of selling their God for thirty pieces of silver so long as there was the faintest hope of making it forty. These have bored him into signing contracts by which they have made enormous profits at his expense as well as the country's."

Lincoln by now felt himself strong enough at least partly to remove the ladder by which he had risen to power. Cameron was sent as Minister to St. Petersburg. There was a hint in this halfway house to Siberia—and Lincoln was a freer man.

XI

Thus ended the year 1861. It had not been a glorious one for Lincoln's administration. Its record was one bad beating, two nasty bits of political corruption, the three chief generals quarrelling like cats and dogs and the avoidance of a foreign war by a public confession to a breach of international law. As Lincoln said, "If something was not done soon, the bottom would drop out of the whole concern." It was very true.

The first months of 1862 were mainly occupied with the fighting in the West for the control of the Mississippi and are interesting for the appearance upon the Northern side of a new general, Ulysses Grant. Grant had served with some distinction in the Mexican War. When the war was over he took, it seems, to the bottle, as his very constant companion, but the outbreak of the Civil War showed him that this was a trade not incompatible with soldiering. He therefore returned to the army. Later, during his Presidency, he took apparently a pledge of teetotalism. It is sufficient to add that he was a very good general and a very bad President.

The Northern strategy was hampered by lack of coöperation between the two responsible generals, and later by preference of the less to the more able as generalissimo. The result nevertheless of the fighting of the first four months of the year was in the West a victory—won at too large a price—at Shiloh and

Abraham Lincoln

the capture of New Orleans and of all the Mississippi except a hundred miles around Vicksburg.

But 1862, if a good year for Lincoln on that front, was one of black darkness for him in the East. After Bull Run the command-in-chief had been given to McClellan, one of the many mistakes which Lincoln made in his judgment of men. McClellan was a man of some ability in the reorganization of a shattered army but over-cautious, ill-mannered, of doubtful honesty, of doubtful loyalty, and possessed of a mania that others did not wish his enterprises to succeed. An interesting story could be made of Lincoln's quarrels with McClellan. Lincoln carried on his side of the controversy in a homely jargon. To send troops to McClellan was, he said, "like shifting fleas across a barn-floor with a shovel." When McClellan complained of the fatigue of his horses, Lincoln wrote, "What have the horses of your army done that fatigues anything?" He called on McClellan and, when the general refused to see him, only remarked that he would "hold General McClellan's horse for him, if only he will give us a victory." But McClellan would do nothing of the sort and for two good reasons.

Until April, 1862, he was entirely inactive though he faced Johnston with 149,000 to 40,000. In April he began his famous Peninsular Campaign. His troops were transported by sea to Fortress Monroe at the end of the peninsula that lies between York River and James River. Thence they were to march upon and capture Richmond.

Lincoln understood McClellan to have promised him that for the Peninsular Campaign he would not draw off such a number of troops as to leave Washington insufficiently defended, yet he made it his first business to give orders to McDowell to follow him from the defense of "that sink of iniquity, Washington," to that of his own army. He then wrote to Lincoln a memorandum on the duties of a Christian gentleman.

Lincoln's reply was to forbid McDowell to obey McClellan. In spite of this McClellan defeated Johnston on 31st May and 1st June and advanced to within four miles of Richmond. The town was saved, not by an attack on his forces but by the brilliant counter-move of Stonewall Jackson, who, marching north, made havoc of the three armies that stood between himself and Washington—the one under McDowell, the second under Frémont, a third under Banks, an influential politician in Massachusetts. To oppose such men to Stonewall Jackson was laughable.

At the end of June McClellan was driven from Richmond by Lee in the Seven Days' Battles. But he had, with great skill, shifted his base from Fortress Monroe to Harrison's Landing on the other side of the peninsula and was thus able to save his army, though at the cost of abandoning the peninsula. "If I save the army now," he telegraphed to Lincoln, "I tell you plainly that I owe no thanks to you nor to any other persons in Washington. You have done your best to sacrifice this army." It was his obsession that with McDowell's troops he could have taken Richmond. Yet, even were that so, as Lee said of a later but exactly similar situation, "We would have swopped Queens." Lee would have entered an undefended Washington. The South would have been enormously the gainer by the exchange.

Pope, a new general, next advanced upon Richmond. His numbers were a hundred and fifty thousand to Lee's fifty-five thousand. Yet Lee divided his forces, sent Jackson round to threaten communications with Washington, and himself fell upon and defeated the wretched man at the second battle of Bull Run. Pope retreated to Washington. His brief career of generalship was at an end.

Washington was too strongly held for direct attack. It was Lee's plan instead to invade Maryland. Maryland was a Southern State. In the early days of the war a Massachusetts Regiment, as has been said, had been mobbed in the streets of Baltimore. The

Southern hope was that she would now rise and throw in her lot with the invaders. Washington, which lay between her and Virginia, would then necessarily fall. Europe would recognize the South and the North be unable to continue the struggle.

It was the high moment of Southern hope. Then, alone in all the war, did success seem reasonably at hand. The glamour of splendid victory was on Lee's army when this company of singing soldiers crossed the Potomac and entered Maryland. They marched to the familiar repertory of Southern songs:

> "Galernipper,
> Mississippi,
> Ohio,"

"Dixie" and the rest were there, but with them another, and the country-people, who turned out to see these strange conquerors pass by, heard for the first time,

> "The despot's heel is on thy shore,
> Maryland, my Maryland."

That Maryland who in an hour of dark fortune for the South had stoned Union soldiers in the streets of Baltimore would now in her triumph join the Confederacy seemed a most reasonable hope. Lee issued to her citizens a restrained and wise proclamation. For some reason there was no response. "Maryland, my Maryland" gave only cold glances to her deliverers. Union flags were even thrust into the faces of the Confederate soldiers.

In Maryland's hands lay certainly the decision of the war. Why she let slip such an opportunity for imposing herself on history cannot be certainly decided. The most ardent Southern sympathizers had already joined the Southern army. Lee's troops, though victorious, were ill-shod and ill-fed. Enthusiasm for secession diminished, the further a State was from the land of cotton. An ancient rivalry with Virginia prevented a step which looked too like putting herself under her rival's leadership. Lincoln had been at special pains to allow no grievances of hers to remain unremedied. All these are no doubt true and help towards an explanation. They are hardly sufficient, nor has a sufficient explanation been given.

Perhaps much may be due to the strength of her chivalrous pity. There was little at that date in Lincoln to suggest the great man or the builder of a nation. It looked as if he would pass down to history as the last and most wretched of the Presidents of the United States. Yet he, having set his hand to the plough, went on doggedly and without complaint at that riot for which he knew that he, by his surrender to the Cameron crew, was partly responsible. The pathetic sadness of this battered man may have touched the imagination of Marylanders.

So Maryland did not rise and Lee fought an indecisive battle at Antietam, then had to retreat again to his own people.

Meanwhile McClellan had not been idle. When he was in the peninsula a certain Fernando Wood, of New York, who at one time had pestered Lincoln with assurances that he had "reliable and truthful authority that the South wished to make peace," had come to offer McClellan the Democratic candidacy for the Presidency of 1864. One of the conditions of the offer had been that he should give to the Democratic politicians a written, but secret, pledge that he would conduct the war in such a way as to conciliate the South. The Northern Democrats wished to be able to fight the election of 1864 on the program that Lincoln's attempt to impose the Northern will upon the South had failed. If they were to make their plans for such a campaign, it was essential to be quite sure that before 1864 the attempt should not have succeeded. There was no better way of being sure of this than that of giving the commanding-general an interest in failure by making him also the candidate. In case of difficulties it was felt better to have McClellan's pledge in writing, to be used, if necessary, for purposes of blackmail. McClellan was about to send off the required pledge from the peninsula, but on the representation of one Smith that it "looked like treason," did not do so. Later he changed his mind, and after the battle of Antietam it seems that he gave Wood such a pledge. As a result Lee returned to Virginia unmolested.

Lincoln has been strangely attacked on the charge that he removed McClellan from command because McClellan was a Democrat. Yet it is quite clear that he removed him because he was a traitor. McClellan once wrote, "I would cheerfully take the dictatorship and agree to lay down my life when the country is saved." His country never asked of him the first sacrifice. It is a pity that it never asked of him the second.

Burnside, who was appointed to succeed McClellan, followed Lee into Virginia only to be driven back by a third of his numbers in the enormous defeat of Fredericksburg on 11th December, 1862.

Hooker followed Burnside in this procession, to fall in his turn in the next May, at Chancellorsville. Yet in her moment of great victory the South lost more than an army. A stray Southern bullet towards the end of the day pierced the great heart of Stonewall Jackson. Thus died the last and incomparably the first of the Puritan captains of history, fighting so nobly and in such a cause, as the champion of a traditional way of European life.

Such was the story of the failure of the North in 1862 to impose her will upon the South by military means. But the military story is not the whole story of that year. During it Lincoln claimed for his side a new weapon. From the beginning of the war Lincoln had been careful to point out that this was not a war against slavery. In the slave States which did not secede he was most rigorous in enforcing the Fugitive Slave Law. To the clergymen from Chicago who told him that it was God's will that he adopt a policy of emancipation he replied, "I hope it will not be irreverent for me to say that, if it is probable that God would reveal His Will to others on a point so connected with my duty, it might be supposed He would reveal it directly to me. Is it not odd that the only channel He could send it by was that roundabout route by that awfully wicked city of Chicago?" Yet it is clear that the progress of the war did create a real problem—that of the deserting slave of rebel ownership. It was not within reason that a slave should be returned to an owner in arms against the Union. Willy-nilly then the Northern army became an invitation to freedom and the escaped slave was confiscated from his master on the ground that he was contraband of war. He was then liberated.

Larger and larger grew the temptation to embarrass the South by the policy of issuing an invitation to their negroes in a general proclamation of freedom to all slaves, the property of rebel owners. To this policy Lincoln gave his adhesion by his famous Emancipation Proclamation of 22nd September, 1862. He had resolved to follow this policy earlier in the year, in July, when he "had about come to the conclusion that it was a military necessity, absolutely essential to the salvation of the nation, that we must free the slaves or be ourselves subdued." He had at that time submitted his plan to the Cabinet. But on Seward's advice it was agreed that such a measure of patent panic could only avoid harm if it was issued after at least an apparent victory. It was therefore kept until Antietam and issued at the beginning of Lee's retreat.

Too large language has been used about this business. Lord Charnwood calls it "one of the signal events in the chequered progress of Christianity." Let us rather call it a political trick, on the whole justified by necessity. Between two European nations it is an underhand blow if the one attempts to strike the other by raising against it an insurrection of non-Europeans within its territory. That is a mere interpretation of the phrase, "the unity of Christendom," by the reality given to which our higher civilization survives. This was such an attempt. It forced the war, in Lincoln's own phrase, to "degenerate into a violent and remorseless revolutionary struggle." Worse than that, it made certain that, after the war and apart from its issue, the prestige of the white race would have to be reimposed by the vilest of all kinds of conflicts. Of all these dangers Lincoln was well aware. He had often pointed them out to the more foolish. The sexual consequences of such an invitation were, to his Kentucky blood, peculiarly abhorrent. He must have known well enough that he had not solved the negro question, but put off, for at least a generation, the possibility of even an attempt at solution.

As military necessity it was defensible; as a social reform it was a fatal half-measure. To give to the slaves the merely negative side of freedom without a scheme for giving them also its positive attributes, such as property, could only bring one of two results. Either it might throw the whole country into the chaos of race-war or else, as Calhoun said, merely "change the form of slavery," substituting for the slavery of individual to individual a crueler slavery of race to race.

What then can be said for Lincoln? Simply that there was nothing else to be done. War is not a parlor-game. He fought because he thought it vital that the Union should be preserved. All means to preserve it seemed to have failed. So, as there was no alternative, he called in the black race to redress the balance of the white. Jefferson Davis did not make things better by expressing his horror in atrocious threats of vengeance. And it is easy to forgive Lincoln everything in his desperation except his fearful prophecy that "there will be some black men who can remember that with silent tongue and clenched teeth and steady eye and well-poised bayonet they have helped mankind on to this great consummation." Indeed there were, and what a consummation!

During these months Lincoln had again to compose differences in his own Cabinet. Chase, the Secretary of the Treasury, was engaged in raising up an opposition against Seward, the Secretary of State. Nine important Senators demanded to see the President in order to force Seward's resignation. When they arrived they found themselves confronted with the whole Cabinet, except Seward who had resigned already. Lincoln put upon Chase, the instigator of the revolt, the task of defending his late colleague—a task which in public he could not decently refuse. The result was that Chase had to add his resignation to that of Seward, and Lincoln was able to arrange that both be withdrawn.

Since the battle of Shiloh the fighting in the West had been in two theaters, one of much, one of little importance. On the one hand there had been an inconclusive invasion of Kentucky by the Confederates and a subsequent retreat to Tennessee, on the other the attempt of Grant to capture Vicksburg and thus make the Mississippi free for Northern ships. On Independence Day, 1863, Vicksburg surrendered and, as Lincoln said, "the Father of Waters again goes unvexed to the Sea." In other spheres the year of 1863 was a good one for the North. At almost the same time as the fall of Vicksburg Lee's second invasion of Northern territory was checked by Meade at the bloody battle of Gettysburg, though the Southern army was allowed needlessly to escape, and in Tennessee the Confederate Bragg, who had held his opponents at Chickamauga in September, was routed and driven right back into Georgia by the battle of Chattanooga in November.

A number of the State Governors combined to erect on the battlefield of Gettysburg a cemetery. This cemetery was opened on the 19th November of this year and at its opening Abraham Lincoln spoke. With that speech all are familiar, nor is it the purpose here to repeat it. It was a speech of great sadness and yet of great triumph. He had held hard to his faith through some of the darkest days through which a man can live. On the cause which he loved a curse seemed to hang. Not only had plans miscarried, but for some time the motives of almost every man to

Abraham Lincoln

whom confidence was given seemed suddenly to turn to vileness. Now at last—it was much—he had been able to find generals who would rather win the war than not. There was good hope. In this good hope Lincoln spoke. Yet for us there is a sadness in the speech. Those who had died, had died, he claimed, so that "Government of the people, by the people, for the people should not perish from the earth." But it is hard to see in what sense it could ever have been pretended that the Northern cause was especially the cause of democracy. Still less, as one looks at the North which has emerged from the war, can it be pretended that the victory has been especially the victory of democracy.

The other problems of this year were those of internal politics, centering mainly around conscription. The Southern Government had introduced conscription early in the war. The North, with her larger and more apathetic population, naturally did not take this step until later. In May, 1863, the Conscription Bill became law. The arguments for the bill were clearly conclusive to anyone who granted the original premise that victory in the war was desirable. They were generally accepted, and serious criticism can only be brought against the provision by which a rich man could buy a substitute for himself—a provision which showed how very partial was even Lincoln's own application of the principle of "government of the people, by the people, for the people." The persons who had made the war were thus able to avoid fighting in it. Yet election-year was coming on. Some riots, say, in New York, and an election-cry were necessary for the Democratic cause. McClellan deplored them and, with a sense of loyalty and honor delicious in a subordinate who was also an opponent, pointed out that "the remedy for political errors, if any are committed, is to be found only in the action of the people at the polls." Yet for the Democratic purpose conscription was most convenient. A few niggers hung in the streets of New York, to prove that Democrats were not bigoted abolitionists, could do nobody any harm.

The American Heresy

With such a program and a general string of complaints against the tyranny of "King Abraham I," the Democrats had been gaining ground throughout 1863. In their complaint against the Government's tyranny and against arbitrary arrest for offenses as vague as "discouraging enlistments," "any disloyal practise," or giving "aid and comfort to the rebels," there was much force—though it was a policy followed rather in spite of Lincoln than by him. Those in power seemed to be captured with an appetite for interference in the affairs of others. Lord Lyons, the British ambassador, wrote with penetration worthy of a de Tocqueville,[1] "The applause with which each successive stretch of power is received by the people is a very alarming symptom to the friends of liberty and law." "A more unlimited despot than the world knows this side of China," was Wendell Phillips' description of Lincoln, and there comes to us an echo from an old world of freedom, when, as the *grand finale* in the *crescendo* of the Government's crimes, that writer records that "for the first time on this continent we have passports, which even Louis Napoleon pronounces useless and odious."

The Democratic program towards the war was summed up by their leader, Vallandigham. "The war for the Union is in your hands a most bloody and costly failure. War for the Union was abandoned; war for the negro openly begun. With what success? Let the dead at Fredericksburg make answer. Ought this war to continue? I answer 'No—not a day, not an hour.' Shall we separate? Again I answer 'No, no, no.' Stop fighting. Make an armistice." To this the reply was obvious. The South insisted on secession. It was necessary either to beat their army or to grant their demands. Even to discuss any third alternative was waste of time. Such an answer was clearly made by Lincoln, by Jefferson Davis and by all sensible people. Vallandigham would not believe

---

[1] Alexis, Comte de Tocqueville (1805–58), author of *De la démocratie en Amérique, De l'Ancien Régime*, etc.

that Jefferson Davis had given such an answer. So with fine humor Lincoln sent him to see for himself, handing him over to the Confederates who soon kicked the silly football back again. Yet in a free country one cannot exile a man for being a bore, nor is a good joke a substitute for good justice.

1864 was the year of Southern defeat. It opened with two Southern armies lying to the north and west of Richmond—one under Lee between Richmond and Washington, the other under Johnston at Dayton in Tennessee, a town as yet untroubled by the problems of descending monkeys. The achievement of the year was the reduction of the two defending armies to one.

In May, Grant and Sherman began to move forward. The record of Grant and the Eastern army was, on the whole, one of victory. Against the Southern success at Cold Harbor could be put the repulse of Early's raid on Washington in the Shenandoah Valley. Yet at the end there was still a Southern army in the East. It was the only one. Farragut's capture of Mobile in August, Sherman's capture of Atlanta in September, his march through Georgia and capture of Savannah in December, Thomas' victory at Nashville had reduced all other warfare to the guerilla. The end could not be far off. And as it drew near Lincoln greeted its approach with conversation that grew daily more and more Rabelaisian.

"Reuben," he once remarked to an absent-minded friend, "you're in bed with the wrong wife." It was a reminder often needed in the political society of Civil War Washington. "A Republican Senator, honored by the Empire State and held in high esteem by the religious denomination of which he is a member," was "reported to have left the President's presence because his self-respect would not permit him to stay and listen to the language which he employed."

Yet, incredible as it may seem, even in this year it appeared for a time that the gift of victory would be refused by the victors themselves. The year had begun for Lincoln with a quarrel with Horace

Greeley, the impossible editor of the *New York Tribune*. Greeley, deceived by an adventurer called Jewett, called on Lincoln to stop the war, though, like the Democrats, he also demanded that the Union be preserved, and failed, like them, to explain what you were to do with Lee's army if you were not to fight it. Indeed he was even more impractical than they, for, added to the rest, he was a fanatical abolitionist. His fantastic program amounted to this; he demanded of Lincoln that he should lay down his arms, disband his army and then ask of the triumphant South if she would be so good as kindly to concede every point for which she had been desperately fighting for the last four years. Lincoln, whatever his faults, was not the man to think a thing wrong in 1864 because it was difficult, which he had thought right in 1860 when it appeared that it would be easy. Greeley, whose infallibility was as constant as his opinions were various, was such a man.

Lincoln's other quarrel was with his Secretary of the Treasury, Chase, who had been ambitious to supplant him. Chase had no high opinion of Lincoln. "The spigot in Uncle Abe's barrel is twice as big as the bunghole," he said. "He may have been a good flat-boatman and rail-splitter but he certainly never learned the true science of coopering." It was another—the last—of those continual bickerings about corruption with which Lincoln's Cabinet was full. This time the accusation was made by Chase against Lincoln—of favoritism in appointments—and Chase resigned. Yet Lincoln afterwards appointed him Chief Justice, returning good for evil.

XII

Chase's repudiation by Ohio removed Lincoln's only serious rival within the party but, though he received the nomination as the Republican candidate, he found in the field against him

Abraham Lincoln

Frémont as a Radical Republican and McClellan a Democrat. Frémont's candidature was supported by Governor Andrew, whose grievance against Lincoln was that "while the Governor was setting forth a matter he had at heart, the President, by way of putting him off, told him in illustration a smutty story, which turned the manner of his presentation into ridicule and caused him disgust."

In the country there was no general recognition that its President was a great man. Dana[1] expressed a common judgment when he said, "He likes rather to talk and tell stories with all sorts of persons who come to him for all sorts of purposes than to give his mind to the manly and noble duties of his great post. . . . He has a kind of shrewdness and common sense, mother wit and slipshod, low-level honesty, that make him a good Western jury-lawyer. But he is an unutterable calamity where he is."

Frémont eventually withdrew on condition that his enemy, Blair, resigned from the Cabinet, but McClellan remained and for a time his chances of election were thought very good. His program was: "Resolved that the war is a failure"—a proposition to the truth of which he had himself very considerably contributed. That this was true, in the sense that Northern hopes had been disappointed, cannot be denied. Whether an academic record of discreditable historical fact is an adequate party program may be doubted. McClellan at least had not himself drawn up the program. Other men had put him forward and he, in his speech of acceptance, explained that such an excursion into veracity was entirely contrary both to his own wishes and habits. He took no responsibility for it and almost promised that it would not be repeated.

Before election day news had come of the fall of Atlanta, Shenandoah and the rest. The Democrats' phrase recoiled fatally

---

[1] Richard Henry Dana (1815–82), prominent Massachusetts lawyer of Radical Republican opinions and author of *Two Years Before the Mast*.

upon their own heads and Lincoln was easily re-elected. The election of Lincoln shattered the last hope of the South—a hope that the North would weaken in her determination. The Constitutional Amendment to prohibit slavery was passed in January, 1865. But slavery was, as Jefferson Davis admitted, already dead. By the campaigns of Sherman and Sheridan the last Southern armies around Petersburg and Richmond were being squeezed to death within one dreadful iron ring. In February Lincoln and Seward had met three commissioners of the Confederacy, of whom Alexander Stephens was one, upon a ship in Hampton Roads. There had been some fantastic discussion of a combination of the armies for an attack upon the French in Mexico. But the talk showed that the Confederacy was not yet ready for submission. The end was not far distant.

Slavery was not the issue at the last, any more than it had been at the first. "You have already emancipated nearly two millions of our slaves," said Jefferson Davis, "and if you will take care of them you may emancipate the rest. I had a few when the war began. I was of some use to them; they were never of any to me. Against their will you 'emancipated' them; and you may 'emancipate' every negro in the Confederacy, but we will be free."

On 4th March Lincoln took the oath of Presidential office for the second time. What were the thoughts that chased one another through his brain as he waited to deliver his inaugural address? It would be fascinating to know. Four years before, to the day, he had stood in the same place. On that day Douglas, the man whom he had defeated and ruined, had stood beside him and held his hat—Douglas who, when the war broke out and many who should have been Lincoln's friends jumped only at an opportunity for pilfering, came and asked nothing but how he could best serve his country, left Washington for ever and was now dead three years ago in Illinois. Would Lincoln ever see Illinois again—Illinois, his home-state, which, when all America

Abraham Lincoln

was going for him, had gone against him? "A prophet"—how does it run? Willy was here four years ago—his young son, who had died two years afterwards. And they were all wondering what to do about Fort Sumter. Four years ago the flag had been shot away from Fort Sumter. Three weeks ago it had been put back there. No, it had not been put back yet, had it? But Charleston was captured. Seward had turned out better than he feared. Grant and Sherman did fight at any rate. They were the sort of men he wanted. How trying Mrs. Lincoln sometimes was! At times he thought that she would go mad before the end.

There had been black days, but somehow things seemed to have turned out all right in the end. Or had they? It had all seemed so clear once. Now he sometimes wondered if he was at the end or the beginning of his troubles. Would the North ever allow the South her freedom again? Could he hold the people? Sumner was a strong man—and he could understand nothing. The first mumbles of the quarrels with the Radicals could even now be heard. White and black could not cohabit. It made one shudder all over to think of it. He must save the South from that.

It is certain that in these days his chief concern was with plans for reconstruction after the war. And it is characteristic of this extraordinary man that in this moment of its utter ruin the whole strength of the Southern case comes most clearly home to him. There comes, too, a great humility. Even where something seems to him plainly wrong he now feels more and more that fallible man cannot know for certain. "Both," he said, "read the same Bible and pray to the same God, and each invokes his aid against the other. It may seem strange that any man should dare ask a just God's assistance in wringing their bread from the sweat of other men's faces; but let us judge not that we be not judged. The prayers of both could not be answered—that of neither has been answered fully. The Almighty has his own purposes." In the days of Fort Sumter, or when Lee marched into Maryland, he did not hesitate for an instant. The news from Appomattox Court House alone found him wondering where right lay. Were the Democrats right after all? Was the war a failure—because it was a success?

His speech concluded with the fine passage: "With malice towards none, with charity for all, with firmness in the right, as God gives us to see the right, let us strive to finish the work that we are in, to bind up the nation's wounds, to care for him who shall have borne the battle and for his widow and his orphan, to do all which may achieve and cherish a just and lasting peace among ourselves and with all nations."

This speech was not very popular. Of the reason for its unpopularity Lincoln truly wrote: "Dear Mr. Weed,—Men are not flattered by being shown that there has been a difference of purpose between the Almighty and them." No more they are.

It would be unfair to leave the impression that Lincoln, at this last, felt it in any way necessary to apologize for his past policy. It would also be too greatly to simplify his metaphysics. His idea seems rather to have been that the whole Civil War, a suffering shared by North and South, was a divine punishment for the sin of slavery of which North and South were both guilty. In order that this purpose might be achieved Divine Providence had narrowed the capacity of the leaders of both sides to comprehend right. Lincoln had done right "as God gave him to see the right." So had Jefferson Davis. But God had given to both only a partial vision.

XIII

On 2nd April Jefferson Davis abandoned Richmond. On 5th April Lincoln landed from a small tug-boat at one of the city wharves. Picking up as a guide a negro who happened to be loitering nearby and escorted by ten sailors, the President walked for a mile and a half along a hot and dusty road to the city. Thus did the mighty master of war make his triumphal entry into the captured capital of the enemy.

Three days later—it was Palm Sunday, the day upon which the people of Jerusalem had come out shouting for a King—Lee met Grant and Meade in a small farm-house near Appomattox. Lee had fought a fight which places him in the company of the great captains of history. Both Grant and Meade seem to have been great enough to realize the greatness in whose presence they stood. This Sunday was not a day for triumph.

Lee began by greeting Meade and commenting on how gray his hair had grown since they last met. Meade replied that Lee himself was the cause of its grayness.

Lee then turned to Grant and they exchanged reminiscences of the old days at West Point. According to the first draft the Confederate generals were to surrender their side-arms, but, as he looked up, Grant caught sight of the handsome sword by Lee's side. Without a word he picked up the pen and drew a line through this clause.

Lee had only one more request to make. Grant might not know that the Confederate cavalry troopers owned their own horses. Grant said that they would be useful for the plowing and added the concession.

"This will have the best possible effect on the men," said Lee. "It will do much towards conciliating our people."

They shook hands and went out. A little way off stood Lee's troops. The general rode up to them.

"We have fought through the war together," he said. "I did my best for you."

Grant posted off at once in order to take his little son back to school.

Lincoln was on that same day on board ship, sailing back from City Point to Washington. He sat on the deck and read

Macbeth to those gathered around him. It is recorded that when he came to the lines:

> "Duncan is in his grave;
> After life's fitful fever he sleeps well;
> Treason has done his worst; nor steel, nor poison,
> Malice domestic, foreign levy, nothing
> Can touch him further,"

he stopped and read them over again and then repeated "Duncan is in his grave."

On the Tuesday he reached Washington and was welcomed by a cheering crowd. To them he made a speech, outlining his plans for the reconstruction of the South. When the crowd called on him to name a tune, he answered, "The songs of the South are now our songs. Bid the band play 'Dixie.'"

XIV

On Good Friday morning he held a Cabinet meeting. He spoke to it of his hope that "there will be no persecution, no bloody work after this war." He prophesied to them that some great thing was about to happen, for he had dreamed that he was sailing in a ship of a peculiar build and being carried with great speed towards a dark shore in the distance. This dream he had had before every Federal victory—Antietam, Murfreesborough, Gettysburg and Vicksburg. Grant bluntly said that Murfreesborough was not a victory and no one else paid much attention to the talk.

That night he and Mrs. Lincoln went together to the theater to see a comedy, *Our American Cousin*. The theater was crowded and Lincoln received a great ovation. Some time after ten o'clock a shot rang out. The President was observed to lurch forward in

Abraham Lincoln

his box. A man who had entered unobserved from behind jumped down from the box on to the stage, there turned and shouted "*Sic semper Tyrannis*"—the motto of Virginia—and vanished into the wings. The murderer of Lincoln, John Wilkes Booth, a weak-minded actor, was afterwards shot in a barn, whither he had been pursued. Lincoln lingered on until the morning of Easter Eve. At 7.22 a.m. the life left him. "Now he belongs to the ages," said Stanton, who was standing by his bedside.

I have spoken with one who was a Confederate soldier and in prison in Washington on that Good Friday night. He has described to me how he heard the people around his prison yelling like wild beasts for blood. One can well believe it. Hardly ever in history has a deed been done so wicked and also so senseless. There was horror upon the whole city that night, and next day its decorations were all draped in black. Yet few things are more disreputable than the attempt to fasten the responsibility upon the leaders of the Confederates. Jefferson Davis was arrested for murder on the order of Andrew Johnson, who had succeeded Lincoln in the Presidency. He defended himself. "There is one man, at least, who knows this accusation to be false. Whatever else Andrew Johnson knows, he knows that I preferred Mr. Lincoln to him." It is a certain irony of justice that Johnson, in his turn, should have had afterwards to defend himself against this monstrous charge.

On Easter Day in almost every pulpit in the North sermons were delivered upon Abraham Lincoln, and many suggested that God, in His inscrutable wisdom, had removed him from the earth because his policy towards the defeated rebellion was too lenient.

So ended the great experiment of free America. The principle of the equality and independence of the States upon which it was built has never again received more than lip-service. Whether Lincoln would have been strong enough to restore it we shall

The American Heresy

never know. He must always remain, for those who judge wisely, a tragic figure. Few souls are strong enough to bear the temptations of power. But Lincoln grew from power, not more proud but more humble, not more solemn but more humorous. Yet with a thousand noble humors and virtues, had he not through all his life been on the wrong side? by refusing to accept the Dred Scott decision shaken the confidence of the South in the whole constitutional mechanism? by driving Douglas out of public life robbed the Union of the last man who might have saved it? by rejecting the Crittenden Compromise made war inevitable? by refusing to allow secession undermined the foundations of freedom? by his proclamation of emancipation wantonly aggravated racial problems? And yet, even if it be true that this gallant gentleman had fought nobly through all his life for the wrong, still at his death he had found an issue, greater perhaps than all of these, upon which he was gloriously and chivalrously in the right—the issue of Southern freedom.

Abraham Lincoln was a man who died with his work before him. But, if history cannot pass here a verdict of accomplishment, let it, thinking on the dark days of the war and the men around him, record this. Others, through the mud of abuse, calumny, malice, have yet been seen to be noble men. Lincoln's has been a harder test. Even in spite of hero-worship he still remains a hero.

Woodrow Wilson

I

JEFFERSON DAVIS, after his arrest, was bundled into a carriage, along with Alexander Stephens, his Vice-President, and sent off to jail, where it was intended that he should remain until after his trial for the murder of Abraham Lincoln. On his way thither, as he was being driven through the streets of Augusta, in Georgia, a small boy, aged eight, peered through the blinds of an upper window of a Presbyterian manse that he might see the sight. The name of the boy was Thomas Woodrow Wilson, the son of the Rev. Joseph Ruggles Wilson, Pastor of the First Presbyterian Church of Augusta.

Five years later this same Thomas Woodrow was a pupil of Professor Derry's Academy for the Sons of the Best People in Augusta. One day, in the May of 1870, there was a holiday and Thomas Wilson and the rest of Professor Derry's charges were dressed up in their best clothes and paraded in crocodile. With them went the boys from the Richmond Academy. And, when at last the signal was given, all had to file past a kind old gentleman with a beard—General Robert Lee. "I have only the delightful memory," Wilson was to write, "of standing, when a lad, for a moment by General Lee's side and looking up into his face. I have nothing but a child's memory of the man."

In 1874 the Rev. James Ruggles Wilson received a call to be Professor of Pastoral Theology at the Theological Seminary of Columbia, in South Carolina. Thither his son went, too, and of mental development at this maturing age the loving father soon found evidence.

"Says Tommy to me at breakfast this morning after he had been reading until way after midnight last night:

"'Father,' says he, 'Eureka,' says he.

"And I says, 'Eureka, Tommy. And why?'

"'Eureka,' he repeats, all fine and gay. 'Eureka. I have found it,' says he.

"'Found what?' says I.

"'A mind, sir. I've found I have an intellect and a first-class mind.'"

II

Thus equipped, Wilson, at the age of eighteen, went to Princeton, where, one can but conclude, first-class minds were that year very plentiful. For, of his class, forty-two were at graduation placed on the roll of honor and of these Wilson was forty-first. Still, as a contemporary wrote, "Tommy seemed to have an uncanny sense that he was a man of destiny. When he walked alone, it was, as he explained, to have an opportunity for calm reflection." Yet he did not refuse to recognize existences other than his own. For "Wilson soon began to use the word 'comradeship' as expressing his idea of the best part of college-life."

After leaving Princeton he went first to study law at the University of Virginia, less peculiar then than in the days of its founder, afterwards, to practice it in Atlanta, where he found little practice but a wife. In order to secure a settled income he determined to return to the academic world, went to Johns Hopkins to earn his Doctor's Degree and thence was appointed professor at Bryn Mawr in 1885.

Woodrow Wilson

Bryn Mawr was a new college and he did not remain there long. "The social advantages were inadequate," he said. He moved on to Wesleyan University at Middletown, Connecticut. In the life there he made for himself the unexpected place of football-coach. "Professor Wilson told them," says a writer in the *Wesleyan Alumnus*, "that he was referee . . . of the Princeton team in its championship days, and was kept from being on the victorious team only by a prolonged illness." And, though these claims were certainly untrue, he was perhaps none the worse a coach for that.

Let us observe a first-class mind at work.

"Suddenly from the Wesleyan bleachers a man walked out in front, clad in heavy rubber-boots and a raincoat. He shouted to the Wesleyan contingent, reproaching them for not cheering for their team, and at once began to lead them in the Wesleyan yell, beating time for them with his umbrella. He continued this violently until the Wesleyan cheers heartened Slayback's men in spite of their handicap, and the tide of the game turned. . . . After the game, the Lehigh players, inquiring about the magnetic cheer-leader, were informed that he was Wesleyan's Professor of History, Dr. Woodrow Wilson."

The important words are surely "in front."

III

In 1889 Wilson returned to Princeton as Professor of Jurisprudence. For thirteen years he was to hold that chair. They were his years of leisure and during them the greater part of his score of books was written. If a politician is not utterly unlettered it is among some people the fashion grossly to overpraise his literary skill. Few politicians of this century have possessed more than a competent command of written language. Wilson certainly had hardly that. If he was, as is often said, the slave of phrases, they were not very good phrases. The story is told that Wilson at Princeton once dismissed his class for the day because he was unable at the moment to think of the exact word in which to express his thought. If it is true, as it well may be—it is to be hoped that his pupils demanded the return of their tutorial fees—it is an example only of arrogant affectation. For a man who could write in a revised and published book, "What he did it is idle to speculate, being confident that he did whatever he pleased," can have had very little sense of grammar, nor one who could write of Washington that he "fared forth, very bravely caparisoned in proper uniform," much ear for language.

Wilson's twenty books are not important as Jefferson's one book is important. For Wilson's thoughts do not matter as Jefferson's thoughts matter. Jefferson was a philosopher, trying to think out an ethical scheme for himself and through politics to give that scheme to his country. It is impossible therefore to study his politics without studying his philosophy. It is impossible to study American history without studying his politics. The works of Wilson make no such demand upon us. For he wrote of none of those ends which he was afterwards to attempt to realize. He was by nature an autocrat. And the natural autocrat is often an aristocrat in his library, but, in the leadership of practical politics, if he cannot be an emperor, becomes—the next best thing—a democrat. In an aristocracy the rest of his class are his equals. In a democracy all are equal—except himself.

At the back of Wilson's mind was always a feeling that he was an intellectual peer, superior to the herd. "I do sometimes wish that people were not so damned stupid," he was afterwards to say. Yet at the same time he could not bear that any of this despised herd, low as they had sunk, should sink so low as not to know the name of Woodrow Wilson. "Popularize, but do not vulgarize," we can always feel him saying to himself. Through such work as his he felt that the people might be raised from materialism to idealism. And with a consciousness of some virtue he was to write to Harper and Brothers from the White House in 1912 to suggest that he be given more favorable royalty terms on his *History of the American People*. The publishers agreed, advising him that "it was their belief that his *History of the American People* had brought financial return many times larger than any similar number of words ever written by any historian anywhere in the world." A blow to Macaulay!

He wrote twenty books on various subjects of American and English history. They were all autobiographies. There are character sketches of Washington and Lee, of Burke and Chatham, but they all tell only of two characters, of Woodrow Wilson as he was, the quiet and not exuberant scholar, of Woodrow Wilson as he would be, the champion smashing worlds and remolding them nearer to his heart's desire. "Often in those days," says his brother-in-law, "I have heard him cry out, 'I am so tired of a merely talking profession. I want to do something.'"

IV

In 1902 Wilson was appointed President of Princeton University. For four years his rule was of peace and solid success. "Altogether everything was moving up," writes Mr. Kerney.[1] "Millions of dollars, and the number of instructors," doubled. What could be more satisfactory? How unimportant beside it that the number of students slightly decreased!

His appointment to the Presidency had been largely due to Moses Taylor Pyne, multi-millionaire and New York financier, one of the most prominent of the Trustees. By his advice Wilson

---

[1] *The Political Education of Woodrow Wilson*, by James Kerney. The Century Company. New York, 1926.

was selected. This service the new President recognized in grateful language. "Mr. Pyne," he said, "has been the ideal friend of Princeton. He has given her money . . . and what is better than that, he has given her constant service of thoughtful counsel." Another among his important supporters was Grover Cleveland, the only Democrat except Wilson to have been President of the United States since the Civil War, now an old man who had come to live in his retirement at Princeton. Wilson was his friend. "It has been one of the best circumstances of my life that I have been associated with you in matters both large and small," he wrote to Cleveland in a letter of birthday congratulations. At first Wilson was content to be grateful to the powerful interests which had raised him from a chair of Jurisprudence to that of President. But as time passed and confidence grew he seems to have begun to feel that there was a certain indignity in walking through the conventional duties of a University head as the puppet of a financier and an ex-statesman. Was this worthy of the twentieth-century heir of Chatham and Burke and Gladstone, of Washington and Robert E. Lee? "When you come into the presence of a leader of men," he was to say of Lee, "you know you have come into the presence of fire." Pyne and Cleveland must be taught their lesson.

He determined therefore to deliver an original attack which should make his name memorable. For its objective he chose the Princeton clubs. At Oxford there are a number of professedly exclusive dining-clubs, to obtain election to which is, I have been told, the ambition of certain undergraduates. At Princeton there was of course no so fully developed residential system as at Oxford. The club was therefore not only dining but residential. After a year all students were driven out from the College commons and those—more than one-half—who were unable to obtain election to any club, were shut out from much of the general college life, from that "comradeship" of which Wilson used to speak. Some, thus excluded, would even leave the University.

Wilson made up his mind that the clubs had grown into an intolerable abuse. He determined to abolish them and to substitute "the quadrangle system of Oxford." The trustees agreed with him in principle but for financial reasons delayed action. All changes in a seat of learning are inevitably opposed by the old boys. For every change necessarily violates a tradition. Therefore it was only to be expected that Wilson's plan would be denounced. He was clearly attempting to remedy a real evil. Yet for the violence of the opposition he had only himself to blame—or praise. For, not content that it be fought out privately in ordinary academic warfare, he carried his battle to the public and shouted to the public that it was one between democracy and plutocracy. The plutocrats huddled together in their clubs and formed a class, while Woodrow Wilson was out on the wind and "no class can serve America," he told the audiences of Pittsburgh.

The cry against plutocracy was at that time becoming popular. It was the latest and most original of the "stunts" of the plutocratic press. Theodore Roosevelt broadcast it from the White House. Liberal professors cried out for academic freedom. It won Wilson his headlines. Yet as a classification of his quarrel it was only a half-truth. Doubtless there were richer and poorer at Princeton, as was inevitable so long as the wealth of America was unequally distributed, and on the whole the average income of the half who entered the clubs was larger than that of the half who did not. Wilson's dishonesty lay in pretending that wealth was the only qualification required for election. It was one of the qualifications. No doubt the member would have to maintain a certain standard of living. But he was elected because of his general social qualities. The clubs formed not a plutocracy but an aristocracy. The enemy of an aristocracy is often the plutocrat who cannot get admission to it. His perhaps was the battle that Wilson chiefly fought.

With this controversy soon came to be combined another and a more bitter. The degree of an American requires less advanced scholarship than does that of an English University. Therefore the American who wishes to complete his education usually takes a post-graduate course and, to provide for him, many universities have a Graduate School. The Dean of the Post-Graduate School at Princeton was Dr. Andrew West, at one time a friend of Wilson. Dean West was an ambitious man. He foresaw a great future for his school, and, in order to obtain the money necessary for his ambition, published a brochure of explanation. To this brochure Wilson contributed an introduction in which he wrote that it was his ambition to see "a community of scholars set at the heart of Princeton."

Yet soon Dean West could not help feeling that Wilson, in spite of the introduction, was hostile to his plans. Money began to be diverted from the Graduate School to the quadrangle and Wilson to express anxiety lest the Graduate School should become too nearly independent of the University. When therefore the Massachusetts Institute of Technology invited Dean West to become its head at double the salary which Princeton was paying to him he went to Wilson and asked whether the President would prefer that he accept the offer. Wilson begged Dean West to remain. The offer was therefore refused and Wilson himself wrote a resolution of confidence in Dean West. Cleveland Dodge, one of Wilson's friends among the Trustees, even promised, in the enthusiasm of the moment, as the Dean thought, to find financial support for five professors at the Graduate School at a salary of five thousand dollars a year. But this, it was afterwards explained, was "not a promise but a verbal expression of opinion."

Grover Cleveland and Pyne were both West's friends and took his side in the quarrel. In their opinion Wilson, having persuaded Dean West to refuse the Massachusetts offer, was under a moral obligation to support him in carrying out his plans at Princeton. When such support was not given Cleveland felt that Wilson was behaving dishonorably and, in June, 1907, he vigorously attacked him at a meeting of the Board of Trustees. Of the President's honesty he was becoming more and more suspicious, of his vague ideology more and more impatient. The quadrangle-system, he said, "has neither reason nor common sense to sustain it. It has produced no such effect at Oxford as is predicted for it here"—a judgment most certainly just. To an elaborate panegyric on greater democracy at Princeton he rapped out, "Sounds good. I wonder what he means." He prophesied that if Wilson entered political life he would go far and would wreck the Democratic party.

Cleveland died in 1908 and was succeeded as Chairman of the Trustees by Pyne. Three hundred thousand dollars had been subscribed in 1906 towards the building of the Graduate School and in 1909 William Cooper Procter, of Cincinnati, offered a further $500,000 on the conditions that another $500,000 were raised to meet his gift and that he was allowed to choose the site where the school was to be built. There was no difficulty in satisfying the first condition. The second was to be the occasion of great battle.

Procter was a friend of Dean West's party. His demand was that the school be built on its present site, some distance from the other buildings, or, as Pyne put it, "where they would have room to expand and where the studious life of the college should not be subject to undergraduate distraction." "I cannot accede," Wilson wrote to Pyne, "to the acceptance of gifts which take the educational policy of the University out of the hands of the Trustees and faculty and permit it to be determined by those who give money." This was harsh language to use to "the ideal friend of Princeton who has given her money . . . and what is better than that, has given her constant service of thoughtful counsel."

On 13th January, 1910, the Committee for the Graduate School met in Nassau Hall. Wilson addressed it, asking it to refuse Mr. Procter's offer. But after his speech a letter was produced and read from Mr. Procter, withdrawing his condition concerning the site.

Amid silence Wilson rose again. He was white and agitated. "This offer," he stammered, "is too—too—too complicated. The time has passed for compromise. At any rate—I can't accept this. The matter of the site is not essential. Under proper auspices my faculty can make this school a success anywhere in Mercer County. The whole trouble is that Dean West's ideas and ideals are not the ideas and ideals of Princeton." He sat down.

This story has been denied. But certainly it represents the truth, even if it does not report correctly the facts. The quarrel between Wilson and Dean West was not a quarrel between the poor man's friend and the plutocrat, for, as Mr. Annin[1] has shown, though it is true that Pyne was a rich man, yet on the whole the power of wealth was on Wilson's side. "The anti-Wilsonians were chiefly lawyers, clergymen and teachers, Mr. Pyne being the only one of really large means. On the other side there were eight whom common report placed in the millionaire class; three were certainly multi-millionaires; and two of these probably possessed wealth in excess of all the rest of the Board combined." Still less was the quarrel concerning the site of a Graduate School. This was "not essential." Wilson had made no especial point of it when he wrote the introduction to Dean West's brochure at the time of the gift of the $300,000. The explanation is more simple. "The effect," Mr. Annin writes, "of Wilson's first four years at Princeton was to build up what in politics would be called a personal machine." "The teachers added in furtherance of the Preceptorial system had no delusions as to the power on which depended their tenure of office." The ideas and ideals of Dean West were not the ideas and ideals of Woodrow Wilson. His fear was that another name than his might be sometimes mentioned at Princeton. To

---

[1] *Woodrow Wilson: A Character Study*, by Robert Edwards Annin. Dodd, Mead & Company. New York, 1924.

prevent this he was willing to upset America by the story of a fight between the rich and the poor, which existed, if it existed there, only in his imagination. Yet it would be a mistake to call him a liar. For, as Mr. White[1] explains, "his excuse dramatized itself best for the public upon the issue of the interference of money in academic affairs."

After Wilson's defiance of Dean West the debate was continued in Nassau Hall. Wilson was asked why, if he disapproved of "the ideas and ideals of Dean West," he had written an introduction to his brochure. Wilson replied that he had written the introduction without reading the book. But this "dramatization" was not assisted by Dean West's possession of a copy of the proofs annotated in Wilson's own handwriting. Forced to acknowledge this, Wilson afterwards explained that he had not previously seen the illustrations and, as he once said to the Dean, "we must not lay too great stress upon commitments."

Once more Wilson carried his quarrel to the country. In its final form the Procter offer was virtually unconditional. It had now therefore to be explained that a Graduate School was, as such, an engine of plutocracy. Wilson was equal to the task. "Will America tolerate the seclusion of Graduate students?" he asked the alumni of Pittsburgh in tones of ringing scorn. "Will America tolerate the idea of having Graduate students set apart? America will tolerate nothing except unpatronized endeavor. Seclude a man, separate him from the rough-and-tumble of college life, from all the contacts of every sort and condition of men, and you have done a thing which America will brand with its contemptuous disapproval."

O democratic Gadarene swine, who ran, so nobly together, down a steep place into the sea, you at any rate America will not brand with contemptuous disapproval. Yet to abolish privilege

---

[1] *Woodrow Wilson, the Man, His Times and His Task*, by William Allen White. Houghton Mifflin Company. Boston, 1924.

does not necessarily mean to abolish privacy. A right to liberty, as Jefferson spoke of it, implies a right on occasion to bang one's door and lock it, and that, too—impious thought—in spite of the disapproval of America. And was there not in the Princeton class of '79 a delicate boy in spectacles, who "had an uncanny sense of destiny? When he walked alone, it was, as he explained, to have an opportunity for calm reflection." Had this delicate boy by now reflected so much and so calmly that it was never again necessary for a post-graduate student to reflect any more?

Yet the end was at hand—an unforeseen end. On 18th May died a wealthy old man, Isaac C. Wyman. A few days later David Lawrence, a student-reporter, knocked at Wilson's door and handed him a telegram from the *New York Times*.

"Isaac C. Wyman, of Salem, Massachusetts, died, leaving an estate valued at over ten million dollars to the Graduate School at Princeton, naming his attorney, John H. Raymond, and Dean Andrew F. West executors. Ask President Wilson for statement to use in connection with tomorrow's paper."

"Lawrence," said Wilson, "this means defeat."

To fight plutocracy in the shape of a million dollars was a noble crusade. To fight her in the shape of ten million was to ask too much of any man, however uncanny his sense of destiny. "The size of the gift," he explained to Dean West, "entirely changes the perspective." How often before in the chequered history of the human race this had been most sadly true, the historian of the United States, if any one, must have surely known.

It is perhaps a misfortune for Princeton that her very ordinary academic quarrels should have become the common subject of international discussion. It is the penalty she must pay for driving her President into public life in order to be rid of him. For Woodrow Wilson played the game of life on principles opposite to those upon which a man takes his part in a golf or tennis tournament. After each round, though he had won no victory, he yet moved up to the next. From defeat at Princeton he took refuge in New Jersey, from New Jersey in the White House, from America in the adulations of Europe, and from the disasters of Versailles he found the ultimate refuge. As the flood rose he saved himself by always climbing one step further up the ladder.

V

Colonel George Harvey was the head of Harper and Brothers, Wilson's publishers, and the editor of *Harper's Weekly*. The firm and the magazine were both of high standing and in the eyes of the uninquiring world entirely independent. Yet in truth neither had lately been prosperous and J. P. Morgan had thought it wise to take advantage of their embarrassments by an advance of four hundred thousand dollars. The magazine was thus continued on the Morgan subsidy.

In this magazine began to appear during the early months of 1909 an insistent demand that Wilson be nominated as Democratic candidate for the Governorship of New Jersey in the next year's election. In Colonel Harvey's opinion Wilson would be the best candidate for the Democrats to put forward. For newspaper "stunts" had aroused talk against plutocracy. Such talk might have a certain voting power. And Wilson was an ideal man with which to capture such a vote. The story of his fight against plutocracy could easily be given attractive publicity, while, since the fight itself was quite fictitious, success need cause no anxiety.

The Democratic machine in New Jersey was at that date under plutocratic control. Its masters did not personally descend into the arena but preferred to work through "bosses." These "bosses" were genial, well-spoken people, players of the game, as its rules were handed down to them, with no large visions of remaking society nor with any mean ones of enslaving it; corrupt, no doubt, but when the outcry threatened, as one of the first among them said, "pandering a little to the moral sense of the community," friendly, humorous, without malice, neither solemn nor self-righteous—taking it all in all perhaps the best type that representative government in America produces. The chief of them at this time in New Jersey were the "Jim-Jim crowd" and "little Bob Davis." The "Jim-Jim crowd" were the followers of two cousins, James Smith and James Nugent. Davis was the sheriff and friend of the poor man, upon whom he saw that the law did not press too hardly.

Colonel Harvey made it his business to induce Wilson to escape from the difficulties of Princeton by running as candidate for the Governorship and to act as go-between from Wall Street to the "bosses" in order to arrange for his support. Smith was frankly puzzled at the selection but loyally obeyed orders, passing it on to his followers in vague commendation that "Wilson was the man of the hour"—a phrase which conveyed, if little more, at any rate the information that he was to receive the vote. Of Wilson's political opinions it is improbable that Smith was interested in much more than the sentence in his book, the *State and Federal Government*. "They are the political bosses, whom the people obey and affect to despise. It is unjust to despise them." It seemed sufficient.

Just before the end of the University term, in June or the last days of May, Colonel Harvey asked Wilson if he would accept the nomination should it be offered to him. Wilson answered that he would be glad to consider it. On 9th July a reporter of the *Newark Evening News* went to Lyme, in Connecticut, where Wilson was spending his holiday, to ask if there were any truth in the rumors which connected his name with political ambitions. Wilson had been much annoyed by these rumors and met them with indignant denial. "Make it just as forcibly plain as you can, so that it may perhaps put an end to all these stories, most of them absurd, which have made me appear as being a candidate for office."

On 12th July Wilson went to New York. In a New York club he met Smith, Nugent and a third leader of the gang named Ross, and also Davis, Hudspeth and Kinkead of the other gang. There were also present Colonel Harvey and Richard V. Lindabury, counsel for the Steel Corporation, J. P. Morgan and other large trusts. At this conference Wilson was told that there was a real demand for his candidature. At first he was puzzled. He asked whether it were true that the bosses had "seen the dawn of a new day" and wanted a leader. The bosses agreed. Naturally such unexpected news altered the President's decision and, returning to Lyme, he announced that, though "I do not wish to be drawn away from my present duty and responsibilities," yet—always it is the stern Calvinist—"my wish does not constitute my duty. If it is the wish of a decided majority of the thoughtful Democrats of the State that I should consent to accept the party's nomination for the great office of Governor," he would bow and obey. "I should not feel personally disappointed if it should turn out otherwise.

The battle was not yet won. Wilson had never taken any part in the political life of Mercer County, the county in which he lived. After this announcement the Democratic League of that county had sent him an invitation to their annual outing on 27th July. Wilson wrote in refusal, "May we not hope that after this outing our party may soon have an inning?" Yet, in spite of the repartee, the "thoughtful Democrats" of Mercer County were unanimous in their preference for Mayor Frank S. Katzenbach to Wilson. Others, too, in spite of the bosses were on Katzenbach's side.

On 14th September the nominating convention met at Trenton. "It will be Wilson on the first ballot," said Smith to the reporters. "Wilson will have eight hundred of the fourteen hundred and thirteen delegates." "We can win with Wilson, a man of high attainments, not an office-seeker—a man who rose from the people." Wilson, a Virginian gentleman who had often argued that it was necessary for gentlemen to go into public life, the descendant, as Mr. White so often says, of Irish kings, was not pleased with the compliment.

Smith was almost right in his prophecy. On the first ballot Wilson received seven hundred and forty-seven-and-a-half votes and the nomination. By what methods these votes were collected has never wholly been revealed. After the election Westcott, who nominated the defeated Katzenbach, told Wilson how a block of Camden delegates had been bargained for in the nominating convention. "Wilson," writes Mr. Kerney, "was so shocked that he expressed a doubt as to whether he could honorably continue to hold an office that had come to him through such methods." Yet he did continue to hold it.

According to one story, Wilson was on the golf links when the news came to him of his nomination. He returned home, changed his clothes and motored to Trenton where he delivered to the Convention his speech of acceptance. The speech, it seems, aroused at the time great enthusiasm. He said that he accepted the nomination free of all pledges. The bosses did not feel uneasy.

If Wilson was to succeed it was necessary to win for him some popularity with the Democrats of his home-county of Mercer. So four days later Smith and Mr. Kerney, the editor of the *Trenton Evening Times*, took a delegation from the county to visit Wilson at Princeton. Wilson and the delegates conversed in the study. Smith and Mr. Kerney strolled outside in the garden.

"Jim," said Smith, as he looked around him at the beautiful view, "can you imagine any one being damn fool enough to give this up for the heartaches of politics?"

Yet Wilson had as yet no regrets. Within he was charming his neighbors of Mercer County. When they left the house, they reported that "that's a go-through guy." It was his first victory.

The campaign soon started and it became evident that Wilson would make a good fighter. The eagerness with which the Trustees of Princeton snapped up his resignation hurt him but it was almost the only blot on this early triumph. With triumph came the twin dangers of confidence and verbosity, and one day in a forgetful moment Wilson in one of his speeches challenged any opponent of his policy to meet him in public debate.

The challenge was at once accepted to the dismay of Wilson's managers by a Mr. Record. Mr. Record was an independent Republican, a radical and a most able man, who had obtained some reputation from his exposure of the "boss" system and the plutocratic control of politics. Wilson's managers advised him that it would be dangerous to submit to public questioning from such a man and Wilson therefore at first ignored the answer, but in the end, being forced to take some notice of it by Mr. Record's demand that he either accept or publicly withdraw the challenge, wrote to say that he was very sorry that all his evenings until the election were already filled with engagements. Yet he agreed to answer in writing whatever questionnaire Mr. Record might choose to send him. In Mr. Record's questionnaire the most important request was: "If, as you say, the Republican leaders are the representatives of the railroads and the utilities and other interests, which I admit, is it not a fact that the Democratic leaders, such as Jim Smith, also represent the same interests?"

To this Wilson answered with an uncompromising "Yes." Among some of the bosses there was anxiety but Smith professed to regard it merely as a move in a regular game, and dryly observed that, to a direct question demanding a "Yes" or "No," no other answer was possible. Wilson had spoken, it seems, on the advice of Mr. Kerney, who had told him that thus "you will win hands down." This advice proved good for at the poll Wilson received a majority of forty-nine thousand.

VI

Wilson had been made Governor by Smith and Colonel Harvey. Yet it was not in his nature to remain under an obligation long. He could not bear to feel that he owed his success to anybody other than himself. He was also acutely over-sensitive about his academic past. On the one hand this gave him a great feeling of superiority over other politicians. He resented it when Smith said that he "had risen from the people" and was to prefer greatly the deferential tact of Colonel House to the manners of Colonel Harvey, "who addressed the candidate familiarly as 'Wilson' and treated him as an equal."[1] On the other hand he was always determined that he should not be thought a bookworm and incapable of the conventional Machiavellianisms of twentieth-century politics. Of this his fear was probably exaggerated. A third reason, which made him part company with Smith and Colonel Harvey, was certainly the desire to obtain the favor of Western opinion. The Governorship of New Jersey was only a stepping-stone. The White House was the final goal. Financial support could make a man Governor of New Jersey, but no man could become President without some backing from the West of the Mississippi and, owing to the campaigns of Bryan and Roosevelt, it was only possible to gain that support by, at least, appearing to defy finance.

Smith early gave the opportunity for a quarrel. At that time the members of the United States Senate were elected by the Legislatures of the States. But the candidate for the Senatorship in each State was popularly nominated by a direct primary vote. Obviously such a nomination to a politician whose party was in a minority in the Legislature was purely complimentary. Smith had not foreseen a Democratic victory in the Legislative, as well as in the Gubernatorial, elections and had therefore refused to

---

[1] J. Kerney.

be a candidate at the primaries. In his absence a certain Martine had been victorious.

Yet the Democrats had succeeded in capturing the Legislature. Still the primary elections had no legal existence. The party in the majority in the Legislature was not at all bound to accept the people's nominee, and Smith, finding a Democratic majority in control, wished it to set aside the primary as a joke and send him to the Senate. The primary had been largely a joke and Martine was not well qualified to be a United States Senator. Once before Smith had been returned to the Senate in defiance of a primary election. Still it would have been more sporting in him to have allowed Martine his good luck. Wilson was at first inclined to agree with Smith, but afterwards came to see that this was a good cause for which to fight. He said that Martine should be the candidate. Smith replied that the campaign had been too much for Wilson and he needed a rest. Smith, though he was a Catholic, was unable to secure wholehearted Catholic support. The attitude of many was expressed by Mr. Kerney who said: "Now see here, Bishop, I believe your candidate is a crook. And I'm not above supporting a crook but he must be a Protestant crook. I don't propose to have my Church loaded up with him." Wilson determined to divide Smith more completely from his co-religionists and, in order to do so, went out of his way to eulogize three of his own Catholic supporters, "who illustrate in their lives . . . the teachings of the great Church of which they are members. Men sometimes forget that religious truth is the one solid and remaining foundation." How very, very true!

In the same speech Wilson went on to accuse Smith of a plot to get himself elected by the help of Republican votes and told a story of a secret meeting between him and two Republican bosses in Philadelphia. This story was afterwards proved to be false but Wilson did not contradict it and Smith was easily defeated.

In his first three months of office Wilson succeeded in adding to the Statute Book a mass of useful and vigorous legislation, suggested largely by Mr. Record. They were bills intended not so much to please New Jersey as to please the West. The arrangement was that Mr. Record drafted the bills which Wilson caused to be presented to the Legislature, but, since Wilson did not like to have to admit an obligation face to face, Mr. Record deposited them in an outer room and left without seeing the Governor. Wilson used the bills and afterwards wrote to Mr. Record, "We are working for the same end though along somewhat different lines which policy dictates and principle does not condemn." Mr. Record took the hint and did not again call on Wilson.

The mere problems of New Jersey could not long hold such a man's attention. More and more he gave his mind to the furthering of his Presidential chances for 1912. It was necessary somehow to capture the West. His friends were all in the East and he was at a loss to know how to set about his task. Solution came as from Heaven. At the Texas State Fair at Dallas in October, 1911, a Colonel House heard and was impressed by Wilson's speech. This Colonel House was a strange, quiet man of velvet, who lived for the "arranging of situations." In his schooldays it had been his habit "to incite disputes between his schoolmates in order to have an opportunity of settling them." The second habit, at any rate, had lingered. He had determined to arrange the present situation. He was on the lookout for some one to make President. His first favor had been given to Mayor Gaynor, of New York, but the Mayor had proved unsuitable. Of Wilson he had a better hope. Wilson was to lead, Colonel House only asked to be allowed to admire and serve. A meeting was arranged in New York and on these terms agreement was easily reached.

In May, 1911, Wilson made his first big speaking-tour in the Western States. He found that there the referendum and the popular initiative were the questions which filled men's minds. For one perilous and forgetful minute at Kansas City he almost committed himself to these measures. He was warned by his terrified friends in the East, who wired to him that a Presidential candidate who favored the referendum was a candidate already beaten, and, warned, he did not mention it again. The problem was, he saw clearly, to find a program upon which he could unite the Conservative Democrats of the East and the Radical Democrats of the West. It was at first difficult to invent one, but after some thought he concluded that "all were interested in the uplift of mankind in general."[1] His friends' telegrams of warning ceased.

Wilson had gone off for his Western trip on 13th April and returned on 3rd June. During his absence Mr. Ackerman, the president of the Senate, was acting Governor. And, since during the month of May Wilson had not set foot in the Senate nor performed any of the governor's duties, the state comptroller insisted that he was legally bound to pay that month's salary to Mr. Ackerman. Wilson was very shocked, but Mr. Ackerman to whom the difficulty was explained offered to endorse the cheque and hand it over to Mr. Wilson, who thenceforth held a very high opinion of Mr. Ackerman's abilities. "I want to express my personal appreciation," he wrote to him, "of the thorough and thoughtful way in which you have fulfilled the duties of the Governorship during my absence. It gives me comfort to feel that the office was in such safe hands."

Wilson's campaign for the Presidential nomination was by now very definitely organized. It was his purpose to smash the financial control of politics. For this he seemed to be able to command unlimited funds. Even Democratic papers were beginning to ask where the "Wilson money" came from. There was no one source. It came, as do all party funds, from a variety of sources. Wilson's only large advantage over his rivals was in the support of the Jews. On 6th January he had "delivered a very inspiring

---

[1] J. Kerney.

address on the Jews" in New York, and thenceforth received four thousand dollars a month from Henry Morgenthau, the millionaire Jew banker, whom he subsequently made American Ambassador to Turkey. His manager, Mr. McCombs, seems to have received and spent about a quarter of a million dollars up to the time of Wilson's nomination and other friends certainly handled a great deal more. This sum was needed for discrediting rival politicians in Wilson's own party.

Roosevelt was at this time touring the country uttering the same menaces, if not using the same language, as Wilson. Both were determined to check "the insolence of aggrandized wealth." Roosevelt's manager was Mr. George Perkins, while Wilson's campaign was being assisted by a newspaper, called the *Trenton True American*, which was kept alive by subsidy for the purpose. Its nominal backer was Mr. Cleveland Dodge, Wilson's old friend and supporter among the Princeton trustees. During the investigation by Congress into the origins of party funds, Mr. Dodge was asked if any one was coöperating with him in this subsidy. He answered that he had received a loan, to be used for the support of the paper, from Mr. Perkins. Mr. Perkins was the head of the Harvester Combine which had been indicted by President Taft for violation of the anti-Trust laws. Wilson and Roosevelt then, who were to submit themselves to the people as opponents and as alternative liberators of America from financial control, were not only living at the subsidy of financiers but living at the subsidy of the same financiers. "The incident," as Mr. Kerney says, "is amusing."

Colonel House was a friend of Bryan and he insisted that Wilson needed Bryan's support if he was to gain victory. Wilson had a low opinion of Bryan and had previously described him as a man "foolish and dangerous in his theoretical beliefs." But, being present with Bryan at a Democratic rally at Burlington on 5th April, he declared there: "Mr. Bryan has shown that stout heart which in spite of the long years of repeated disappointments has always followed the star of hope, and it is because he has cried 'America, awake,' that some other men have been able to translate into action the doctrines that he has so diligently preached."

Bryan was flattered, but as yet unconvinced. Colonel Harvey had clung to Wilson in spite of his treatment of Smith, and every week *Harper's Weekly* appeared with the heading: "For President, Woodrow Wilson." Bryan looked on Colonel Harvey as the spokesman of the Wall Street, which he feared. And, though Colonel House wrote to Bryan to report that Harvey had told him that he was backing Wilson in spite of the opposition of Morgan and Wall Street, Bryan was skeptically unconvinced. Wilson began to see that, if he wished for the friendship of Bryan and the West, he must pick a quarrel with Colonel Harvey. As Walter Hines Page advised him: "The right sort of enemies often turn out to be more valuable than the wrong sort of friends."

Colonel Harvey had heard rumors that Wilson was complaining that the support of *Harper's Weekly* was doing him no good. Therefore, meeting Wilson with Colonel Watterson, of Kentucky, in the Manhattan Club in New York towards the end of 1911, Colonel Harvey asked him whether this was so. Wilson answered that it was.

"Harvey asked: 'Is there anything I can do, except of course to stop advocating your nomination?'

"Governor Wilson answered: 'I think not. At least I can't think of anything.' . . . A long pause—it must have been icy. Governor Wilson said: 'Good-by, gentlemen.'

"The two insulted Colonels, Harvey and Watterson, nodded responses.

"W. W. exit."[1]

Soon after it was stated in a newspaper that Wilson had broken with Colonel Harvey because he had refused to accept the

---

[1] J. Kerney.

financial support of Colonel Harvey's friend, Mr. Ryan, a Wall Street leader, and of other Wall Street interests. Colonel Watterson wrote to the paper to explain that he had been asked by Wilson to coöperate with Wilson's managers in raising money, that he had suggested to the managers that Mr. Ryan might provide some and that they were delighted with the suggestion.

Wilson wrote in reply: "The statement that Colonel Watterson was requested to assist in raising money on my behalf is absolutely without foundation." To this Colonel Watterson answered that he possessed proofs of the request and would submit them to a court of honor. Wilson then wrote that Colonel Watterson was "a fine old gentleman" and that he must "decline to discuss the matter further."

"The sole issue," answered Colonel Watterson, "is whether I have lied, as Governor Wilson says I have, or he has lied, which I have engaged conclusively to show. He dare not face the facts."

Wilson did not reply. It had been his intention to make it appear to Bryan that there had been a noble gesture of the refusal of financial aid. The gesture had not been wholly successful. Nor were his chances of gaining Bryan's support improved by the publication of a letter, written by Wilson to a Mr. Joline at the time of the previous election, in which he hoped "that something dignified and effective might be done to knock Bryan once and for all into a cocked hat."

Yet Bryan was playing a game too deep for him to be able to afford to take offense easily. On 8th January, 1912, the two met at a Jackson Day dinner in New York and it was observed by the reporters that Bryan not only shook hands with Wilson but "even put an arm round his neck." To what purpose?

Wilson's tireless campaign was beginning to cause amusement. In March he was entertained at dinner in Atlantic City by the New Jersey Senate. The menu "took the form of a railroad time-table and was very cleverly done. It caricatured Wilson's flights over the country chasing the Presidential nomination. It made no great hit with Wilson."[1] He was wise enough nevertheless to accept its hint and from that date until the meeting of the nominating convention in June at Baltimore kept himself more quiet.

VII

Before that convention were four strong candidates—Champ Clark of Missouri, Speaker of the House of Representatives, Governor Harmon of Ohio, Senator Underwood of Alabama, and Wilson. Of these four, Governor Harmon and Senator Underwood were representative of the old Conservative Cleveland Democrats, while Champ Clark had, it seems, no particular political opinions but was a good party man, having supported in turn Cleveland and Bryan, when they were the regular nominees.

Bryan was to go to the convention as one of the delegates from Nebraska and he wished to discover which of the candidates could be counted on as supporter of his radical policies. He therefore made a test case of the appointment as temporary chairman of a Conservative, Alton B. Parker, and sent telegrams to the four candidates, asking for their support if he challenged this appointment. Wilson alone supported him and, with the vote of the Wilson men and others, he was able to muster five hundred and eight votes against five hundred and seventy-nine for Parker. The vote showed that the Middle and Far West were behind Bryan, the East and South behind Parker.

When the balloting began, on the first ballot Clark received four hundred and forty-and-a-half and Wilson three hundred and twenty-four. The remaining three hundred and fifty were divided among Senator Underwood, Governor Harmon and

[1] J. Kerney.

others. A two-thirds majority was necessary for nomination. On the tenth ballot Clark received an absolute, though not a two-thirds, majority. On the thirteenth the seventy-six votes of New York switched across to him. Bryan's intention was to bring about a deadlock between Clark and Wilson. With the support of New York Clark was now uncomfortably strong. Bryan therefore moved a resolution, standing in the name of his brother, demanding "the withdrawal of any delegate under obligations to J. Pierpont Morgan, Thomas F. Ryan, August Belmont or any other member of the privilege-hunting and favor-seeking class." Such a resolution was angrily declared inadmissible but in its place Bryan was allowed to move another, declaring the convention "opposed to the nomination of any candidate for President who is the representative of or under any obligation to J. Pierpont Morgan, Thomas F. Ryan, August Belmont or any other member of the privilege-hunting and favor-seeking class." This was passed.

Bryan was not merely a sentimental and gaseous fool. He had been sent to the convention as a delegate from Nebraska and with instructions to vote for Clark. Now he announced that Clark, since he was openly supported by Tammany Hall, was in effect condemned by the resolution. Bryan would therefore consider himself absolved from his instructions and would transfer his support to Wilson. He called upon others to follow his example and sufficient did so to prevent a stampede to Clark.

Bryan was thus able to spin out the convention through the week. On the sixteenth ballot, on Saturday night, Clark received four hundred and sixty-three-and-a-half votes and Wilson four hundred and seven-and-a-half. The deadlock seemed complete. At that moment Bryan dropped his first hint of a possible escape. He professed that he himself was "not a candidate" but, "if the convention should regard his nomination as necessary, the regular party leaders would find him easier to deal with than Wilson."

That same day, he had as a friend advised Wilson to withdraw, doubtless neglecting to point out some of the advantages of such a plan. After considering it over the week-end, Wilson, largely because of his wife, according to one story, according to another, of his manager, Mr. McCombs, rejected the advice. Bryan's first plan was therefore defeated.

The convention dragged on through the next week. By the adjournment on Monday, 2nd July, the positions of Clark and Wilson had been reversed. Wilson had now the majority of the convention, though not yet the necessary two-thirds majority. It was probable that on the Tuesday he would be nominated, and to prevent such an end to the deadlock Bryan on that morning, before the convention met, sent for Colonel Harvey to whom he gave an interview in his bathroom. Bryan's suggestion was that Colonel Harvey should get the supporters of Clark, before any further balloting could take place, to propose the adjournment of the convention for thirty days. Bryan, assuming the leadership of Wilson's supporters, was to second the proposal which would thus be carried. Bryan was confident that he could use the interval to make the nomination of Wilson as impossible as that of Clark. In order to help forward his plan he told a reporter of the *World* that there would be such an adjournment.

But Colonel Harvey was well aware that Wilson had repudiated *Harper's Weekly* at Bryan's demand and had no mind to help Bryan to the achievement of his ambition. He therefore did not give the message and the proposal was not made for Bryan could hardly make it himself without appearing to be insincere in his support of Wilson.

The forty-third and forty-fourth ballots were taken. On the forty-fifth Wilson received six hundred and thirty-three and Clark three hundred and six. Senator Stone, Clark's floor-leader, thereupon rose and released the delegates who had been pledged to Clark. On the next ballot Clark had therefore only eighty-four votes and Wilson nine hundred and ninety, easily sufficient for nomination. Clark told a reporter; "I lost the nomination solely through the vile and malicious slanders of Colonel William Jennings Bryan of Nebraska." Mrs. Bryan wrote to Colonel House; "I was never so proud of Mr. Bryan. . . . Will said all the time that he did not think it was his time, and when we found the way things were set we were sure of it. . . . As to the possibilities in case of Democratic success, I . . . believe he would do anything to help the cause."

VIII

Owing to the split of the Republican votes between Roosevelt and President Taft the Democratic nomination in this rare year was tantamount to election. Yet the campaign was not without its personalities. Violent attacks were made upon Wilson's sexual morality. These attacks Roosevelt repudiated, calling them contemptible. He added; "What's more, it won't work. You can't cast a man as Romeo who looks and acts so much like the apothecary's clerk."

Wilson's victory in November was overwhelming. Though he did not receive a plurality of the popular vote, he gained four hundred and thirty-five in the electoral college, Roosevelt eighty-one and President Taft only eighteen. Mr. McCombs, his manager, who was almost wholly responsible for the organization of victory, came to offer Wilson his congratulations. It is said that Wilson replied: "God ordained that I should be the next President of the United States. Neither you nor any other mortal could have prevented that."

Some of Wilson's friends thought that on his election he should resign the Governorship of New Jersey at once. If he did so the Democrats would have a very good chance of recapturing it. But Wilson insisted that he should continue to draw the salary for as long as possible and did not resign until 1st March, three days before his inauguration as President.

Almost immediately after the election Wilson had gone to Bermuda with his wife. Thence he returned in December. Before leaving New Jersey he had one especial business to fulfill. He had, as has been said, been most annoyed that the state comptroller had refused to pay to him the Governor's salary for months during which he was totally absent from the State. It happened that at this time the comptroller, whose name was Edwards, was seeking election to the state-treasurership. Wilson therefore returned from Bermuda in order to secure Edwards' defeat. Edwards "complained that in refusing to pay the salary he had only done his duty," and pleaded that he had always loyally supported Wilson. Wilson wrote; "I feel very strongly indeed that it is unwise and inexpedient that a banker should be elected to the post of Treasurer of the State." In preventing Edwards' election Wilson, with his new prestige, was successful.

Wilson took very little interest in the appointments to his Cabinet. Patronage always bored him. Certain people, who had in some way opposed him, he might wish to ruin but it was contrary to his nature to further another's interests. The Cabinet-making and the diplomatic appointments were therefore left largely to Colonel House and Mr. Tumulty, his private secretary. Later, after he had secured his own position of Secretary of the Treasury, Mr. McAdoo also was able to exercise a considerable influence—an influence which was greatly increased when he afterwards became Wilson's son-in-law.

The most important appointment in Wilson's gift was the Secretaryship of State. To that, largely by the advice of Colonel House, he determined to appoint Bryan. Bryan's wisdom in refraining from a public desertion of Wilson was thus justified and he was able to fill many posts with friends of his who had been supporting him with that hope for some years. Bryan's interest in patronage was as large as Wilson's was small. His only embarrassment in dispensing it came from the large number of his clamorous friends. To satisfy them all it was necessary that those first served should agree to resign their preferment after a decent period of enjoyment in order that a second group of fortunates might receive an innings. When it came to light that Mr. Pindell, of Peoria, Ill., had been offered the Embassy at St. Petersburg on the condition that he would resign it again in "say, October, 1914," and with the promise that in the meanwhile "there will be no treaties to adjudicate and no political affairs to bother with, for the administration will see to that for a year," it was widely felt that the statesmen of Europe had behaved in August of that 1914 with a regrettable lack of consideration towards the prophecies and arrangements of a distinguished American theologian and politician.

The only difficulty in Bryan's appointment came from his refusal to serve anything more stimulating than grape-juice at diplomatic dinners. For Bryan, though a large eater, was a very fervent teetotaller. To his fad Wilson made no objection. Indeed he himself was later to earn unpopularity with Senators because "when they go to the White House for conferences they are offered nothing to drink except water and nothing to smoke."[1]

IX

Wilson secured the passage through Congress during his first Presidential term of five most important measures—the Federal Reserve Act, the establishment of the Federal Trade Commission, the establishment of the Tariff Commission, the eight-hour

---

[1] *The Intimate Papers of Colonel House.* Houghton Mifflin Company. Boston, 1926–28.

day on the railroads, and the facilitating of rural credits. The Federal Reserve Act set up a Federal sinking fund which, it was hoped, would prevent financial panics and stabilize the rate of interest. It was a great banking reform. Yet the manipulation of this sinking fund was put into the hands of commissioners of whom three out of five were direct representatives of big business. "The tyrannies of business, big and little, lie within the field of credit," Wilson had once truly said. Such power of tyranny was thus greatly increased.

The newspapers had expected that one of the commissioners would be Mr. Record, the man who drafted Wilson's bills in New Jersey. Yet Mr. Record was a man of sincerely radical opinions. His presence on the commission might prove inconvenient. So Mr. Perkins, Roosevelt's manager and the financier of Wilson's *Trenton True American*, head of the Harvester Corporation, used his power to prevent it. Wilson, desiring to shift the responsibility to other shoulders, sent a message to Mr. Record that it would be useless to appoint him as he had heard that the appointment would not be confirmed by the Senate. "Senator Boise Penrose, Republican floor leader, subsequently stated that he could not find any Senator on either the Republican or Democratic side who knew anything about the Record matter with the single exception of Hughes, of New Jersey, who was ardently in favor of the appointment."[1]

The Radicals took their revenge by blocking the appointment to a commissionership of Wilson's old Princeton friend, Jones. Jones, who had contributed $10,500 to Wilson's pre-nomination campaign fund, was a colleague of Perkins in the directorship of the Harvester Corporation which was, as it happened, at that time being prosecuted by the Government. But Wilson explained that Jones had only joined the trust "to withdraw it from the control which had led it into the acts and practices which

---

[1] J. Kerney.

have brought it under the criticisms of the law-officials of the Government. . . . His connection with the company was a public service, and he has won additional credit and admiration for his courage in that matter." Perkins answered that "there was no suggestion by Jones or any one else that he should come on the board to assist in reforming the company." Nor did Jones deny this.

The rest of Wilson's legislative policy needs little explanation. The Tariff Commission was set up in order to alter the tariff from an absolute to a lower and flexible one. The South, which has even today comparatively few manufactures but lives by the export of cotton, is of course opposed to a high tariff, but, since she gives no political support to the Republicans, her interests are apt to be neglected by them when they are in power. A Democratic President will therefore always have to modify the tariff policy of his Republican predecessor. The eight-hour day on the railroads was introduced to avoid a threatened strike. The granting of rural credits was a sensible and necessary concession.

Yet it was his Mexican policy which during these early years attracted most attention and gave most difficulty to the administration. In Mexico the long reign of Porfirio Diaz, who had ruled the country autocratically for almost forty years, had just come to an end. He had been succeeded by Francesco Madero, a spiritualist, a vegetarian, a millionaire and a revolutionary, who held power for eighteen months. Just before Wilson's inauguration Madero had been forced to resign and had been later assassinated. General Huerta, the leader of the Diaz party, had seized power, first as President and afterwards as Dictator. President Taft had given no recognition to Huerta, against whose government, in Wilson's first month of office, a revolution began under the leadership of General Carranza, Governor of Coahuila. In his inaugural address Wilson did not mention Mexico but later, in the month of March, issued a statement that his policy towards the Republics of Central and South America would be one of coöperation. In

August he proposed definite terms of Mexican settlement. They were, first, the cessation of fighting under an armistice; second, a free election; and third, that in that election General Huerta should not be a candidate for the Presidency; fourth, that all parties should agree to abide by the result of the election.

Of these four terms all but the third were at least pious. They sounded constitutional. Yet Wilson should have understood that a Mexican election is decided not by the politics of the voter but by the politics of the soldier who guards the polling-booths. On that important question he had said nothing. More serious was the third term. This was interpreted by Mexico as interference in internal affairs and it is hard to see how it could have been interpreted otherwise. Wilson's complaint against Huerta was that the methods by which he had obtained power were immoral. In a sense this was doubtless true. Very few people do attain Presidencies by moral means. Huerta, who had frankly seized power from Madero, a man whom he had maintained to be incapable of governing the country, looked on himself as the leader both of the army and of the party of Porfirio Diaz. That he had a very fair chance of restoring to Mexico such a Government as, for good or bad, Diaz gave her, is now obvious. That he was prevented from doing so by Wilson's hostility and later by his embargo on arms for Huerta and permit for those to be used by generals in rebellion against him, is also obvious. Almost wantonly the Government of Wilson plunged Mexico back into a chaos from which she had a certain chance of emerging. For that Wilson must bear the responsibility. His motive it is less easy to guess.

He seems to have thought that Huerta was responsible for the murder of Madero. If that was his opinion he preferred his own disinterested conclusion to the report after investigation of his ambassador, Henry Lane Wilson, and of an American eye-witness, named Ryan, who were both convinced that Huerta was not responsible. "At least we know that Huerta was not responsible for *his* death," wrote Mrs. O'Shaughnessy,[1] who was on the spot. Yet Wilson hardly ever listened to his regular diplomatic representatives. Instead it was his habit to send personal messengers to report on foreign countries in which he was interested. The messenger whom he sent to Mexico was one John Lind. Lind after a short investigation reported that "prostitution and the Catholic Church are the chief causes of the Mexican trouble." From the first therefore Lind put himself in vigorous opposition to Huerta, a Catholic, though by no means a clerical. Bryan, too, threw his influence on to the anti-Catholic side. In financial circles also there remained a tradition of anti-clericalism, dating from the middle of the last century when, as a result of liberal legislation, various interests had been able to get hold of lands previously the property of the Church and had acquired the habit of opposing the clerical party both for fear that, if it returned to power, it would restore the lands to their former purpose and from a more vague feeling that Catholicism was "bad for business." Under these three influences Wilson received his instruction that General Carranza ought to be supported and General Huerta opposed. A great weight of opinion was on the other side. Pointedly Sir Lionel Carden, the British Minister, presented his credentials to General Huerta. The American ambassador in Mexico was recalled for venturing to point out some inaccuracies in Wilson's interpretation of Mexican history. He would listen to no advice.

Colonel House records that once "I told him that all the really big men I had known had taken advice, while the little men refused to take it. . . . He remarked that he always sought advice." Yet it is generally agreed that this was the opposite of the truth. Here, at any rate, the professor was aroused. He was "the authority"; the opinions of others were "journalistic."

---

[1] *A Diplomat's Wife in Mexico*, by Edith O'Shaughnessy. Harper & Brothers. New York, 1916.

The American Heresy

Wilson did not intend to interfere in Mexican internal affairs. Nevertheless Lind was authorized to announce that "if Mexico acted at once"—that is, deposed Huerta—"President Wilson would express to American bankers assurances that the Government of the United States would look with favor upon an immediate loan to Mexico." It was an attempt to bribe the electorate over the head of the Government and, had there been an electorate, might very well have succeeded. Wall Street had made up its mind that, Wilson or no Wilson, Huerta, the friend of Lord Cowdray, must go. Huerta's crime was that he was a friend of England. Mexico had always needed foreign capital for her development. America, since at the time of the building of her transcontinental railways her capital was all needed for internal use, was, until the European war, a debtor nation. The earliest capital in Mexico was English, but under Porfirio Diaz a considerable quantity of American capital came into the country. In 1913 the American capitalist was, for the first time, able to challenge the English for the control of the country's government.

Since Mexican investments were not of sufficient importance to Great Britain to dominate her foreign policy, America, owing to her geographical position and the Monroe Doctrine, was certain to win in such a struggle. Yet under General Huerta's régime English investments were increasing fast, those of Lord Cowdray, according to Mr. Randolph Wellford Smith,[1] by forty thousand pounds a month. The Mexican people strongly resented any foreign capitalist control, and more particularly that of the American capitalist, who was the more effective because the nearer. They who had under Diaz been autocratically governed were to be allowed under the democratic reforms of Madero to express from time to time at the polling-booths a preference for one group of foreign financial masters over another. This, Wilson

---

[1] *Benighted Mexico*, by Randolph Wellford Smith. John Lane Company. New York, 1916.

explained, was known as "ordered freedom." The question was, it seemed, "Who was it to be ordered by?"

An election was held in October. But its results, being favorable to General Huerta, were, Wilson decided, not a genuine expression of the will of the people. Whenever the people expressed opinions other than those which Wilson had previously made up his mind that they wished to express, he was apt to conclude that democracy, that fine instrument, had been degraded into mere mob rule. Yet in his complaint that the elections were "irregularly conducted" he was right, but it only showed his ignorance of Mexico that he should have troubled to make such a complaint. The electoral machinery was treated by both sides as a tired and flagging joke and was kept in existence only out of a puzzled good nature because, for some reason quite incomprehensible, it seemed to give pleasure to the President of the United States. To General Huerta and his opponent it appeared—and was—mechanism so ludicrously unsuitable that neither side ever dreamed of using it properly. Yet General Huerta probably had the support of the majority of the people of Mexico, for he alone seemed able to give to them any promise of peace.

On 9th April, 1914, some American bluejackets attempted to get oil from a prohibited area in Tampico and were consequently arrested. They were afterwards released with apologies, but Admiral Mayo demanded in addition a salute to the American flag. American interests determined to use the opportunity and on 21st April troops landed at Vera Cruz. There were a few casualties in street-fighting and, on 15th July, General Huerta was forced to resign and sailed away to Europe. With him sailed the hope of Mexican peace. "We have gone into Mexico," said Wilson, "to serve mankind, if we can find a way." The difficulties were soon discovered to be insuperable, and for the nine years of civil war which followed Wilson is largely responsible.

The American Heresy

For the rest of Wilson's Presidential term three rival brigand-chiefs, Carranza, Villa and Zapata, disputed the succession to General Huerta's power. Only a very small proportion of the Mexican people took sides with any of the three. Nevertheless the conflict was carried on with indescribable brutality. It became more and more obvious that, before expelling General Huerta, Wilson had given no thought to the problem how a stable government was to be established under anybody else. His policy was described as one of "watchful waiting," but in truth he had no policy. He preserved a sort of peace only because he was at his wits' end to know on whom he should make war. Argentine, Brazil and Chile—the leading South American countries—had eventually to take the problem out of the hands of North American statesmen who were clearly incapable of solving it. On 9th October, 1915, a significant day, the first in history upon which North America had had to accept the leadership of the South, a conference met at Niagara which decided that the only hope of peace lay in a recognition and support of one of the rival brigands. Carranza was picked almost by methods of Ena-meena-mina-mo, and recognized on 19th October. Villa was naturally furious at this and showed his anger by a series of raids on American border towns and barbarous massacres. At one time, according to Senator Lodge, Villa had possessed considerable popularity in the Middle-West owing to a rumor that he neither smoked nor drank. But afterwards, the Senator said, it was discovered that he both smoked and drank and his popularity waned.

X

Meanwhile the outbreak of the larger European War distracted men's minds from the Mexican quarrels. Individual Americans had their personal sympathies with the countries of their origin but hardly anybody, at its beginning, suggested that the United States should enter the war on the one side or the other. They had not been a party to the guarantee of Belgian neutrality. Its violation then obviously could commit them to nothing. There was therefore general approval of Wilson's declaration of neutrality. Even Roosevelt, the tune of whose song was afterwards to be so very different, wrote in those early days that "what has been done in Belgium has been done in accordance with what the Germans, unquestionably sincerely, believe to be the course of conduct necessitated by Germany's struggle for life," and he discovered in his veins some German blood of which he boasted himself proud.

Two things changed the policy of the American Government and brought it eventually to declare war. On the relative importance of these two there is great room for difference of opinion. The newspaper version of America's entry into the war concentrated on the story of Germany's submarine policy. Unquestionably it was this policy which aroused American hostility against Germany. An intellectual school in America, in reaction against the large nonsense of war-time propaganda, today continually insists that Great Britain, by her blockade, interfered with American commerce as drastically and illegally as did Germany by her submarine campaign. Everybody knows that the United States had at one time very serious cause of complaint against British naval policy. Still the argument of the intellectual tells only a half-truth—and the less important half. American opinion was aroused not by the technical illegality but by the brutality of German policy. It is said that Germany, owing to her naval inferiority, had no weapon with which to meet the British blockade except the submarine. It is an answer to that argument that Germany refused a proposal to abandon her campaign on condition that Great Britain abandoned the blockade of foodstuffs. Yet, even if it had been true that Germany could only save herself by the murder of American citizens, that is no reason why America should have been indifferent to such a murder.

In February, 1915, the German navy began its submarine warfare on neutral commerce. It proclaimed a war-zone around the British Isles and informed neutrals of their danger within it. In May of that year came the sinking of the *Lusitania* with the loss of a hundred and twenty-four American lives. Wilson sent a note of protest in which he committed himself to the "sacred duty of maintaining the rights of the United States and its citizens and of safeguarding their free exercise and enjoyment"— words which sounded ominously like a periphrasis for war. The *Lusitania* controversy fortunately cost Wilson the resignation of Bryan, who throughout insisted that the *Lusitania* carried munitions worth $152,400 and that "Germany had a right to prevent contraband going to the Allies." It is curious in what desperate shifts of militarism the international pacifist is sometimes forced to indulge. Bryan had signed the note of protest to Great Britain against her interference with neutral shipping. In Bryan's logic Great Britain might not "prevent contraband" by taking a ship peaceably into port, Germany might "prevent" it on the high seas by a torpedo at two minutes' notice. By what justification? Because Germany was potentially more hostile to the United States than Great Britain and therefore protest against the more violent interference was more likely to lead to war than protest against the less violent. From the safe distance of Lincoln, Nebraska, he continued consistently, for the duration of the war, to turn other people's other cheeks to the menace of the German submarine.

Bryan was succeeded as Secretary of State by Lansing and, after the change, began that apparently interminable series of notes that was to exasperate to madness the frayed nerves of a Continent. Wilson was by temperament a pacifist and, though he saw the country drifting towards war under his leadership, he

Woodrow Wilson

was determined, if possible, to preserve her neutrality—at least until after the Presidential election. The bellicose vote he hoped to gain by the "preparedness" policy of Garrison, his Secretary of War, which he adopted in his speech before the Manhattan Club in New York in November, 1915, in which he said that he would give America incomparably the greatest navy in the world. The pacifist vote he hoped to retain by shortly afterwards dismissing Garrison from office.

It had been his ambition as a neutral mediator to put himself into history as the great peacemaker of the world. Recognizing the drift of the United States towards war, he saw that if peace was to be made and kept it must be made early. Colonel House was therefore sent on a confidential mission to Europe. His instructions were to induce the belligerents to lay down their arms and accept the mediation of Wilson. The mission of Colonel House was in the early days of 1916. Wilson in his eagerness had even gone so far as to promise France and Great Britain that, if they would agree to a conference which Germany refused, "the United States would probably enter the war against Germany." Why such forwardness?

The popular reason for America's entry into the war was a real reason. American opinion was genuinely aroused by German barbarities, and the Germans were genuinely barbarous. It is futile to murmur "propaganda" with a superior sniff and walk away, as is becoming the habit of certain intellectual persons when confronted with a historical fact that is not definitely and merely economic. Yet it would be equally futile to neglect the economic reason. We cannot forget its existence today. It would be foolish to forget that it existed also in 1916. Great Britain had been able, in the early days of the war, to extract from American financiers large loans both for herself and for her Allies. These loans, owing to the enormous superiority of British and French over German propaganda, had been made in the expectation that the Allies would win the war. As time went on this was seen to be more and more doubtful. An Allied victory, if it was to come at all, seemed only likely to come after so long a time that the victors would be economically too exhausted to pay their debts.

Therefore there grew a stronger and stronger financial pressure upon America to enter the war on the Allied side. Finance controlled, among other things, the press. It made it its business to see that the real grievances of America at the German submarine campaign were known throughout the country and that the excuses for it, such as they were, were not known. It controlled also the Foreign Affairs Committee of the Senate. It came in the end to control, unchallenged, every coming and going to the White House until Wilson broke beneath the pressure.

Wilson was not crudely bribed. On no particular day did a rich man walk into his study and buy him for $100,000, but he was as much the tool of financial interests from 1917 onwards as if that had happened. He was too great a gentleman ever to stoop to take a bribe. For that reason he spent a great deal of his life doing other people's dirty work for nothing.

In May of 1916 Wilson seems to have made up his mind that the pressure could no longer be resisted. He met Claude Kitchin, the Democratic leader, Flood, of the Foreign Relations Committee, and Champ Clark, Speaker of the House, at a secret conference, which, because it took place at seven-thirty in the morning, came to be known as the Sunrise Conference. He told them, it seems, that he had determined to commit the country to war. To his surprise they opposed him and, taking heart and advice, he resolved to resist the pressure a little longer and to fight the election of November as "the man who kept America out of the war," rather than as "the man who brought her in." It proved to be a wise political chance.

Until the election therefore Wilson was still officially the puzzled and professorial spectator, critically unable to make head or tail of the pell-mell of Europe. "I wish someone would tell me what the Allies are fighting for," he said in August.

XI

The Democratic nominating convention met in St. Louis soon after the Sunrise Conference. Glynn, of New York, proposed Wilson. "Neutrality is America's contribution to the laws of the world," he said. "The Wilsonian policy satisfies the mothers and all those who worship at the Altar of the God of Peace." Yet this was but mild talk to the speech of Senator James of Kentucky, a very great racing expert and the permanent chairman of the convention.

"Without orphaning a single American child, without widowing a single American mother, without firing a single gun or shedding a drop of blood, he has wrung from the most militant spirit that ever brooded over a battlefield the concession of American demands and American rights."

There was deafening applause and loud cries that he repeat the sentence, which—it is almost incredible—he did. He continued:

"I can see the accusing picture of Christ on the battlefield, with the dead and dying all around Him, with the screams of shrapnel and the roll of cannon, and I can hear the Master say to Woodrow Wilson: 'Blessed are the peacemakers for they shall be called the children of God.'"

It is only fair to remember that at that date Woodrow Wilson had not yet made a peace.

The election was fought on Wilson's claim to be "the man who kept you out of war." The Democrats had the initiative and used it cleverly, for thus the Republican candidate, Mr. Hughes, was made, almost necessarily, to appear a supporter of war. The contest was the closest in American history. All turned on the result in California, the last State to send in her returns. At one time it appeared that Hughes had won. Wilson even prepared a formal—very formal—message of congratulation and his defeat was, it will be remembered, reported in many English newspapers and offensive articles, accounting for it, published. Yet in the end California's vote was found to have gone for him. He received in the electoral college two hundred and seventy-seven against Mr. Hughes' two hundred and fifty-four.

Wilson's stern Calvinistic faith had taught him to be an individualist and a democrat—a democrat when the majority was on his side, an individualist when it was not. Today *vox populi* was *vox Dei*. And, when President Hibben, his successor at Princeton, hearing that he would return to his old home to vote in a municipal election, wrote to offer him the hospitality of the University, the elect of God did not deign even to reply to the impertinence of a mortal. Meeting Hibben on a railway-station platform, he cut him dead. Though it is true that Wilson disapproved strongly of everything that had been done at Princeton since he left, yet it might have been better to have shown the normal courtesies.

XII

The date of the election was November, 1916. On 12th December the Germans made an offer to negotiate peace. In reply, on 18th December, Wilson suggested that both parties state clearly their war-aims. If Germany had been willing to say, publicly and without prevarication, that she would evacuate Belgium and make restitution to her for the wrong which she had done, she might even at that date have prevented intervention. Neutral opinion was apt to feel dazed before the volume of rival propaganda and emerge from it with a very vague, and not very unjust, feeling that between the Great Powers it was six to one and half a dozen to the other. The German invasion of Belgium alone did not fit into that easy and comprehensive formula. Belgium at least was not responsible for the war. There was a clear and unprovoked wrong. Until it was confessed, whatever may have been the peccadilloes of the allied diplomatists, there was no equality in fault.

The Germans missed their chance as, in their amazing stupidity, they missed every chance which they were given during the years of the war. They replied to Wilson on January 2nd, giving no terms but making vague proposition of a conference. They sent postscripts of equal futility on 11th January and 13th January. On 22nd January Wilson replied with his Message to Congress in which he laid down what were, in his opinion, the foundations of peace.

He proposed that the nations should "adopt the doctrine of President Monroe as the doctrine of the world." Such a sentence by no means explained itself nor was it wholly fortunate. But it meant, as he went on to say, that territorial boundaries should be drawn on the "principle of self-determination" and that, when they had been so drawn, no nation should interfere with anything that happened beyond its frontiers.

In the second paragraph appeared the dangerous phrase "entangling alliances." It was, I fancy, no more than a phrase and, if so, it was certainly a dangerous one. The peace of the world, Wilson felt, was to be found in nationalism and an absence of entangling alliances. But what is a nation but an entangling alliance? German troops marched into a French village. *All* France resisted them. Why? Because all Frenchmen were united in the entangling alliance of nationhood. By far the best example in history of an entangling alliance is of course the Constitution of the United States. If it is not immoral for individuals to band themselves together into a nation why is it immoral for nations to band themselves together into an alliance? Was it wrong of the nations of Christendom to unite in entangling alliance before the menace of the Moslem? Would the world's peace have been more fully attained if each little prince had stood against the invader as an isolated ninepin, and waited obediently his turn to be knocked down? "There is no entangling alliance in a concert of power." If "all" agree, their agreement is not wicked. But how can all agree in practice when all do not agree in morals? And why should those who do agree in morals deny themselves sane measures of self-preservation?

In Wilson's hope of peace by dividing the world into water-tight compartments there is a difficulty which he would never face. What was to be the attitude of the Government to its citizen who goes abroad? Should Washington say to the American citizen who invests in Mexican securities, "I am sorry, but it is no business of mine how the Mexican Government administers its laws?" or to the victims of the *Lusitania*, "If you choose to travel on a British ship, you do so at your own risk?" There is much to be said for such an attitude. It is certainly much better than a Palmerstonian alternative. Yet it was not an attitude, as he well knew, that Wilson's masters would ever let him use in practice. More and more the business of the poor countries of the world is carried on by capital loaned to them by citizens of the rich countries, and the rich citizens demand and receive the support of their Government if in those countries they meet any treatment inconvenient to themselves. Wilson knew this very well. And, unless he was willing firmly to refuse such support, his claim that "every people should be left free to determine its own polity, its own way of development unhindered, unthreatened, unafraid, the little along with the great and powerful," was mere words. General Huerta, it may be remembered, had tried it. He died from an illness contracted in an American Federal prison, where he had been confined without trial, almost exactly a year before this Message was delivered to Congress.

The German reply to Wilson was to announce a renewal of the submarine warfare within a larger zone. On 3rd February the United States therefore severed diplomatic relations with the German Empire.

Two more months passed by before they took the next and logical step of declaration of active war. It was not necessarily implied in a severance of diplomatic relations. With Austria-Hungary, for instance, the United States had had no such relations for some time. Yet they did not declare war on the Austrian Empire until long after they had declared it on the German. Still few people can have had any doubt after 3rd February that war with Germany would follow in a very short time. It could only be avoided if Germany were to take this last, terrible hint and modify her policy. It was almost impossible to hope for such a modification, not because the political or diplomatic leaders of Germany were men ignorant of the necessary effect of adherence to such a policy or of the meaning of war with the United States—no man could have been more keenly aware of its meaning than Germany's most intelligent ambassador in Washington, von Bernstorff—but because the military and naval leaders of Germany were so stupid and ignorant as to be almost insane, and so arrogant and insubordinate that they would obey no command of their political masters. It is impossible not to feel as one reads such a book as the *Intimate Papers* of Colonel House or Herr Ludwig's *Wilhelm II* that the German Empire fell because of the Prussian soldier's utter lack of a sense of discipline. Prussianism could manufacture everything except a superior officer who knew how to obey orders.

A soldier or sailor who demands that he, as a soldier or sailor, should dictate policy is a menace to civilization. "The purpose of war," as Marshal Foch has said, "is to obtain results." Or, in other words, military means must be used to secure political ends. A militarist is not a man who demands that his country should maintain a large army or that certain methods of discipline be used to make that army efficient. The necessary size of an army depends entirely on circumstances and the demand that it be made efficient is simply an evidence of sanity. A militarist is a man who cannot see that force can properly be used only for a purpose. To fail to see this is a form of madness—a form from which the great soldiers of the world—Hannibal or Napoleon or Cæsar—have been most notably free but which took hold in the dark years of the war upon the barbaric and half-witted minds of Berlin's Admirals and Generals, whom the politicians of Germany could not or dared not check. In a mad passion to impose a rule of force upon the world the militarists defied even their own masters.

By the end of March Wilson seems to have made up his mind that it was no longer possible to preserve peace. His friend, Frank Cobb, of the *World*, has told the story of how on the last night of March Wilson sent for him. Cobb arrived at one o'clock in the morning and found the President in his office. Wilson was restless and agitated. He saw—and it was clearly true—that American entry into the war would mean the end of such a thing as a neutral opinion and that the danger to the future welfare of the world in such a destruction was enormous. No nation can remain sane through the organized effort of a modern war. Least of all is this possible to a nation which possesses, like the American, an efficient system of elementary education and therefore lacks capacity for judgment. And it was possible, even at such a date, for a wise man to foresee that the terms which the victors of such a war, unchecked by neutral opinion, would impose on the vanquished, might well be such as to manufacture only the causes of new wars.

Wilson feared also that the war would mean the destruction of all American domestic liberty. This fear proved very just. Yet owing to the absence in America of an instinct for liberty such destruction perhaps would not have been long delayed even had there been no war to hasten it.

Woodrow Wilson

Anyway for these two reasons Wilson dreaded the notion of war. Nor was he under any illusion of the effect which it would have upon his own career and place in history. He foresaw for himself only a small period of adulation followed by contempt, as the excessive hopes upon which propaganda would have to feed the people were found plainly exaggerated or wholly false.

Yet before German madness what alternative was there? "If there is an alternative, for God's sake, let's take it!" he exclaimed. But Cobb had to admit that he could see none. And in such doubt and despair did Wilson go before Congress and ask it for a declaration of war.

The question why the United States went to war with Germany, is one too complicated to be answered in a phrase. As has been said, the causes seem to have been two—the German submarine campaign and the desire of the financiers to keep the Allies solvent. Of these causes the latter was not mentioned in more formal orations, and even the former, once war was declared, dropped more and more into oblivion. Its place was taken by that vaguer phraseology which it is the fashion to describe as "idealism." Those politicians who, a few months before at St. Louis, had heard "the Master say to Woodrow Wilson: 'Blessed are the peacemakers,'" now turned instead to congratulating the Almighty upon the opportunity of witnessing, from a position of some advantage, the sublime spectacle of "the American nation girding itself for Service." The war-aims of the United States were defined from time to time in a variety of "idealistic" phrases. These may be summed up in the most expressive and popular, which told her Allies that the United States were "fighting" in order "to make the world safe for democracy."

This phrase received enthusiastic and not very critical adulation. But from the comparative detachment of the 1930's it is impossible not to apply to it a certain measure of examination. Was the Allied cause supported only by the friends of democracy?

Was the cause of the world's democracy adequately upheld by the Russia of M. Sazonoff, the England of Lord Curzon, or the France of M. Charles Maurras? If by "democracy" Wilson meant, as he did mean, this system of voting, election and representation from which it has been the main aim of post-war politics in most of the Allied countries to free their Governments as far as possible, it is hardly credible that whole nations were laying down their lives for an electoral arrangement, in support of which only a small proportion of them could be bothered, in time of peace, to walk across the road and make a cross on a piece of paper.

Yet the phrase, false as political philosophy, was valuable as propaganda. It would never have induced a single Frenchman, Italian or Englishman to take up arms in defense of Parliamentary Government, for the French, the English and the Italians had such a Government already. But the Germans—poor fools—had not got it and had not found it out. And therefore the phrase might—and did—induce some of them to lay down their arms. If democracy was not a cause to fight for, it was at least a cause to stop fighting for.

At the same time, if it is hard to twist the issues of the war into terms of democracy and autocracy, yet Wilson was right in feeling that there was a united culture of Western Europe, which France, England and Italy shared and which Prussia menaced, and that of this culture one of the bases was, if not democracy, at least the proposition that one of the titles of a moral government must be that it possesses the consent of the governed. Russia, it is true, was quite outside this culture. And Russia was a lesser menace to Europe than Prussia, not because her morals were better, but only because her railway system was worse. Europe, in its desperation, had to use the lesser barbarian in order to defeat the greater. But the essential fight was that of France and Great Britain against Prussia, and, however defective his phrasing, Wilson was right in seeing that in that fight France and Great Britain represented a spiritual principle of civilization, a capacity for European loyalty which Prussia wholly lacked and which Prussian victory would, perhaps disastrously, threaten.

Yet such general arguments were as true on 4th August, 1914, as on 3rd April, 1917. The Prussian who was a barbarian when he sank the *Lusitania* was equally a barbarian when he marched into Belgium. What Wilson, it seems, failed to see, was that, the more "idealistic" he made his reasons for entry into the war, the harder was it to justify himself for having remained neutral for two and a half years. So far as he merely argued that America had gone to war in order to safeguard American rights when it was at last patent that there was no other remedy, no one could complain of her conduct. So far as he argued that America had gone to war in order to save humanity, humanity had the right to ask why its salvation had to be so inconveniently postponed until after the American Presidential elections.

In the two answers—that, if possible, it was far better that the Allies should win the war for themselves and that American moral support would be more valuable as neutral than as belligerent opinion, and that Wilson wished to wait until a united nation would follow him—there is much sound sense. Yet there was another reason for delay less publicly trumpeted. A war creates many jobs. And to Democrats it seemed a better plan that in time of war patronage should be in Democratic than that it should be in Republican hands. There were demands that a coalition Cabinet be formed but Wilson wrote to Mr. Tumulty, "You will know how to create the impression on the minds of the newspaper men that I regard it merely as a partisan effort to hamper and embarrass the Administration."

It is generally agreed that the corruption at Washington during the war was amazing. "Beware," said Roosevelt in a master's phrase, "of the Y.M.C.A. banditti down at Washington." Even the sentimental Mr. White, who does not as a rule think that muck-heaps are things that should be spoken of in polite society, bears witness to this. There is no suggestion that Wilson had a hand in it and much of it was no doubt inevitable. But it was not the less good fun for that.

Apart from corruption, the war in America, as in England, increased vastly the dominance of finance and big business over public affairs. Wilson's claim to stand against "the insolence of aggrandized wealth" had always been flimsy. Before this menace of reality it wholly collapsed. The government of the country was almost made over to the house of J. P. Morgan. One of its partners, Henry P. Davison, who had previously had the control of all purchases to be made in the United States for the Allies, was put at the head of the Red Cross. The Morgan house recommended that all Allied and American purchases be consolidated and a second partner, Edward R. Stettinius, was put in charge of the consolidation. He was also made Assistant Secretary of War and surveyor-general for war supplies. Two more Morgan partners, Dwight Morrow and Thomas W. Lamont, were made the Government's advisers on European finances. John W. Davis, the firm's attorney, soon afterwards went to England in order to succeed Page as ambassador to St. James'.

Such facts should be recorded in blame neither of Wilson nor of J. P. Morgan and Company but as illustrations of a general law to which people are too wantonly blind. So far as Wilson used his vague ideology in order to conceal from himself and from others the truth, he is to blame. That he called in financiers in order to win the war, he is not to blame. For he had no alternative. Nor under the circumstances of modern war will any statesman ever have any alternative. The war was not, as is often said, between democracy and autocracy, but between plutocracy and militarism, in which plutocracy won. France, alone of the Allied countries, avoided a submission to plutocratic rule as the price of victory—and she avoided it by the simple but pleasing plan of getting other people to finance her war and not paying them back.

Modern societies are industrial and victory in war depends upon the efficiency of a country's industrial system. No way has yet been discovered of having industrialism without also having plutocracy. And the hold of finance over an industrial country, while not yet quite unassailable, is yet so large that to attack it inevitably involves some dislocation of the country's business. In time of peace when efficiency need not be the sole aim a country may be able to afford such an attack. In time of war it dare not risk the dislocation and, as the experience both of England and the United States shows, can only adopt towards the financial magnate the policy of Henry VII to the Earl of Kildare. To those who fear the accumulation of vast power in the hands of a few men of whose sense of moral responsibility there is no guarantee, this will add one more to the reasons why war should only be undertaken as a last resort and before most extreme provocation.

XIII

Wilson was soon involved in the quarrels of patronage. Theodore Roosevelt in the first months of the war had, as has been said, boasted of his German blood, justified the German invasion of Belgium by arguments similar to those of von Bethmann-Hollweg, and approved the American policy of neutrality. Yet his opinion had changed. And for some time before America's entry into the war he had been its largest apostle. "High-sounding words, unbacked by deeds," were, he found, "proof of a mind that dwells only in the realm of shadow and shame."

Theodore Roosevelt had collected around him a crowd of men anxious to hitch their wagons to so very convenient a star. Of these the most embarrassing was General Leonard Wood, at that time Chief of Staff in the War Department, and afterwards Governor of the Philippines, an able soldier but one who was apt to look upon military appointments as opportunities for furthering political ambitions.

General Wood used his official position in order to supply Roosevelt with the data for his attacks upon the administration. Before the outbreak of war they had together made public the scandalous condition of the Plattsburg training-camp and after it they certainly accomplished much useful service by their continual and relentless exposure of a corruption and incompetence so complete as almost to justify Senator Chamberlain's complaint that the military establishment of the United States had "all but ceased to function because of inefficiency in every bureau and almost every department." Yet accuracy of fact does not necessarily establish integrity of motive. And it seems to be the general opinion that the object both of Roosevelt and of General Wood was so to force themselves on public attention that Wilson would be unable to resist their desire to be sent to France in command of armies. General Wood wished for such a command in order that, as a military hero, he might be able to impose himself upon the party as Republican candidate at the next Presidential election, Roosevelt perhaps simply from a constitutional incapacity to avoid the limelight.

It is hard to blame Wilson for trusting to the sober and regular sense of General Pershing and refusing to grant the requests of either of these statesmen. He would not allow the Western front to be used either by Roosevelt as an epilogue to Cuba or by General Wood as an election meeting. Between Wilson and Roosevelt little love was lost. And it is impossible to grudge Wilson the ironic humor with which he issued a statement to the Press that "it would have been a pleasure to pay Mr. Roosevelt the compliment of sending to their"—the Allies'—"aid one of our most distinguished public men, an ex-President, who has rendered many conspicuous public services and proved his gallantry in many striking ways. But this is not the time or the occasion for compliment or for any action not calculated to contribute to the immediate success of the war."

Both Roosevelt and General Wood had therefore to remain in America and the whole incident was only made memorable by an open letter which M. Clemenceau addressed to Wilson, asking that Roosevelt be sent to France. Why a man so wise did a thing so foolish it is impossible to explain. M. Clemenceau was not at that time Prime Minister. Yet, none the less, such a wanton interference in the affairs of another country could not fail to be resented, however intelligent was the advice which he had to offer. And the advice was, as M. Clemenceau must have known, extremely foolish. M. Clemenceau was himself the first of the French anti-clerical politicians who had the courage and vision to insist that in the hour of the country's peril it must be asked of a general not whether he was a good Freemason but whether he was a good general. The great realist was the last man to imagine that a war could be won by headlines and perorations, and it is incomprehensible that he should have allowed himself to be used for these purposes of sentimentality.

XIV

The military history of the awful and triumphant year of 1918 it is not to the purpose of this essay to recount. In that year, as all know, our civilization was almost lost and finally victorious. The simplicity of the phrase that "the Americans won the war" is such as to make it sound offensive in European ears. Yet it is certain that, but for the United States, the Germans would have succeeded in capturing Paris, and whether or not the Allied morale could have survived such a blow, it will never be possible to tell. The Allies, even without the United States, were, from their economic superiority, like Mansoul in Bunyan's *Holy War*. The enemy could not enter in save with the consent of some of those of the city. And M. Clemenceau had said, in the high moment of a hero's courage, "We will fight before Paris; we will fight in Paris; we will fight behind Paris." Yet he would be a confident man who can feel certain that, if Paris had fallen, none would have been found to give that consent. That the Allied morale was never put to such a fearful test we may thank the United States.

Yet in an essay on Woodrow Wilson it is more important to trace the fortunes of that war of ideas in which Wilson was more deeply interested than he was in the war of arms. For it was in this war, as General Ludendorff has borne witness, that Germany was primarily defeated.

In the days of American neutrality Wilson had attempted to force from the two sides a statement of their war-aims. Now that the United States were belligerent, consistency required that he himself should state the objects for which they were fighting. They had gone to war because of the German submarine campaign. But, when once they had entered in, neither reason nor Wilson's temperament would permit them to be content with any petty purpose of merely making the seas safe for ocean travelers.

> "The world was out of joint, and it was quite
> As it should be that he should set it right."

Therefore on 8th January, 1918, Wilson, in an address delivered to a joint session of Congress, enunciated the afterwards famous Fourteen Points, containing those terms upon which, with a slight modification, Germany eleven months later laid down her arms. Of these Fourteen Points[1] the first four contained the conventional liberal demands for open diplomacy, the freedom of the seas, free trade and disarmament. The fifth concerned

---
[1] *See* Appendix D.

the difficult colonial question and was so phrased as to be interpreted in any way that might be found subsequently convenient. The next seven hinted at the broad lines of territorial rearrangement which the application of the principle of self-determination would make necessary. The fourteenth demanded the establishment of a League of Nations, a project which now began to lurk in shadowy menace around every dinner-table where peace was debated. There was in the Fourteen Points no mention of any German payment of reparation or indemnity.

The Fourteen Points contain no new principle of politics, for Wilson invented many new phrases but no new thoughts. Yet those who realize the truth of Disraeli's great dictum that you must either govern by force or by tradition, will not think the worse of them for that. They were not foolish because they were old; they were only foolish so far as they were so phrased as to be interpreted as a mere invitation to disruption. And because of their pronouncement Wilson was unquestionably for ten months at the head of the politicians of the world. To him the world looked for peace.

The world was before him, like a class. The sight of it turned the head of the pedagogue made prince. In November of 1918 took place the elections to Congress. As the summer drew to an end there began to trickle in from Democratic candidates throughout the country requests that the President give them a letter of endorsement. It was decided that the best plan would be for him to make a speech at some central Middle-Western town, such as Indianapolis, in which he would appeal to the country not to favor one party rather than the other but to give him a Congress which would support him in his leadership of the national effort of war. "The party," said Burleson, "wanted a leader with guts."

Burleson, the Postmaster-General, had advised this plan and went off to Texas for ten days at the end of September, assured that his advice would be followed. On his return he found that behind his back the party politicians had brought influence to bear on Wilson to cancel his speech at Indianapolis and instead write a letter, appealing for a Democratic Congress. This letter, Burleson found, had already been given to the Press. It was interpreted, as Burleson foresaw that it would be, as an abominable slur upon the loyalty of Republicans. And its publication made certain an overwhelming Democratic defeat. Wilson was at the time, according to Mr. White's explanation, "in the upper spiritual zones of idealism," and therefore not at leisure to correct the popular impression that the letter was sent on Burleson's responsibility. But this impression, while ruining Burleson's political career, did not prevent Wilson's overwhelming repudiation by the American people. Only after Wilson's death was the story of the publication discovered.

XV

On 11th November, 1918, the German army, conquered by the military genius of Marshal Foch, laid down its arms on the promise that peace be made, with one reservation, upon the basis of the Fourteen Points. The people both of Germany and of the Allied countries would have been saved much disappointment if they had understood more clearly that, in the very month in which he set out to dictate to the world, Wilson had forfeited any right to speak for the American nation. He gave to mankind what his country had rejected. As Theodore Roosevelt said, "Mr. Wilson and his Fourteen Points and his four supplementary points and his five complementary points and all his utterances every way have ceased to have any shadow of right to be accepted as expressive of the will of the American people."

By an established convention of American politics the President, during his term of office, did not leave the territory of the

United States. The more important the foreign negotiations in which he happened to be engaged, the more important was it, it was argued, that this convention should be maintained. For no asset is more valuable to the negotiator of delicate difficulties than that of an ever-ready excuse for delay. The excuse of having to refer back to the President had always in the past been present to the American diplomat and had often proved of advantage. There are many who think that Wilson would have more nearly achieved his ends if he had sent Colonel House or Mr. Lansing to Paris and himself remained at Washington, a God, ready, according to circumstances, to appear in or out of his machine. Yet an ambitious actor, unexpectedly cast for the rôle of Messiah, could perhaps hardly be expected voluntarily to relegate himself to that of stage-prompter.

Whether or not Wilson blundered in going to Paris, is open to debate. It is certain that he blundered in refusing to take with him any associates who were not members of the already repudiated Democratic party. From Republican politicians Wilson's war policy had received some criticism but much patriotic support. By his letter on the eve of the Congressional elections he had gratuitously and outrageously insulted the Republican party. And the Republican party, whether right-headed or wrong-headed, had a majority in the Senate by whom the Constitution demanded that the Treaty should be ratified. Common sense therefore suggested that Wilson, if he wished for the ratification of his Treaty, should associate the Republican party with the responsibility for it. The saner of his advisers, such as Colonel House, urged this. And to refuse was to issue to the Senate an invitation to reject the Treaty.

Yet Wilson would have none with him unless their "minds went along" with his. Therefore of older men none but the unique Colonel House could approach his intimacy. And he fell back for company and advice more and more upon the younger Professors who, too junior either to feel or to arouse envy, found in contemplation of and obedience to the President a comfortable proof that the academic life, pursued until middle age, did not necessarily bar a man from the highest posts of the practical world.

The Peace Conference was not to meet until the middle of January, 1919. Wilson, who had reached Europe in December, 1918, therefore packed off his Professors to Paris and himself set out for a month's tour of the Allied countries. It is the fashion to pretend that at that time the whole opinion of the world was at his feet. Those who possess a more accurate memory, and, having chanced to overhear a few conversations in any place, public or private, rich or poor, in England during that month, can still recall them, know that it was by no means so. In silence and in secret places broken and battered men thought within themselves, "Peace we know and war we know, but what is the meaning of this nonsense?"

It will be remembered that Wilson was entertained to luncheon by the King at Buckingham Palace and the curious noted that the King in his speech did not use the personal pronoun at all, while in Wilson's it appeared twenty-two times, the American nation being referred to as "my people." That day was the day of greatest shame in the history of England. For, as Wilson drove off in his motor-car from the luncheon, there began to trickle in the first returns of the British General Election. The Government had appealed to the country to give it a mandate to break that faith to another and a helpless power which a little more than a month before it had solemnly and publicly pledged, and the British electorate had returned it to power with a majority overwhelmingly greater than that ever given to any other Government which appealed to it for an honorable purpose. It is not necessary to have any feelings of tenderness towards the Prussian militarist in order to denounce the unnecessary and abominable perfidy of the 1918 election. Had Wilson been wiser, he would have learnt a lesson from that election. Yet he accepted the flattery of a few politicians' phrases rather than the plain evidence of facts, and, unabashed in confidence, went off to Milan, from a box in whose opera-house he blew kisses to the assembled people one famous Sunday evening.

XVI

Neither in England nor in Italy did Wilson meet the man who was to oppose to him idea against idea, to meet his dream and to shatter it. That man was at Paris at the Peace Conference. The future of the world lay between Wilson and Clemenceau.

Of this remarkable man, the final conqueror of Wilson, it is necessary to say a few words. It is not in the nature of Parliamentary Government that it should easily produce great men. And least of all is it likely to produce them in a Latin nation, to whose genius it is peculiarly unsuited. Yet somehow, out of the dirt of mediocrity which is French politics, there was thrown up this one man, unquestionably great, the only one among the statesmen of Western Europe of imagination sufficient to serve an idea. In the Invalides, in Paris, are two pictures. The first is the handing over of Alsace-Lorraine to the Germans after the war of 1870. One of its figures is a young man named Clemenceau. The second is of the handing back of Alsace-Lorraine by the Germans in 1918. In it, too, there is a Clemenceau. It is the story of his idea. "We are ruled by our dead," Clemenceau once said with penetrating truth. The dead by whom he was ruled were the dead of the war of 1870. From their memory he had built up a coherent theory of European politics, an idea to oppose to the Wilson idea.

The two can be stated thus. Both Wilson and Clemenceau professed themselves democrats—that is, professed a certain belief in the capacity of human beings to use liberty. Now a capacity to use liberty implies a capacity for loyalty. The war had shown a disease in Europe, had shown that somewhere in Eastern Europe were certain people incapable of that general European loyalty without which they would be unsafe members of European society. The two differed in their location of the disease. Wilson ascribed the evils of Germany to militarism. Germany, he thought, was under the dominance of a small military clique. It was this clique alone and not the German people which was incapable of European loyalty. Once destroy the power of this clique and the German nation could be accepted as the equal of any other.

It was, as Clemenceau saw, too superficial a diagnosis. "The good God has only His Ten Commandments," he barked out. "Who is this Wilson with his Fourteen?" Wilson called his solution a solution of Liberalism. But Clemenceau, a Liberal, knew well that Liberalism is often merely the excuse of the man who is too idle to find out the facts, finding it so much easier to apply ready-made formulæ. The German people, as he was aware, had not possessed democratic government before the war because they had not wanted it. The military government not only existed but was accepted. The result of imposing upon Germany the forms of representative institutions would be indeed to put Marshal von Hindenburg to the trouble of having to be elected before he could begin to rule the country, but would be very little more. You do not change the nature of a nation by calling it a Republic.

Clemenceau therefore, rejecting the easy Liberal formulæ, thought that there was in Eastern Europe a population quite alien from the general culture of Europe, incapable of loyalty to Europe and a menace to European life whenever it acquired too great strength. For the general well-being this population must be kept in suppression. Its home was Germany.

Now if one examines history it is impossible honestly to conclude that the inhabitants of the geographical area, Germany, have been consistently less moral than those of the rest of Europe.

Nor does reason show us any cause why this should be so. A nation's character is formed by its philosophy and shown by its history. The ideas that have ruled the life of South Germany and Austria are the ideas upon which our common Christian civilization has been built. The history of these countries is stained with crimes, no doubt, as is the history of every country, but it does not tell of a people notably less capable of European loyalty than any other. Only when we turn to Prussia do we find a population clearly alien to Europe. Men today are frightened from telling the truth by fear that what they say will sound like the echoes of the stuff that the newspapers used to print during the war. Yet it would be fatal if, merely from such a fear, we today allowed ourselves to neglect the barbarian nature of Prussia.

Clemenceau's mistake was to ascribe this barbarian nature to all Germans, unable to see that the crime of the Austrians and South Germans was only the much smaller one of being deluded by the very temporary success of Prussian militarism into accepting its leadership. The cause of Prussian barbarism and the cause of Clemenceau's mistake are both worthy of examination. The belief of nineteenth-century Liberalism was that human nature, left to itself, was noble. This belief Wilson, according to Mr. White, held firmly—though how he reconciled it with Calvinism it would be interesting to know. In the amazing vagueness of modern thought such a belief is sometimes spoken of as Christian, simply because it is sentimental. It is flatly anti-Christian. The Christian belief is that human nature, left to itself, is prone to evil.

According to Christian doctrine then, a nation will only be capable of a wider European loyalty if it has been thoroughly educated in a philosophy which imposes such a loyalty on its mind. The natural man would lack such a loyalty. And Prussia, alone among the great nations of Europe, since she was never Roman, practically never Catholic and has had since the Reformation a

Protestantism too weak to act as a restraining influence upon the policy of her rulers, has never had such an education in loyalty. If therefore Prussia is in a position to menace the general well-being of Europe she will do so. For the Prussian mind is unable to see that well-being as a thing at all valuable.

Clemenceau, a European, was then right to despise the mere sentimentalist who pleaded that Prussia, being down, should be allowed to get up again and have another try. Yet he himself had a blind spot. He had a hatred for religion and had been accustomed throughout a long life to assert over and over again that men's conduct was not at all influenced by their religion. Because of this large prepossession he was unable to realize that the frontiers of European civilization are its religious frontiers, and tried instead to draw them along the much less real lines of nationality. This error vitiated the whole settlement which he tried to impose on Europe and made it in result quite doubtful whether the peace of Clemenceau was any better for the world than that which Wilson, unhampered, would have dictated. It is curious to notice how, when a good man refuses to submit his will to authority, in nine opinions out of ten upon the ordinary affairs of men he may be right, but often upon the tenth he will so exaggerate some side of the truth that the whole value of his work is wrecked.

It is impossible not to sympathize with Clemenceau in the contempt which he must soon have learned to feel for his fellow-negotiators. He himself had spent his life in the study of Europe and was familiar with every detail of its history. Neither Mr. Lloyd George nor Wilson had until a very few years previously given its problems their serious attention. Even when they did turn to them they found easy and inapplicable formulæ a substitute for the acquisition of knowledge. And again and again, as every story of the Peace Conference shows, Clemenceau had to listen to large pontifications, unsupported, as a short question or two soon revealed, by acquaintance with facts. "I suppose that this man can read," he said of Mr. Lloyd George, "but I doubt if he ever does." "One of them thinks himself Napoleon and the other Jesus Christ."

If any security for peace was to be won, wise statesmanship should have striven to find for Central Europe three major territorial solutions. Its aim should have been to re-create a strong, independent Poland—to preserve the unity of the Austro-Hungarian Empire—perhaps the greatest single bulwark of civilization that pre-war Europe possessed—to destroy the unity of the Prusso-German Empire with a view to the eventual reunion of the German States under the natural leadership of Vienna. Of these aims the first, by an amazing chance, was achieved. If it had not been for the providential breakdown of Russia it would presumably have been impossible for the Allies to have given Poland her independence and thus to have righted the wrong of a hundred years. As it was she re-emerged, a strong barrier between the non-European powers of Russia and Prussia. France was able to strengthen herself by transferring from the unnatural alliance of Russia to the natural alliance of Poland. The change was sheer gain to Europe. Both Wilson and Clemenceau wished for a successful solution of the Polish problem—Wilson because of his devotion to the principle of self-determination and Clemenceau because of his devotion to France. The re-created Poland has already saved us once—at the time of the Bolshevist invasion—and it will save us again.

In this aim alone did they succeed. The problems both of Austria-Hungary and of Germany they bungled. The rights and wrongs of the war were not as clear as it was the fashion and necessity of propaganda to make out. In truth, as should have been recognized, two wars were being fought. France and Great Britain were defending the civilization of Western Europe against the Prussian barbarian. Austria-Hungary, at the same time, was defending the civilization of Central Europe against the Slavonic barbarian from Serbia and Russia, more murderous in his methods, more clearly barbaric even than the Prussian. Rightly choosing the lesser of two evils, civilization concentrated upon the destruction of Prussia, taking the risk that the fall of Prussia would necessarily involve Austria also in ruin. Yet once Prussia was destroyed, it would have been sane statesmanship to see how much of Austria could be salvaged from the wreck. Instead Wilson encouraged disintegration. In his Fourteen Points he had only made the moderate and statesmanlike demand that the peoples of Austria-Hungary should be accorded "the freest opportunity of autonomous development." With such a demand victory was won and only at the moment of victory, when his efforts should have been turned to the preservation of that Empire, did he wantonly insist on its disruption. He thus took upon himself the responsibility for the Balkanization of Central Europe.

This responsibility the other Allied countries must share. Indeed France, by her support of the Protestant Princes in the Thirty Years' War, of Prussia in the War of the Austrian Succession, by Napoleon III's failure to support Austria in the Austro-Prussian War of 1866, has much to answer for. Prussia is the creation of a France anxious to raise up a power strong enough to menace Austria within Germany and, all too successful, raising up one strong enough to menace the whole world. If Austria-Hungary was to be destroyed, the least that wise statesmanship should have done would have been to insist that Austria should join the German Empire and thus increase the strength of South Germany against North Germany within the Empire. By a failure of imagination the French did not do this. Instead Clemenceau put a clause into the Treaty forbidding Austria to join Germany. His motive was, it seems, simply a surrender to the fetish of head-counting. If Austria joined Germany there would be more souls within the German political unit at the end than there had been at the beginning of the war. Germany would therefore, he foolishly thought, have emerged victorious from defeat. Yet that Germany should again be powerful in Europe was both inevitable and desirable. The problem which statesmanship should have faced was how to arrange the affairs of Germany so that the right sort of German had power rather than the wrong sort.

The third aim—the destruction of the German Empire—Clemenceau failed to achieve because of his anti-religious bias. This bias forced him to make no difference between Catholic and non-Catholic German. The Rhinelander had no reason to love the Prussian rule. He had tolerated it only because it seemed to be successful. In many ways it was more alien to him than had been the rule of Jerome Bonaparte. And on Armistice Day, when even the success of Prussianism had been shown a cheat, the French had a great opportunity to undo the work of the Congress of Vienna a hundred years before. They should have marched into the Rhineland and the Ruhr not as conquerors but as liberators. Instead, by weakly abandoning their first demand for a West Prussian Republic and by treating the population of the occupied territories as if they were as guilty of the war as any other Germans, they forced them back upon that Prussian leadership which they were so ready to repudiate. Only when they had compelled every German willy-nilly into loyalty to Berlin did Clemenceau's meaner successors, in order to make the solidarity of the Prussian Empire doubly sure, let out a gang of anæmic jail-birds and parade them through the streets as a Rhineland Separatist Government. It is a record of wretched tragedy.

From Clemenceau alone could understanding of the problem be expected. Mr. Lloyd George and Wilson were ignorant of it and, as is natural to all men when they are ignorant, accepted the newspaper opinion. The newspapers, while insistent that Germany should pay the cost of the war, also insisted that she should remain united. Partly this came, no doubt, from mere ignorance. They thought of the arrangement of Germany under Prussian leadership as normal, when it was grossly abnormal. Partly it came from the financial and commercial interest to whom it is always convenient that industrial states should be strong and agricultural weak. The Treaty of Versailles has been much criticized, but mainly because of its economic clauses. Yet it is clear that it also sinned in its territorial arrangements, and in them its worst crimes came not from its violation of the Wilsonian principle of self-determination but from its too rigid adherence to it.

Of its economic clauses so much has been written that little need be said here. Wilson himself told the American delegation, in somewhat naïve confession, that he was "not interested in the economic questions." That these clauses were a gross breach of faith and that Mr. Lloyd George by wantonly injecting the indemnity as an issue into an unwanted British General Election was more responsible for them than any of the other statesmen cannot be denied. It would no doubt have been economically possible to levy some small and fixed indemnity from Germany, had it been desired to do so. It was not so desired. Mr. Lloyd George was only anxious to keep satisfied the stupidest British Parliament of history. Clemenceau, Prime Minister of France, a self-supporting country and one that shared a land frontier with Germany, cared nothing about payment and everything about security. If the trade of Germany were ruined he was indifferent. Wilson, soon learning to despair of the Treaty and to care only for the League of Nations, was satisfied to have found the ready wit of General Smuts and Clemenceau capable of explaining how every phrase of the Treaty could be proved in conformity with the Fourteen Points.

Wilson must not then be directly blamed for the reparation clauses nor for the honoring of the Secret Treaties with Italy and Japan. These were to him the price to be paid for the League of Nations. In his opinion, if the League were established, it would be able to correct every injustice in the Treaty. Therefore injustices in the Treaty were for the moment not worth fighting for. He failed to see that submission to a League of Nations was submission to an authority who should regulate conduct, and that it is impossible to expect that men shall accept an authority to regulate the details of their conduct until they are first agreed in philosophy concerning its ends, concerning, that is to say, the sort of society at which they are aiming. There is today no such agreement.

If Wilson only accepted the Treaty in order that he might get the League of Nations, Clemenceau only accepted the League of Nations in order that he might get the Treaty. He knew the diversities of Europe too well to believe in it. Writers—especially American writers—are apt to speak of the conflict between Wilson and Clemenceau as a conflict between idealism and Machiavellianism. Mr. Ray Stannard Baker, for instance, in his *Woodrow Wilson and the World Settlement* habitually uses such a phraseology. Even such a writer as Mr. Kerney, full of admirably cynical realism as he describes Wilson's rise to power in American politics, drops into the language of this preposterous contrast when he comes to speak of European affairs. Truth gives no warrant for it. Clemenceau was a man who had unstintingly given his whole life to the great service of his country. Even his admirers do not deny that almost every action of Wilson was influenced by his egoism. In what was he the superior of Clemenceau except in the facility of his self-deception? "If we say that we have no sin we deceive ourselves." If we say it often enough we even begin to deceive other people. Yet it is a great mistake to think a man necessarily honest only because he is not cynical. It is said that Wilson wished to give the world peace and Clemenceau wished to give it war. The antithesis is unfair. Both wished to give the world peace. They differed concerning the means. Clemenceau's plan was based on laboriously observed fact, Wilson's on "idealism." They were both, no doubt, partly wrong. It has yet to be proved that Clemenceau was more wrong than Wilson.

Wilson had brought with him to Versailles the Allied promissory notes to the United States, worth between eight and ten billion dollars. It was the bland expectation of this man, once the enemy of plutocracy, that by waving them in the face of the statesmen of Europe in the intervals of perorations upon moral idealism, he would be able to induce the Italians to agree to forego the Secret Treaties, of which he had heard, but which, according to Mr. Ray Stannard Baker,[1] he had never put himself to the trouble of reading, and Europe in general to agree to such a peace as he might dictate to it. Whether or not it would have been to Europe's gain to have done so, is open to debate. At least she emerged from the Versailles Conference with a tattered remnant of dignity by refusing, like Jefferson, one hundred and twenty years before, to sacrifice the free life of a continent merely in order to be rid of a debt.

Most of the attempted explanations of Wilson's failure to give the world the peace which he desired fail by setting themselves too large a task. They assume that behind wicked diplomats and politicians there was a mysterious "people"—not to be confused with the people who were "so damned stupid"—an "enlightened conscience of humanity," yearning for Wilson's leadership. Neither in America nor in Europe was there any such conscience, nor, in the mercy of God, will there ever be. The people of the world wanted peace, but they had no confidence that Wilson knew how to give it to them. Both in his own and in other countries they were only anxious for an opportunity to repudiate him and his idealism and, as soon as such an opportunity came, they took it.

---

[1] *Woodrow Wilson and the World Settlement*, by Ray Stannard Baker. Doubleday, Page & Company. Garden City, 1926.

Yet Wilson did by his behavior make a difficult task even more difficult. He could have conquered the world only by personal magnetism. He treated it instead with arrogance, appealing continually over the heads of the people to whom he happened to be talking to an imaginary public opinion, which did not exist but which was supposed to be consumed with a hero-worship for Woodrow Wilson. To a man with the sense of humor of a Clemenceau this was amusing, to others infuriating. Wilson, it is true, is not to blame because the Peace Conference did not debate with open doors. Yet at least it might be thought that the enemy of secret diplomacy would have had the sense to reap the advantages of his convictions and treat with generosity the requests of journalists for news-items. On 16th November—five days after the Armistice—the Government had "for war purposes" suddenly taken control of the cables. On 18th November Wilson announced his attention of going to Paris. It was soon discovered that he believed in "open covenants openly arrived at"—provided that they did not get into the newspapers. Wilson was more grudging in his publicity than was the oldest of old-world diplomats. Only once during all his time in Paris did he consent to meet any reporters.

XVII

It was a February afternoon in 1919 and the scene the Hall of the Clock in Paris. Wilson rose from a seat at the head of a long horseshoe table and read to the delegates of the world the Covenant of the League of Nations. It was a stiff, formal affair. After he had sat down Lord Robert Cecil, as he then was, spoke, and, after Lord Robert, M. Léon Bourgeois. But on Wilson's left-hand there sat a little bald-headed old man in gloves—always in gloves—who did not speak. From this meeting Wilson and

Mrs. Wilson drove off to the station and took the train for Brest and America.

On landing at Boston he delivered a speech in which he said, "I have uttered as the objects of this war ideals and nothing but ideals, and the war has been won by that inspiration." It is hard not to feel that a certain contribution to victory was made by such things as shells, the British navy or the British and French armies, and that, since these things had to bear the burden of the war for some years before the allies were privileged to have the "inspiration" of Wilson's oratory employed upon their side rather than upon that of their enemy, it would have been tactful, at least, to have alluded to these contributory causes. Doubtless he did not seriously mean that he alone had won the war, but there was a tactless carelessness in his phraseology which might have been avoided.

His trip to America taught Wilson for the first time the strength of the opposition to him in his own country. He had stupidly refused to take warning from the Congressional elections of 1918 and hitherto, it seems, always assumed that whatever bargain he managed to bring back from Paris would be obediently ratified by the Senate. The opposite was the truth. The Senate was outraged by the treatment which it had received and was—to borrow an admirable phrase from Mr. Guedalla—"like an inverted Mr. Micawber, anxiously waiting for something to turn down." Wilson was met with a round-robin from Republican Senators containing just sufficient signatures to ensure the rejection of the Covenant and announcing that they could not accept it "in its present form." Changing from godlike arrogance to a panic for concession, he threw himself into the arms of a body of prominent Republicans, known as the League to Enforce Peace. Elihu Root, ex-President Taft and Hughes, Wilson's opponent of 1916, were the leaders of this League. His desire was to find from them what amendments would make the Covenant acceptable to the Republicans. And, with their amendments in his pocket, he returned to Paris in order to force them upon the Peace Conference.

If he blundered in going to Paris for the first time it is certain that he blundered even more badly in returning thither. Colonel House had been left in charge of the American Peace Delegation and Colonel House was a much better negotiator than Wilson. He could easily have secured the passage of whatever amendments were necessary. But whether it was that Wilson, while shrinking from publicity himself, could not bear that another should get it, or whether some other was the reason, he returned to Europe and unceremoniously dismissed Colonel House from the Peace Delegation. From his first entry into politics Wilson's record had been one long list of personal quarrels with those who had served him. He could not bear to be under an obligation to another. And by this date he had consequently only two friends left in the world—Colonel House and Mr. Tumulty. Colonel House had retained his friendship by a fortunate talent for obsequiousness. But in an evil moment a London newspaper published an article in which he was referred to as "the brains of the American Peace Delegation." Mrs. Wilson got hold of the paper and Colonel House's career and friendship were at an end. He was dismissed to London. Only once again did he see Wilson.

Wilson on his return to Paris found two main territorial problems awaiting solution—the problem of the Italian demand for Fiume and of the Japanese demand for Shantung.

The port of Fiume was in dispute between Italy and Jugo-Slavia. On the principle of self-determination both sides laid claim to it with about equal justice. But the strength of the Italian claim is often misjudged because of the impression which many people have that the Jugo-Slavs had been our gallant Allies during the war, whereas they had been rather the main and most efficient part of the Austro-Hungarian army opposed to the

Italians. Jugo-Slavia is a Triune kingdom. Of its three nationalities the Serbs had fought on our side, or—since they started it—we might perhaps more justly say that we had fought on their side, during the war. But of the Croats and Slovenes, who were alone concerned in Fiume, this had been by no means true. Their conduct had been more cunning. They had fought the Italians until the game was patently up, then thrown away their arms and, when the Italians marched in, fondly imagining themselves conquerors, the Croats had poured into the streets, and, with many embraces, cried out, "Our gallant Allies, how noble of you to liberate us! We also have thrown off the yoke of the oppressor." Yet the Jugo-Slavs, it was decided, were to have Fiume because it was necessary for their development that they be given an Adriatic port. The Italian delegation in disgust withdrew from the Conference. But Wilson, who had on his desk a request from Italy for a loan of fifty million dollars in order to buy coal, knew well that they would soon return. They did so and Wilson appeared to have won.

The Japanese had been watching the crisis with interest. They saw that the prestige of the Conference would not stand the strain of another public withdrawal, and therefore chose this moment to present their demand for Shantung, backed by the appropriate threat. Wilson and the Conference collapsed and conceded. History can hardly offer another example so admirable of a man straining at a gnat and swallowing a camel. There was much justice in the Italian claim to Fiume. There was no pretense of justice in the Japanese claim to Shantung. Yet Wilson, outwitted by the astute Japanese diplomacy, granted the latter and refused the former. The Chinese had no weapon but propaganda. Soon their pamphlets began to trickle around the United States. The Republicans saw to it that they received a proper publicity.

It seems that it was the Shantung agreement which finally broke Wilson's pride. He had laboriously engineered through the Conference the first set of Root-Taft-Hughes amendments. After the Shantung settlement they cabled to him a second set on whose inclusion they insisted. In weariness he refused to touch them and the fate of the Treaty was from that moment settled.

It is said by his apologists that he behaved thus because he knew that the Republicans had made up their minds to force amendment after amendment on him, until at last he should refuse one and thus give them an excuse for rejecting the whole Treaty. There seems no exact proof of this, but it may well be true. He had behaved to the Senate with such offensiveness that many of its members would have thought the whole world well lost if only they could humiliate Wilson. If Wilson realized that his Treaty was to be rejected anyway, his lack of courtesy is intelligible in allowing Senators to read its details in the newspapers before it was officially communicated to them. If he still had hope, it was stupid.

XVIII

Wilson on his return to America entertained the Foreign Relations Committee of the Senate at dinner in the White House. It was by Colonel House's advice, and the last time that he ever followed that advice. The purpose of the dinner was that Wilson might explain to the Committee the Covenant and the Treaty, but it was not a success. Wilson was in arrogant and Olympian mood. He proudly claimed that he had never read the Secret Treaties—to which the obvious, if discourteous, retort should have been that, if this were true, he had gravely neglected his duty. But it was not true. In the previous December Colonel House had stated in a public interview that Wilson knew of the Secret Treaties, and there is documentary evidence that this was so. To be caught out in a schoolboy's lie was not an auspicious beginning. "It was," as Talleyrand would have said, "worse than a crime. It was a blunder."

Yet even at this date it is certain that Wilson could have secured the Senate's ratification of the Covenant if he had allowed certain modifications which, in the opinion of many, were not vital to his plan. Lord Grey, for instance, stated on the authority of the British Prime Minister that such reservations were not vital. As a punishment he was not received at the White House. God on Mount Sinai had not been willing to accept an amendment to the Ten Commandments.

Wilson determined therefore to "appeal to Cæsar" and set out on the famous speaking tour which was to bring to a dramatic close his active political life. Strain and disappointment had been too much for him. His health was not good. And continual railway-traveling coupled with continual speech-making does not improve broken health. Nearer and nearer came the inevitable breakdown, until at last one terrible night in Pueblo the President of the United States burst into tears before the whole country during his speech. His next engagement was at Wichita, in Kansas. But, when he arrived there, it was clearly impossible that he should fulfil it. News went out through the town that the President was ill. The great train turned sullenly eastward and, hardly stopping except to change engines, it whirled him back across the plains of America to Washington and to bed. So he remained for days until one September morning he was struck in his bathroom by an apoplectic stroke and found lying as if dead.

The world was left to guess how seriously the President was ill. And, as is its habit, it was not idle in its guessing. There were in the White House some low windows looking out upon the lawn. When the Roosevelts were living there it was found that the balls of the young members of the family had the habit of straying through the panes of those windows. It had therefore been thought wise to guard them by some thick bars. These bars had for twelve years looked out unnoticed upon the lawn. Only now, for the first time, did any one observe them and men whispered to one another that behind them raged impotently a mad President and that those who knew did not dare to tell the world. So safe, they thought, the world was for democracy.

The truth, though bad, was not so bad as that. Yet Admiral Grayson, his physician, despaired of the President's recovery and of his ever again being fit to perform his duties. It was therefore clearly necessary at least to inform Vice-President Marshall unofficially of Wilson's condition and of the likelihood that he himself might suddenly be called upon to take the Presidential oath. Mr. Marshall declared that he would do nothing unless the President resigned or was publicly declared incompetent by medical certificate.

Wilson recovered and heard of the suggestion. Colonel House had written to submit a plan by which Wilson should send a message to the Senate explaining that he was under international obligation to submit the Covenant and Treaty to them as they stood, but that whatever amendments they chose to insert in it would be resubmitted to the European powers. At the same time Colonel House suggested that, in order to prove that personal ambition was not his motive, Wilson should make the excuse of his ill-health to resign the Presidency. The letter was not even acknowledged, and it was the last communication that ever passed between the two friends.

Mr. Lansing, his Secretary of State, had loyally stood by Wilson all through the Peace Conference in spite of the continual jeering and scarcely veiled personality that "this was not to be a lawyer's peace." But on his recovery Wilson learned that Mr. Lansing, too, had suggested that Wilson be replaced by Mr. Marshall. Mr. Lansing also had therefore to go. "Is it true," Wilson wrote, "as I have been told that, during my illness, you have frequently called the heads of the Executive Departments of the

Government into conference?" And again: "While you were still in Paris I felt, and have felt increasingly since, that you accepted my guidance and direction on questions with regard to which I had to instruct you with increasing reluctance and, since my return to Washington, I have been struck with the number of matters in which you have apparently tried to forestall my judgment." The present was "an opportunity to select some one whose mind would more willingly go along with mine." Between Mr. Lansing and Wilson there had never been any question of personal friendship, such as there was between Wilson and Colonel House. This but makes it the worse that service of unswerving loyalty should be so rewarded. Only Mr. Tumulty was left.

The rumors of Wilson's insanity were so persistent that Senator Fall, a Republican, and Senator Hitchcock, a Democrat, were sent to the White House to discover whether they were true or not. Wilson was determined to prove himself sane. "They had from Wilson," writes Mr. White, "thirty minutes of the gayest, blithest, sanest talk they had heard in months. . . . He gibed Fall about trying to get a war with Mexico to protect his local interests." The gibe was sane, certainly, and very just. It seems strange that it should be called gay and blithe.

In March, 1920, the Covenant had been defeated in the Senate by a vote of fifteen Republicans and twenty-four Democrats against twenty-three Democrats and thirty-four Republicans. It thus failed to receive the necessary two-thirds majority. Yet even now Wilson could easily have got the Senate to accept the Covenant with reservations. He refused, preferring to appeal to the people.

Wilson's amazing miscalculation of public opinion in believing that the people would support him against the Senate needs some explanation. The explanation is, no doubt, primarily medical. His doctor, during his illness, had necessarily given orders that no disturbing news be brought to the sick-room. Wilson therefore, not informed of his own growing unpopularity, dramatized the situation to himself. He imagined, though all knew it to be false, that America was yearning for his leadership and insisted that the Democratic party should fight the election of 1920 on the issue of the League, confident that it would thus be victorious. He had thrown the Democratic politicians into consternation by his public message to the Jackson Day dinner on 8th January, 1920, in which he had demanded that the League issue be submitted to the people "to give the next election the form of a great and solemn referendum"—the one thing which they were anxious to avoid—and Bryan had taken the opportunity of that very dinner to repudiate Wilson's policy.

The Democratic convention to select a Presidential candidate met in the summer at San Francisco. Wilson had hoped that it would offer him a complimentary nomination. His name, as that of a candidate, was not even mentioned. Nor was a suggestion which he had sent to the convention of a plank of opposition to the Volstead law discussed. Yet Wilson had at least one small consolation. Governor Cox of Ohio, the selected candidate, paid him a visit in Washington and pledged his support to the League of Nations. Wilson assumed that he would be elected. To do otherwise would be "to break the heart of the world."

Even today Wilson's friends, such as Mr. White, are but too apt to say that he failed because "humanity was not ready" for his high ideals. And his enemies, stupidly granting his "idealism" in order to contrast it with their own plain common sense, often almost concede the point to his friends. It is unnecessary and unhistorical to do so. The feeling of the American people in 1920 was that they were asked to abandon a traditional policy of isolation and commit themselves to certain obligations, the implications of which had been very ill thought out; that the League's first advertised business was to save Europe and that yet nobody in Europe seemed to have very great confidence in it;

that they were told that it would give the world peace but they had meekly to take the word of one whom they thought of as an arrogant and dishonest schoolmaster for that, and, by its invitation to everybody to mind everybody else's business, it was just as likely to involve the world in war. Social reformers spoke of its cause as the cause of idealism, but such language has no meaning, unless you can describe and justify your ideal.

The standpat Republicans were not a lovely crowd. Yet there is as much truth in their picture as in Mr. White's. On the one hand certain arrangements between nations have to be made and it is good that a regular machinery should be erected for making them. It will help to prevent the wars which neither side really wants, of which there are a certain number, and is useful for dealing with such matters as tuberculosis. If such a machinery were to exist the United States, provided that they could obtain proper guarantees that it would not fall into the hands of cranks, were probably better inside than outside it. Yet the sane, plain truth is that their tradition of isolation made it certain that the United States would never largely involve themselves in the disputes of Europe and that, if they were not willing so to involve themselves, it did not very much matter whether they came into the League or stayed out.

XIX

On 11th November, 1920, exactly two years since the Armistice was signed, the election results began to trickle in to Washington and Wilson at last knew the truth. In every corner of the United States electors had shown but one desire—to vote against any man who spoke a good word for Woodrow Wilson. Even in the solid South Tennessee went Republican. Every single State outside the South went Republican. Governor Cox was defeated by a majority of two hundred and seventy-seven electoral votes and a popular majority of more than seven millions. Never had there been such a debacle.

Wilson was unbroken by the news. "You can't fight God," he cried. One cannot but think of the contrast of Lincoln, who dared to pray no larger prayer than that "we may be on the Lord's side."

On 4th March, 1921, ended the political career of Woodrow Wilson. It was but ten years since, by his election as Governor of New Jersey, he had first entered political life. Few other Presidents had had so short a public career and few had been called to play so large a part in history. They helped him down the steps of the White House and into the carriage in which he and Harding were to drive together, according to custom, to the Inauguration. Sixty years ago to the day Buchanan and the strange and unknown Abraham Lincoln had made together a similar drive. Then, too, the times had been big with fate. But not of them did these two statesmen talk this day. "The Senator told the President a funny story about elephants, and he told the Senator another story or two that he had heard or read in a book, and they came to the Capitol."[1] Thus does Woodrow Wilson pass from history.

There is little more to record. With his death or his dying history has no business. He went to live in a house in S street in Washington and there he lingered on for another three years, never wholly understanding how completely it was the end. Sometimes he would talk of entering the Senate as a member from New Jersey, or of dominating the Democratic convention of 1924. They let him talk.

They let him talk because there was none to stop him. Only Mr. Tumulty had been left after the wreck. And then, as the end drew near, even Mr. Tumulty fell from grace. In April of 1922 there was a Democratic banquet in New York. To that banquet

---

[1] William Allen White.

Mr. Tumulty gave the message; "Former President Wilson says that he will support any man who will stand for the salvation of America and the salvation of America is justice to all classes." It seems a harmless message enough. The remark had fallen from Wilson in a private conversation with Mr. Tumulty and Mr. Tumulty had repeated it. If it was an indiscretion it was surely a very minor one. But Wilson's name had been used without his authority. He would not forgive.

Mr. Tumulty wrote to apologize. The letter was unanswered. He called in order to apologize. The door was shut in his face. Instead, this letter appeared in the *New York Times*:

> "My dear Sir,—I notice in the issue of the *Times* this morning an article headed:
> 'Doubt is cast on Wilson's Message to the Cox Dinner.'
> I write to say there need be no doubt about the matter. I did not send any message whatever to that dinner, nor authorize anyone to convey a message.
> I hope that you will be kind enough to publish this letter.— Very truly yours,   Woodrow Wilson."

No man in history, I suppose, was ever more nobly and loyally served than Woodrow Wilson. And, one after one, those who had given to him their lives had received as their wages, not honor, nor thanks, nor even civility, but a kick from the room. The last friend was now gone.

For a little less than two years after the quarrel he lived on in the big formal house in S Street. Sometimes the Bishop of the Cathedral at Washington called. But Wilson's "own salvation did not concern him—that was settled with his calling and election."[1] Once Mr. Lloyd George called in order to hear "a repetition of some of the limericks with which Wilson had regaled the European statesmen at Paris and Versailles," once Marshal Foch—but Wilson did not see him.

---

[1] William Allen White.

Woodrow Wilson

At last, on 3rd February, 1924, Wilson died quietly in his sleep. And as the doctors walked away from the house they found outside, waiting for the last news, a small crowd. Prominent in it was a big Irishman whose name was Tumulty.

A few days later they buried the President in the Episcopal Cathedral. Another crowd was in Madison Square Garden in New York, whither the funeral service and sermon were relayed. Among it—though not prominent—was a gentleman in a fur-lined coat and a soft hat. His name was House.

The New State

THE READER who has followed this book through the essays on Jefferson, Calhoun and Lincoln will, I fancy, have had no difficulty in following its thesis, whether to agree with it or to disagree with it. Yet he may legitimately ask in what way the last essay on Wilson is connected with that thesis. It cannot be pretended that the connection is more than negative. The Jeffersonian state, this book argues, which came to birth in the War of Independence, perished in the Civil War. The justification of the essay on Wilson is that it demonstrates this argument by giving a picture of a new state, perhaps better, perhaps worse than that which Thomas Jefferson built, but at least entirely different from the Jeffersonian state, Hamiltonian, as has been said, rather than Jeffersonian, if one must search out for it an ancestor among the American fathers. A certain verbal homage is still paid to the men of 1776 or the men of 1861. There is an apparent continuity, but that continuity is not real.

The root of the change is to be found in the destruction of the State unit. And, as a result of that destruction, power has largely shifted away from its nominal holders and passed into that of wealth. The United States are today a plutocracy, even as England is a plutocracy, though there, as in England, the plutocracy may still work through an apparently democratic mechanism. Against this rule of plutocracy there have been sporadic protests. They have accomplished little and some of them have been hardly sincere. But, if they have not checked the menace, they have at least proved its existence.

The very natural consequence of this shifting of power has been, as might be expected, a collapse of the capacity for political thought. Men today think about money because money matters. They do not think about politics because politics do not matter. Take, in illustration, the philosophy of a man who is perhaps the most remarkable of living Americans and the imitation of whom is the highest ambition of a very large proportion of rising American manhood—Mr. Henry Ford.

I remember very well sitting in the largest hotel of Chicago, listening to the declaration of the results of the American Presidential election of 1924. Never in my life have I seen a more apathetic crowd. Hardly any one seemed to be the least interested even in the result, while in the issues behind the result no one was interested at all. To the American today politics are a game but not nearly so good a game as baseball. It was not thus that Thomas Jefferson thought of them.

I have myself no great love for the person who is "interested in politics." Nor do I necessarily condemn the Americans for having lost interest. I merely record it as a historical fact that they once did take an interest and that they have now ceased to do so. There has been a positive turning away from political interests. It is important to insist upon this in order that we may avoid the vague metaphor of growth which tells us that, though it may be true that political controversy in America is today crude, yet the country is a young country and has still to grow up. To argue by metaphors is always dangerous and this metaphor the facts very easily disprove. It is not true that American political thought has, like M. Coué's pupils, been getting every day and in every way better and better. On the contrary, the level of controversy from the War of Independence to the Civil War was intellectually extraordinarily high—probably higher than in any country of the world. Hamilton and Jefferson, Hayne and Webster, Clay,

Calhoun, Lincoln and Douglas—all were men who knew when a proposition was proved and when it was not proved and who were accustomed to speak before audiences who demanded that propositions should be proved. These men might perhaps tell a lie—I speak not of their morals but of their intellects—but they would not tell the sort of lie that is told today. Hamilton was quite capable of asserting that Jefferson had taken bribes which he knew that he had not taken. He was quite incapable of telling an audience of Middle-Western women that "our American womanhood is the noblest that civilization has yet produced." For he spoke to audiences that demanded to be convinced; the modern politician speaks only to those who demand to be flattered.

It is then the thesis of this book that there went into the Civil War two politically minded nations. There emerged from it, or rather from the period of Reconstruction, one non-politically minded nation, content, and even anxious, to allow the rich to order its life to the smallest detail. Its so-called political life has become little more than an empty ritual against which Roosevelt, alone among modern Presidents, has made a vigorous, if partial, protest. The real life of America is lived elsewhere. Where Jefferson and Calhoun were masters and Lincoln at least dared to struggle for mastery, even Wilson was a servant and such men as McKinley and Harding were almost puppets. Wilson was arrogant before McCombs or Lansing; he was not arrogant before J. P. Morgan.

There seems no reason to think that the near future will see any large change. What the distant future holds—whether there will be a reaction towards democracy or whether its empty forms will be abolished or even whether the great unit will some day split up—is a question which only the very foolish would attempt to answer.

APPENDICES

Appendix A

THE DECLARATION OF INDEPENDENCE

4th July, 1776

The unanimous declaration of the thirteen United States of America.

WHEN IN THE COURSE of human events it becomes necessary for one people to dissolve the political bonds which have connected them with another, and to assume among the powers of the earth the separate and equal station to which the Laws of Nature and of Nature's God entitle them, a decent respect to the opinions of mankind requires that they should declare the causes which impel them to the separation.

We hold these truths to be self-evident, that all men are created equal, that they are endowed by their Creator with certain inalienable rights, that among these are life, liberty and the pursuit of happiness. That to secure these rights governments are instituted among men, deriving their just powers from the consent of the governed. That whenever any form of government becomes destructive of these ends, it is the right of the people to alter or to abolish it, and to institute new government, laying its foundation on such principles and organizing its powers in such form as to them shall seem most likely to effect their safety and happiness. Prudence, indeed, will dictate that governments long established should not be changed for light and transient causes; and accordingly all experience hath shown that mankind are more disposed to suffer, while evils are sufferable, than to right themselves by abolishing the forms to which they are accustomed. But when a long train of abuses and usurpations, pursuing invariably the same object, evinces a design to reduce them under absolute despotism, it is their right, it is their duty, to throw off such government, and to provide new guards for their future security. Such has been the patient sufferance of these colonies; and such is now the necessity which constrains them to alter their former systems of government. The history of the present King of Great Britain is a history of repeated injuries and usurpations, all having in direct object the establishment of an absolute tyranny over these States. To prove this, let these facts be submitted to a candid world.

He has refused his assent to laws, the most wholesome and necessary for the public good.

He has forbidden his governors to pass laws of immediate and pressing importance unless suspended in their operation till his assent should be obtained; and when so suspended he has utterly neglected to attend to them.

He has refused to pass other laws for the accommodation of large districts of people, unless those people would relinquish the right of representation in the legislature, a right inestimable to them and formidable to tyrants only.

He has called together legislative bodies at places unusual, uncomfortable and distant from the depository of their public records for the sole purpose of fatiguing them into compliance with his measures.

He has dissolved representative houses repeatedly for opposing with manly firmness his invasions on the rights of the people.

He has refused for a long time, after such dissolutions, to cause others to be elected; whereby the legislative powers, incapable of annihilation, have returned to the people at large for their exercise, the State remaining in the meantime exposed to all the dangers of invasion from without and convulsions within.

He has endeavoured to prevent the population of these States; for that purpose obstructing the laws for naturalization of foreigners, refusing to pass others to encourage their migration hither, and raising the conditions of new appropriation of lands.

He has obstructed the administration of justice, by refusing his assent to laws for establishing judiciary powers.

He has made judges dependent on his will alone for the tenure of their offices and the amount and payment of their salaries.

He has erected a multitude of new offices, and sent thither swarms of officers to harass our people and eat out their substance.

Appendices

He has kept among us, in times of peace, standing armies without the consent of our legislatures.

He has affected to render the military independent of and superior to the civil power.

He has combined with others to subject us to a jurisdiction foreign to our constitution and unacknowledged by our laws; giving assent to their acts of pretended legislation.

For quartering large bodies of troops among us:

For protecting them, by a mock trial, from punishment for any murders which they should commit on the inhabitants of these States:

For cutting off our trade with all parts of the world:

For imposing taxes on us without our consent:

For depriving us in many cases of the benefits of trial by jury:

For transporting us beyond the seas to be tried for pretended offences:

For abolishing the free system of English laws in a neighbouring province, establishing therein an arbitrary government and enlarging its boundaries so as to render it at once an example and fit instrument for introducing the same absolute rule into these colonies:

For taking away our Charters, abolishing our most valuable laws and altering fundamentally the forms of our governments:

For suspending our own legislatures and declaring themselves invested with power to legislate for us in all cases whatsoever:

He has abdicated government here by declaring us out of his protection and waging war against us.

He has plundered our seas, ravaged our coasts, burnt our towns, and destroyed the lives of our people.

He is at this time transporting large armies of foreign mercenaries to complete the works of death, desolation and tyranny, already begun with circumstances of cruelty and perfidy scarcely paralleled in the most barbarous ages, and totally unworthy of the head of a civilized nation.

He has constrained our fellow citizens taken captive on the high seas to bear arms against their country, to become the executioners of their friends and brethren, or to fall themselves by their hands.

He has excited domestic insurrections amongst us, and has endeavoured to bring on the inhabitants of our frontiers the merciless Indian savages, whose known rule of warfare is an undistinguished destruction of all ages, sexes and conditions.

In every stage of these oppressions we have petitioned for redress in the most humble terms: our repeated petitions have been answered only by repeated injury. A prince whose character is thus marked by every act which may define a tyrant is unfit to be the ruler of a free people.

Nor have we been wanting in attention to our British brethren. We have warned them from time to time of attempts by their legislature to extend an unwarrantable jurisdiction over us. We have reminded them of the circumstances of our emigration and settlement here. We have appealed to their native justice and magnanimity, and we have conjured them by the ties of our common kindred to disavow those usurpations which would inevitably interrupt our connections and correspondence. They, too, have been deaf to the voice of justice and of consanguinity. We must, therefore, acquiesce in the necessity which denounces our separation, and hold them, as we hold the rest of mankind, enemies in war, in peace friends.

We, therefore, the Representatives of the United States of America, in General Congress assembled, appealing to the Supreme Judge of the world for the rectitude of our intentions, do, in the name, and by authority of the good people of these colonies, solemnly publish and declare, That these United Colonies are and of right ought to be free and independent States; that they are absolved from all allegiance to the British Crown, and that all political connection between them and the State of Great Britain is and ought to be totally dissolved; and that as Free and Independent States they have full power to levy war, conclude peace, contract alliances, establish commerce, and to do all other acts and things which independent States may of right do. And for the support of this declaration, with a firm reliance on the protection of Divine Providence we mutually pledge to each other our lives, our fortunes and our sacred honor.

Appendix B

The Virginia Statute of Religious Liberty

October, 1785

An Act for Establishing Religious Freedom.

I. Whereas Almighty God hath created the mind free; that all attempts to influence it by temporal punishments or burthens, or by civil incapacitations, tend only to beget habits of hypocrisy and meanness, and are departures from the plan of the Holy author of our religion, who being Lord both of body and mind, yet chose not to propagate it by coercions on either, as was in his Almighty power to do; that the impious presumption of legislators and rulers, civil as well as ecclesiastical, who being themselves but fallible and uninspired men, have assumed dominion over the faith of others, setting up their opinions and modes of thinking as the only true and infallible, and as such endeavouring to impose them on others, hath established and maintained false religions over the greatest part of the world and through all time; that to compel a man to furnish contributions of money for the propagation of opinions which he disbelieves is sinful and tyrannical; that even the forcing him to support this or that teacher of his own religious persuasion is depriving him of the comfortable liberty of giving his contributions to the particular pastor whose morals he would make his pattern, and whose powers he feels most persuasive to righteousness, and is withdrawing from the ministry those temporary rewards which, proceeding from an approbation of their personal conduct, are an additional incitement to earnest and unremitting labours for the instruction of mankind; that our civil rights have no dependence on our religious opinions any more than our opinions on physics or geometry; that, therefore, the proscribing any citizen as unworthy of public confidence by laying upon him an incapacity of being called to offices of trust and emolument, unless he profess or renounce this or that religious opinion is depriving him injuriously of those privileges and advantages to which in common with his fellow-citizens he has a natural right; that it tends only to corrupt the principles of that religion it is meant to encourage by bribing with a monopoly of worldly honours and emoluments those who will externally profess and conform to it; that though, indeed, those are criminal who do not withstand such temptation, yet neither are those innocent who lay the bait in their way; that to suffer the civil magistrate to intrude his powers into the field of opinion and to restrain the profession or propagation of principles on supposition of their ill tendency is a dangerous fallacy which at once destroys all religious liberty, because he being, of course, judge of that tendency will make his opinions the rule of judgment, and approve or condemn the sentiments of others only as they shall square with or differ from his own; that it is time enough for the rightful purposes of civil government, for its officers to interfere when principles break out into overt acts against peace and good order; and finally, that truth is great and will prevail if left to herself; that she is the proper and sufficient antagonist to error, and has nothing to fear from the conflict, unless by human interposition disarmed of her natural weapons, free argument and debate, errors ceasing to be dangerous when it is permitted freely to contradict them.

II. Be it enacted by the General Assembly that no man shall be compelled to frequent or support any religious worship, place or ministry whatsoever, nor shall be enforced, restrained, molested or burthened in his body or goods, nor shall otherwise suffer on account of his religious opinions or belief; but that all men shall be free to profess, and by argument to maintain their opinion in matters of religion, and that the same shall in no wise diminish, enlarge or affect their civil capacities.

III. And though we well know that this Assembly elected by the people for the ordinary purposes of legislation only have no power to restrain the acts of succeeding Assemblies constituted with powers equal to their own, and that therefore to declare this act to be irrevocable would be of no effect in law; yet as we are free to declare, and do declare, that the rights hereby asserted are of the natural rights of mankind, and that if any act shall hereafter be passed to repeal the present or to narrow its operation, such act will be an infringement of natural right.

Appendix C

The Bill of Rights

1. Congress shall make no law respecting an establishment of religion or prohibiting the free exercise thereof; or abridging the freedom of speech or of the press; or the right of the people peaceably to assemble, and to petition the government for a redress of grievances.

2. A well-regulated militia being necessary to the security of a free State, the right of the people to keep and bear arms shall not be infringed.

3. No soldier shall, in time of peace, be quartered in any house without the consent of the owner, nor in time of war, but in a manner to be prescribed by law.

4. The right of the people to be secure in their persons, houses, papers and effects against unreasonable searches and seizures shall not be violated, and no warrants shall issue but upon probable cause, supported by oath or affirmation, and particularly describing the place to be searched and the person or things to be seized.

5. No person shall be held to answer for a capital or otherwise infamous crime unless on a presentment or indictment of a grand jury, except in cases arising in the land or naval forces, or in the militia, when in actual service in time of war or public danger; nor shall any person be subject for the same offense to be twice put in jeopardy of life and limb; nor shall be compelled in any criminal case to be a witness against himself; nor be deprived of life, liberty, or property without due process of law; nor shall private property be taken for public use without just compensation.

6. In all criminal prosecutions the accused shall enjoy the right to a speedy and public trial by an impartial jury of the State and district wherein the crime shall have been committed, which district shall have been previously ascertained by law, and to be informed of the nature and cause of the accusation; to be confronted with the witness against him; to have compulsory process for obtaining witnesses in his favour, and to have the assistance of counsel for his defence.

7. In suits at common law, where the value in controversy shall exceed twenty dollars, the right of trial by jury shall be preserved, and no fact tried by a jury shall be otherwise re-examined in any court of the United States than according to the rules of the common law.

8. Excessive bail shall not be required, nor excessive fines imposed, nor cruel and unusual punishments inflicted.

9. The enumeration in the Constitution of certain rights shall not be construed to deny or disparage others retained by the people.

10. The powers not delegated to the United States by the Constitution, nor prohibited by it to the States, are reserved to the States respectively or to the people.

Appendix D

The Fourteen Points

1. Open Covenants of peace, openly arrived at, after which there shall be no private international understandings of any kind, but diplomacy shall proceed always frankly and in the public view.
2. Absolute freedom of navigation upon the seas, outside territorial waters, alike in peace and in war, except as the seas may be closed in whole or in part by international action for the enforcements of international covenants.
3. The removal, so far as possible, of all economic barriers and the establishment of an equality of trade conditions among all the nations consenting to the peace and associating themselves for its maintenance.
4. Adequate guarantees given and taken that national armaments will be reduced to the lowest point consistent with domestic safety.
5. A free, open-minded and absolutely impartial adjustment of all colonial claims, based upon a strict observance of the principle that in determining all such questions of sovereignty the interests of the populations concerned must have equal weight with the equitable claims of the Government, whose title is to be determined.
6. The evacuation of all Russian territory and such a settlement of all questions affecting Russia as will secure the best and freest co-operation of other nations of the world in the obtaining for her of an unhampered and unembarrassed opportunity for the independent determination of her own political development and national policy, and assure her of a sincere welcome into the society of free nations under institutions of her own choosing; and, more than a welcome, assistance also of every kind that she may need and may herself desire. The treatment accorded to Russia by her sister nations in the months to come will be the acid-test of their goodwill, of their comprehension of her needs as distinguished from their own interests, and of their intelligent and unselfish sympathy.
7. Belgium, the whole world will agree, must be evacuated and restored, without any attempt to limit the sovereignty which she enjoys in

common with all other free nations. No other single act will serve as this will serve to restore confidence among the nations in the laws which they have themselves set and determined for the government of their relations with one another. Without this healing act the whole structure and validity of international law is for ever impaired.

8. All French territory should be freed and the invaded portions restored, and the wrong done to France by Prussia in 1871 in the matter of Alsace-Lorraine, which has unsettled the peace of the world for nearly fifty years, should be righted in order that peace may once more be made secure in the interest of all.

9. A readjustment of the frontiers of Italy should be effected along clearly recognizable lines of nationality.

10. The peoples of Austria-Hungary, whose place among the nations we wish to see safeguarded and assured, should be accorded the freest opportunity of autonomous development.

11. Rumania, Serbia and Montenegro should be evacuated; Serbia accorded free and secure access to the Sea; and the relations of the several Balkan States to one another determined by friendly counsel along historically established lines of allegiance and nationality; and international guarantees of the political and economic independence and territorial integrity of the several Balkan States should be entered into.

12. The Turkish portions of the present Ottoman Empire should be assured a secure sovereignty, but the other nationalities which are now under Turkish rule should be assured an undoubted security of life and an absolutely unmolested opportunity of autonomous development, and the Dardanelles should be permanently opened as a free passage to the ships and commerce of all nations under international guarantees.

13. An independent Polish State should be erected which should include the territories inhabited by indisputably Polish populations, which should be assured a free and secure access to the sea,[1] and whose political and economic independence and territorial integrity should be guaranteed by international covenant.

14. A general association of nations must be formed under specific covenants for the purpose of affording mutual guarantees of political independence and territorial integrity to great and small states alike.

---

[1] It is one of the smaller humors of history that access to the Sea was claimed for Serbia, with a large capital S, but for Poland only with a very small one. Why this should have been I do not know.

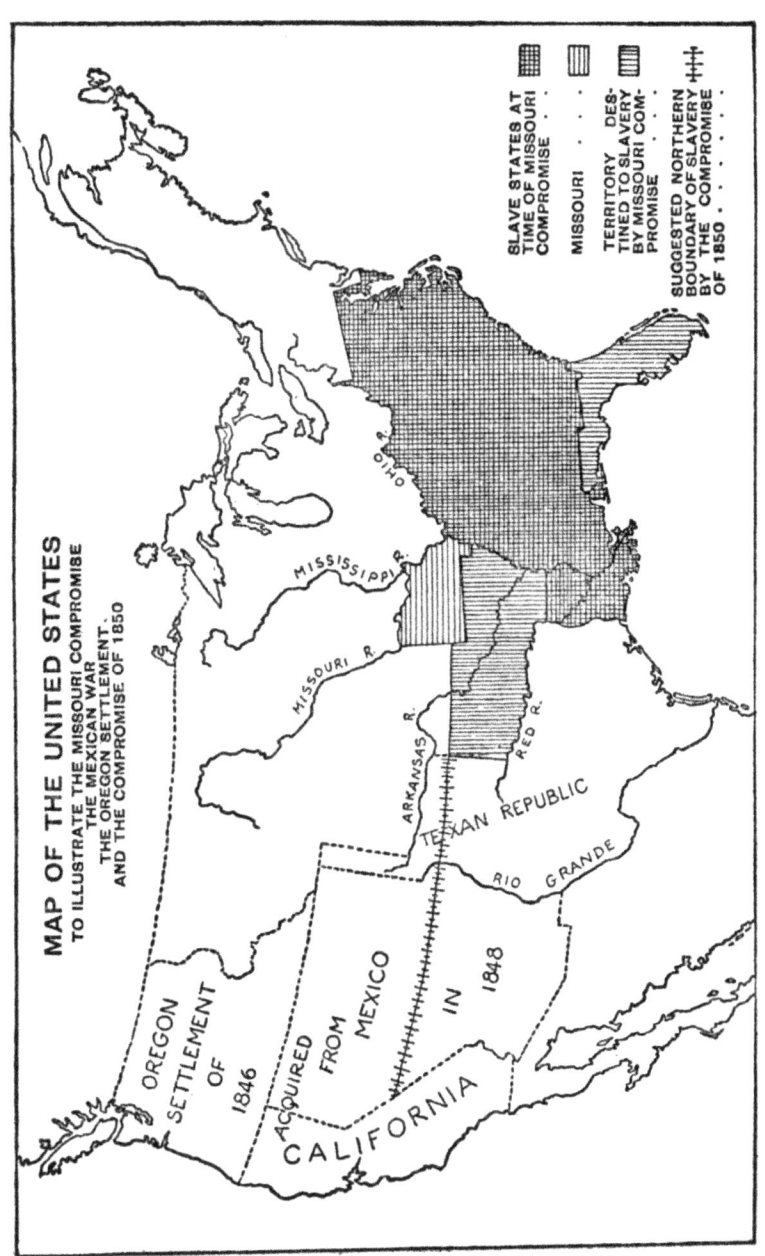

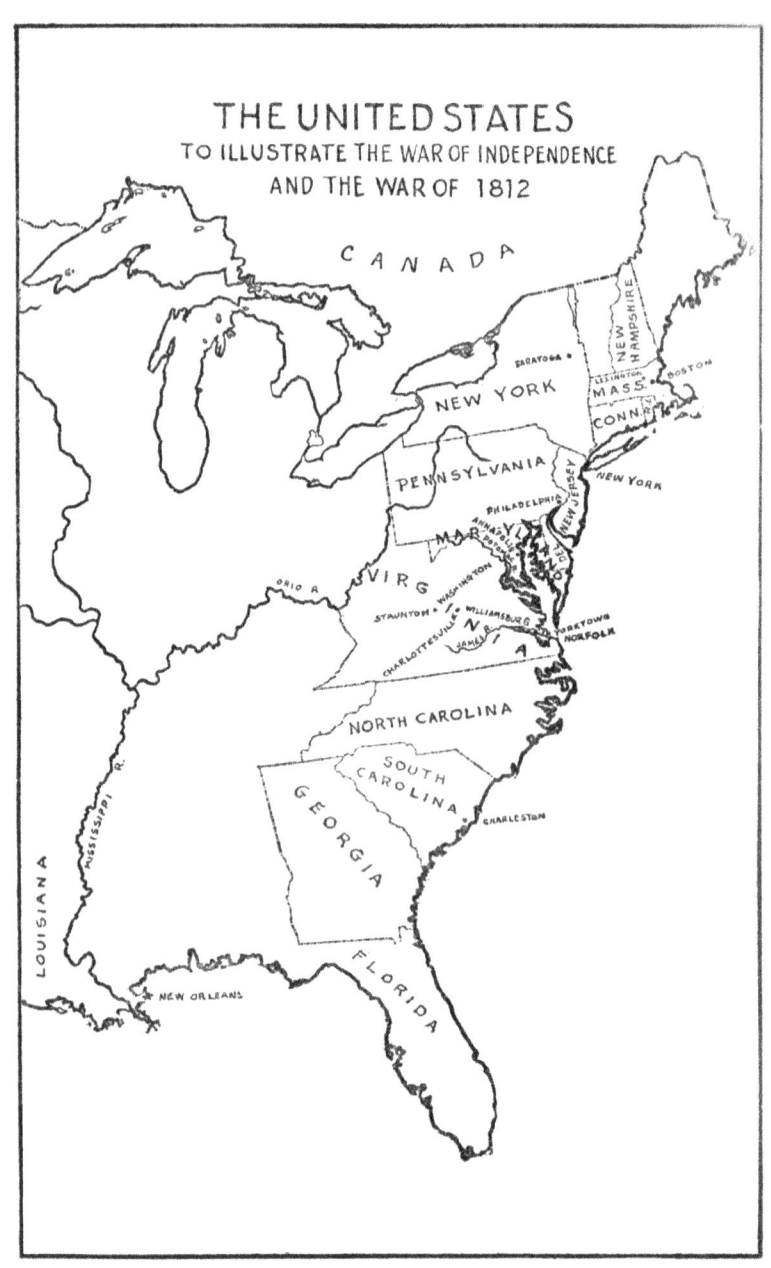

Index

A.B. Papers, 106
Abbeville, Calhoun's birth at, 86
Aberdeen, Lord, Calhoun's correspondence with, 131–132; letter of, 133; Calhoun's conduct not dictated by, 133
Ackerman, acts for Wilson, 246
Adams, C. F., on American Constitution, 37
Adams, John, commercial negotiations of, 33; argument with Hamilton, 41; candidate for Presidency, 54; elected, 55; averts war, 56; again candidate, 57; conduct of, at end of term, 60; corresponds with Jefferson, 74; death of, 83
Adams, John Quincy, quoted on Jefferson's hospitality, 61; reveals Essex Junto's plans to Jefferson, 72; diary of, 93; candidate for Presidency, 94; successful, 95; controversy with Calhoun, 96; diary quoted, 98; on discrediting of Calhoun, 105; quoted on Clay, 110; creates Whig party, 112
Address of the Southern Delegates in Congress to their constituents, 145
Address to the people of South Carolina, 107
Adêt, French Minister to U.S.A., 54
Advantages of Withdrawing from New Colonies in Present Circumstances, by Talleyrand, quoted, 66
Alabama, opposes tariff, 97; secedes, 189

Albemarle, Jefferson's constituency, 19
Alexandria, held by Confederates, 47, 198
Amherst, Lord, Indian policy of, 92
Ampudia, General, in command of Mexican troops, 141
Amsterdam, financial negotiations at, 45
Ana, Jefferson's, 84
Anacreon, quoted by Jefferson, 82
Anderson, Major, in command at Fort Sumter, 188; demands re-enforcements, 191
Andrew, Governor, supports Frémont, 217
Annapolis, Jefferson arrives at, 33
Annin, Mr. R. E., quoted on Wilson, 235
Antietam, battle of, 208; emancipation follows, 210; Lincoln on, 222
Appomattox, Lincoln and, 158; Lincoln receives news from, 220; Lee's surrender at, 221
Aquinas, St. Thomas, doctrine of human equality of, in Summa Contra Gentiles, 16
Argentine summons Niagara Conference, 262
Arizona, slavery in, 188
Arnold, Benedict, treachery of, 27
Atlanta, capture of, 215; political effect of fall of, 217; Wilson practices law at, 226
Atlantic City, dinner to Wilson at, 249
Augusta, Wilson at, 225

Index

Australia, position compared with that of America, 8

Austria, American relations with, 271; and Prussia, 286–287; salvation of, desirable, 289; Napoleon III's failure to support, 290

BAKER, Mr. Ray Stannard, on Secret Treaties, 293–294

Baldwin, Mr. Stanley, defeat of, 125; compared with Southern leaders, 193

Baltimore, Anti-Slavery Congress at, 113; paper demands Texan annexation, 130; Democratic Convention at, 135; Massachusetts Regiment mobbed at, 199, 206, 207; Democratic Convention at, 250

Banks, General, Jackson defeats, 206

Barbé-Marbois, sells Louisiana, 63

Barnes, Professor Harry Elmer, quoted concerning signatories of Declaration of Independence, 5

Bazaine, Marshal, in Mexico, 201

Beauregard, religion of, 158; sent to Charleston, 189; fires on Sumter, 194; "song" of, 196; victory of, at Bull Run, 200

Belgium recognizes Texan independence, 129; Roosevelt defends German violation of, 263; Germany and, 268, 275

Bell, stands for Presidency, 174

Belmont, August, Bryan and, 251

Bentinck, Lord George, argument of, for protection, 33

Benton, Senator, quoted, 95

Berlin Decrees, 71; French arrogance concerning, 88

Bermuda, Wilson goes to, 254

Bernard, General, compares Calhoun with Napoleon, 91

Bernstorff, Count von, intelligence of, 271

Biglow Papers, by Lowell, attacks on Calhoun in, 120

"Birdofreedum Sawin," character in *Biglow Papers*, 118

Black Hawk War, Lincoln and, 159

Blair, advice of, on Fort Sumter, 191; on Frémont, 203; resignation of, 217

Boers, struggle of, compared with the American, 26

Bolingbroke, Lord, Jefferson's opinion of, 4; *Patriot King* by, studied by George III, 9

Booth, John Wilkes, murders Lincoln, 223

Boston, demands a higher tariff, 97; Wilson's speech at, 296

Bourgeois, Mr. Léon, and League of Nations, 295

Bowers, Mr. Claude G., quoted on Calhoun-Jackson quarrel, 106

Brazil, summons Niagara Conference, 262

Breckinridge, stands for Presidency, 174; defeat of, 178

British Columbia, in Oregon Territory, 138

Brown, John, Northern opposition to, 124; exploits of, 173; capture of, 173

Bryan, William Jennings, campaigns of, 243; suspects Wilson, 248; Wilson's letter concerning, 249; Clark's support of, 250; at Baltimore Convention, 250; intrigues with Harvey, 252; Secretary of State, 254; resignation of, 264; succeeded by Lansing, 264; repudiates Wilson, 303

Bryan, Mrs., letter of, to House, 253

Bryn Mawr, Wilson, Professor at, 226

Buchanan, President, and Dred Scott, 167; and Leavenworth Convention, 169; weakness of, 187–188; at Lincoln's inauguration, 190; and Fort Sumter, 193; supports Lincoln, 197; and Lincoln, 305

325

Buffon, Comte de, criticized by Jefferson, 4
Bull Run, Northern defeat at, 200; second battle of, 206
Bunyan, John, *Holy War* of, 280
Burgoyne, General, surrenders at Saratoga, 27
Burke, Edmund, on taxation of America, 8; on French Revolution, 36; Wilson's character sketch of, 230, 231
Burleson, Postmaster-General, 281; ruined, 282
Burnside, General, defeat of, 209
Burr, Aaron, candidate for Presidency, 54; again, 57; ties with Jefferson, 58; Jefferson preferred to, 59; shoots Hamilton, 69; tried for treason, 70; acquitted, 70
Butler, Benjamin, conduct at New Orleans, 156

CÆSAR, Julius, and Napoleon, 36; not a militarist, 272
Calhoun, John Caldwell, views of, on slavery, 2; appeals to Kentucky Resolutions, 57; passim, 84–152; importance of, 84; birth, 86; education, 86; inconsistency of, 90; suspicion of North, 91; Secretary of War, 91; Indian policy of, 92; Adams' criticism of, 93; Vice-President, 94; supports Jackson, 95; controversy with Adams, 96; votes against tariff, 97; reference to, in Adams' Diary, 98; on nullification, 99–100; Webster's gibe against, 102; again Vice-President, 103; quarrel with Jackson, 104; at nullification dinner, 104; quarrel with Crawford, 106; quarrels with Jackson, 107; enters Senate, 108; on Clay, 110; on Force Bill, 111; acts with no party, 112; opposition of, to abolitionists, 114; defends slavery, 114–116; slavery on plantations of, 118; on slave-trade, 119; defense of, for slavery, 120; compared with Socialists, 121; on Southern railways, 122; Jackson's desire to hang, 123; resolutions of, 123; contradiction in theory of, 124; on law of nations, 126; supports Treaty of Washington, 127; Secretary of State, 128; on annexation of Texas, 129; and Jackson, 130; difficulties of, 131; correspondence of, with Aberdeen, 131; on British policy, 132; on interference in Texas, 132; on Texan abolition, 134; promises assistance to Texas, 136; threatens the North, 136; for immediate annexation, 137; and balance of the Union, 138; policy of, concerning Oregon, 139; threatens Great Britain, 140; attempts to avoid Mexican War, 140; opposes Mexican War, 142; and Missouri Compromise, 143; on Oregon, 144; Address of the Southern Delegates, 145; Horace Mann on, 146; on Southern Convention, 146; last speech of, 148; despair of, 149; death of, 149; opposition of, to industrialism, 150; religion of, 158; Mexican acquisitions, 160; opposition of, to Clay's compromise, 161; and tariff, 163; and Wilmot Proviso, 164; and the Supreme Court, 167; plan of a "Roman" Republic, 182; on slavery, 183; and necessity for the South to strike quickly, 194
Calhoun, Patrick, brother of John Caldwell, 88
California, American demand for, 141; Calhoun's policy concerning, 145; demands statehood, 147; admission of, 161; negro-policy of, 188; Mexican loss of, 202; supports Wilson, 268
Cameron, candidature of, 175; bargain

Index

with Davis, 176; and Lincoln, 176–177; dismissal of, 203–204
Canada, American hope to recapture, 73
Canning, George, and Monroe Doctrine, 78
Caraccioli, repartee of, 61
Carden, Sir Lionel, and Huerta, 259
Carnot, and French Revolution, 36
Carolina, North, gives one vote to Adams, 54; opposes tariff, 97; secedes, 199
Carolina, South, and slavery, 2; nullification in, 57; importance of, 88; Calhoun's loyalty to, 90, 98; nullification in, 99; Calhoun's advice to, 103; nullifies, 108; acceptance of compromise by, 109; feeling in, 111; Calhoun's claims for, 124; sovereignty of, 125; Calhoun supported for Presidency in, 128; Calhoun's love for, 129; not to lead in Southern Convention, 147; Calhoun and, 150; and Calhoun's epitaph, 152; secedes, 179; declares herself a Republic, 187; example of, followed, 189; claims Sumter, 191; and Lincoln, 198
Carranza, General, revolts against Huerta, 257; recognized, 262
Centinel, The, of Boston, quoted on Constitution, 38; quoted on Burr, 59
Centreville, McDowell retreats through, 200
Chamberlain, Senator, accusation of, 278
Chancellorsville, Stonewall Jackson killed at, 84; battle of, 209
Charlemagne, and Napoleon, 36
Charles I, system of, contrasted with the Parliamentary, 7; refuses to allow Parliament to tax America, 9
Charleston, British occupation of, 27; Cornwallis at, 86; remonstrance of Chamber of Commerce of, 97;

nullification suspended at, 110; negro song in, 146; Lincoln on, as port of entry, 177; modern opinion on secession in, 186; situation at, 188; Beauregard at, 190
Charlottesville, Tarleton's raid on, 27–28; University of Virginia built at, 79
Charnwood, Lord, quoted on Lincoln's religion, 157; on John Brown, 174; on emancipation, 210
Chase, Governor, candidature of, 175; advice of, on Fort Sumter, 191; and Seward, 211; quarrel of, with Lincoln, 216; repudiated by Ohio, 216
Chateaubriand, South American policy of, 78
Chatham, Lord, Wilson's character-sketch of, 230, 231
Cherbourg, Wilson lands at, 284
Cherokee, dictionary of, Jefferson compiles, 58
Chesapeake, duel with *Leopard*, 71
Chesterton, Cecil, quoted on Southern nationalism, 184; and state loyalty, 186; on Fort Sumter, 191
Chicago, Republican Convention at, 175; Lincoln chosen at, 198; petition from, 209; and Presidential election of 1924, 309
Chile, summons Niagara Conference, 262
Cincinnati, Washington's toleration of, 53
Clark, Champ, at Baltimore Convention, 250; Bryan and, 251; defeat of, 252; on Bryan, 253; at Sunrise Conference, 266
Clark, Lewis and, expedition of, 67
Clay, Henry, Speaker, 88; candidate for Presidency, 94; Secretary of State, 95; character of, 110; and the tariff, 110; Jackson's desire to shoot, 123; compared with Calhoun, 149;

327

compromise of, 160
Clayton, Oregon Bill of, 144
Clemenceau, M. Georges, letter of, to Wilson, 279; boast of, 280; at Versailles Conference, 285–286; opinion of, on Germany, 286–288; contempt of, for fellow-negotiators, 288; Polish policy of, 289; mistaken policy of, towards Austria, 289–290; towards Germany, 291; and problems of French security, 292; and League of Nations, 293, 295
Cleveland, Grover, at Princeton, 231; supports West, 233; death of, 234; Clark's support of, 250
Cobb, Frank, interview of, with Wilson, 272–273
Cobden, Richard, argument of, for Free Trade, 32
Cold Harbor, battle of, 215
Coleridge, Samuel Taylor, quoted on architecture, 79
Columbia, District of, slavery in, 115
Columbia, South Carolina, Wilson goes to, 225
Commentaries on the Constitution, by Rawle, quoted, 98
"Common Sense," pamphlet by Tom Paine, 12
Connecticut, mythical legal system of, 75
Cooper Union speech, of Lincoln, 182
Cornwallis, General, surrenders at Yorktown, 29; marches through South Carolina, 86
Cowdray, Lord, and Mexico, 260
Crawford, Henry, candidate for Presidency, 94; discredits Calhoun, 105; grievance of, against Calhoun, 106; Mr. Bowers' defence of, 106
Crittenden, Senator, attempted compromise of, 188; Lincoln and, 224
Curzon, Lord, limited democratic sympathies of, 274

DALLAS, Wilson meets House at, 245
Dana, Richard Henry, quoted on Lincoln, 217
Danton, and French Revolution, 36
Davis, David, Lincoln's manager, 176; bargains with Cameron, 176
Davis, Jefferson, religion of, 158; on Missouri Compromise, 164; quarrels with Douglas, 173; and secession, 180; and Stars and Stripes, 184; elected President of the Confederacy, 189; and secession, 192; personal grievances of, 194; Artemus Ward on, 197; on emancipation, 218; Lincoln's theory concerning, 220; arrested, 223; Wilson sees, 225
Davis, John, leg of, pulled, 61
Davis, John W., ambassador at St. James', 276
Davis, Robert, New Jersey sheriff, 239; at New York dinner, 240
Davison, Henry P., at head of Red Cross, 276
Dayton, Johnston at, 215
Delaware, and the Civil War, 199
Derry, Professor, Wilson at Academy of, 225
De Tocqueville, Lyons compared with, 214
Diaz, Porfirio, and Huerta, 257–258; and American capital, 260
Dickens, Charles, Lincoln and, 159
Dickinson, on squatter sovereignty, 144
Discourse on Constitution and Government of the United States, by Calhoun, 147
Disquisition on Government, by Calhoun, 147
Disraeli, Benjamin, argument of, for protection, 33; and methods of government, 281
Dodge, Cleveland, and *Trenton True American*, 247

Index

Douglas, Stephen, Lincoln's contest with, 160; position of, in 1850, 161; splits party, 163; abrogates Missouri Compromise, 164; and Dred Scott decision, 165; and the Democratic party, 168; on Leavenworth Convention, 169; Western opposition to, 169; debates with Lincoln, 170; dilemma of, 172; Presidential candidate, 174; praises Lincoln, 176; imperialism of, 185; at Lincoln's inauguration, 190; on secession, 194; supports Lincoln, 197; Lincoln and, 218, 224

EARLY, repulse of, 215
Eaton, Jackson's Secretary of War, 104
Eaton, Mrs., scandal concerning, 104
Eckenrode, Dr. H. J., criticizes Jefferson, 28
Edwards, Jonathan, grandfather of Burr, 59
Edwards, Ninian, writes A.B. Papers, 106
Edwards, Wilson defeats, 254
Ely, A. B., on Cameron, 203
Emerson, on John Brown, 174
Enterprise, incident of, 126
Eppes, John, Jefferson's letter to, 49
Essex judgment, 68
Essex Junto, 72
Everett, supports Lincoln, 197

FABRY, Adhémar, compact of, with the citizens of Geneva, 17
Fall, Senator, calls on Wilson, 302
Farragut, captures Mobile, 215
Fenno employed by Hamilton, 43; attacked by Jefferson, 44; of small importance, 45
Fitzpatrick, Lincoln's quarrel with, 159
Fiume, question of, 297
Flood, at Sunrise Conference, 266
Florida, frontier of, 68; failure of negotiations for purchase of, 70; secedes, 189
Foch, Marshal, quoted, 271; genius of, 282; calls on Wilson, 306
Foote, Senator, brings in motion, 104
Fort Brown, skirmish at, 141
Fort Sumter, situation at, 188; Beauregard at, 190; Anderson demands reënforcements for, 191; Lincoln's policy concerning, 192; forces a choice, 195; Lincoln and, 219
Fortress Monroe, McClellan occupies, 205
Fox, Charles James, joins British Government, 69
France, enters American War, 26–27; Jeferson's friendship for, 40; purchases Louisiana, 49; Jefferson's attitude towards, 68; Catholic reaction in, 75; arrogance of, 88; recognizes Texan independence, 129; Texan policy of, 131; Southern sympathies of, 200; House and, 265; and entangling alliances, 269; democracy of, 274; the creator of Prussia, 290
Francis, St., and human equality, 16
Franklin, Benjamin, attitude of, to monarchy, 9; commercial negotiations of, 33
Fredericksburg, battle of, 209; Vallandigham on, 214
Frémont, General, character of, 202; Jackson defeats, 206; opposes Lincoln, 217
Freneau, employed by Jefferson, 43

GARRISON, Lindley M., preparedness campaign of, 265
Garrison, William Lloyd, founds *The Liberator*, 112; character of, 113; on the Union, 181
Gaynor, Mayor, House disappointed in, 245

Genêt, agent for French Government, 47; indiscretions of, 50
George III, how far to blame for American quarrel, 6; system of, contrasted with Parliamentary, 7; opposition of, to commercial state, 9–10; position of, weakened by Protestantism, 13; as Pharaoh in American coat of arms, 19; head of Virginian Church, 24; Jefferson's changed attitude towards, 68; Madison declares war on, 88
George, Mr. Lloyd, 1918 election of, 284; M. Clemenceau's contempt for, 288; ignorance of, 291; and British Parliament, 292; calls on Wilson, 306
George Washington, Wilson sails on, 284
Georgia, opposes tariff, 97; secedes, 189; Sherman's march through, 215
Germany, Roosevelt defends, 263; submarine campaign of, 263; hostility of, to America, 264; House and, 265; war with, 273; and Fourteen Points, 280; M. Clemenceau's opinion on, 286
Gettysburg, battle of, 212; Lincoln on, 222
Ghent, Peace of, 74
Gilbert and Sullivan, Tripolitan War worthy of, 62
Gladstone, William Ewart, Wilson and, 231
Glynn, proposes Wilson, 267
Grant, General Ulysses, character of, 204; captures Vicksburg, 212; advance of, 215; Lincoln and, 219; at Appomattox, 221; at Cabinet meeting, 222
Grayson, Admiral, report of, on Wilson's health, 301
Greeley, Horace, on secession, 181; and Lincoln, 215
Grenville, George, and American taxation, 5
Grey, Lord, and amendments to the League of Nations Covenant, 300
Guedalla, Mr. Philip, quoted, 296

HAITI, revolt of, 63
Hamilton, Alexander, attacks Jeffersonian state, 3; and Jeffersonian metaphysics, 17; and the Constitution, 37–38; a monarchist, 37; and Jefferson, 39–40; admiration of, for British Constitution, 41; argument of, with Adams, 41; support of Bank, 41; attacks Jefferson, 43; attacked by Jefferson, 45; policy of, concerning debt, 46; outwits Jefferson, 46; wishes to repudiate French Treaty, 50; gains influence over Washington, 53; loses confidence of Federalists, 54; opinion of, on Adams, 56; quarrel with Adams, 58; supports Jefferson, 59; shot, 69; newspaper controversies of, 96
Hamilton, Governor, Calhoun's letter to, 107, 111
Hamilton, James A., agent of Van Buren, 106
Hammond, George, financial agent for British Government, 47
Hampton Roads Conference, 218
Hannibal, 272
Harding, Warren Gamaliel, President, 305
Harmon, Governor, at Baltimore Convention, 250
Harper and Brothers, Wilson's publishers, 230; and J. P. Morgan, 238
Harper's Ferry, John Brown's invasion of, 173
Harper's Weekly, Harvey edits, 238; supports Wilson, 248; repudiated at Bryan's demand, 252
Harrison, William Henry, President, 127

Index

Hartford Convention, Calhoun's studies of, 87

Harvey, Colonel George, head of Harper and Brothers, 238; at New York dinner, 240; familiarity with Wilson, 243; support of Wilson, 248; Wilson snubs, 248; and Bryan, 252

Hayne, Senator, opposes tariff, 97; debates with Webster, 104; Governor of South Carolina, 108

Henry, Patrick, speech of, 11; Governor of Virginia, 26; opposes Constitution, 37; opposes Virginia Resolutions, 57

Hermitage, The, Jackson retires to, 123

Hibben, President, Wilson's rudeness to, 268

Hindenburg, Marshal von, effect of democracy on, 286

Hirst, Mr. F. W., quoted on Jefferson, 7; quoted on Declaration of Independence, 15; quoted on Virginia Statute of Religious Freedom, 19; defends Jefferson's Governorship, 28; attacks Hamilton's methods of controversy, 44

History of the American People, by Wilson, 230

Hitchcock, Senator, calls on Wilson, 302

Hooker, General, defeat of, 209

House, Colonel, deference of, 243; meets Wilson, 245; and Bryan, 247–248; Mrs. Bryan's letter to, 253; influence of, in Cabinet making, 254; on Wilson's capacity to take advice, 259; mission of, to Europe, 265; and Versailles Conference, 283; dismissed, 297; advises dinner to Foreign Relations Committee, 299; plan of, 301; at Wilson's funeral, 307

Hudspeth, at New York dinner, 240

Huerta, General, Mexican dictator, 257; Wilson believes responsible for murder of Madero, 258; British policy towards, 259, 260; resigns, 261; and self-determination, 270

Hughes, Charles Evans, Wilson's opponent, 267; and League to Enforce Peace, 296

Hughes, Senator, supports Record, 256

Hugo, Victor, on John Brown, 174

Hull, General, failure of, 74

Hyer, Tom, supports Seward, 176

IDAHO, part of Oregon Territory, 138

Iliad, quotation from, on Mrs. Jefferson's tomb, 82

Illinois, Lincoln a Congressman from, 160; Senatorial contest in, 160; Congressional Districts of, 170

Indianapolis, Wilson's suggested speech at, 281

Inquisition, compared by de Maistre with U.S.A., 75; compared with the University of Virginia, 80

JACKSON, Andrew, opposition of, to nullification, 57; contempt for State, 65; victory of, at New Orleans, 74; Calhoun's defiance of, 90; candidate for Presidency, 94; marriage of, 104; at nullification dinner, 105; question of his arrest, 105; quarrels with Calhoun, 107; tariff of, 107; conduct of, concerning nullification, 109; denounced in South, 109; a democrat, 112; willing to prohibit abolitionist literature, 121; retirement of, 123; and the mails, 124; and Van Buren, 130; spoils-system of, 156; and the Bank, 166; on the Constitution, 167; and secession, 180; contempt for the State, 185; Cecil Chesterton's admiration for, 186

Jackson, Camp, 199

Jackson, Stonewall, death of, 84;

religion of, 158; on John Brown, 174; counter-move of, 206; death of, 209

James I, refuses to allow Parliament to tax America, 9

James II, Jesuit's defense of, 9

James River, Peninsular Campaign and, 205

James, Senator, Chairman of St. Louis Convention, 252, 267

Jay, John, Governor of N. Y., 59

Jefferson, Thomas, political philosophy of, 1; preference of, for an agricultural state, 2; attitude of, towards slavery, 2; passim, 4–83; description of, 4; on Bolingbroke, 4; and natural rights, 6; theory of Empire, 8; attitude of, towards King, 9–10; his pamphlet "A Summary View of the Rights of British America, 9; in Virginia Convention, 10; supports warlike policy, 11; drafts reply to Lord North's proposition, 12; drafts Constitution for Virginia, 13; drafts Declaration of Independence, 14; on natural rights, 15; debt of, to Sidney, 16; and democracy, 18; and slavery, 18; and religious freedom, 19; and political intolerance, 20; on truth, 21; compared with Mill, 23; attacks Established Church, 24–25; Governor of Virginia, 26; British attacks during Governorship of, 27; escape of, from Tarleton, 27–28; *Notes on Virginia* of, 29; comments on Raynal, 30; on political corruption, 31; a free-trader, 32; wife's death, 33; in Paris, 33–34; opinion of, on French Revolution, 34–35; on American Constitution, 38; and Bill of Rights, 38; Secretary of State, 39; and Hamilton, 40; Hamilton's dislike of metaphysics of, 40; accepts Constitution, 41; opposition of, to Bank, 42; Hamilton's attack on, 43; defense of, 44–45; on the debt, 45; negotiations with Hamilton concerning, 46; on international debts, 47–48; foreign policy of, 49; stands by French Treaty, 50; retires, 51; opinion of, on politicians, 52; fondness of, for shows, 52; Presidential candidate, 54; defeated, 55; as Vice-President, 55; candidate for Presidency, 57; elected, 58–59; Hamilton's conduct towards, 59; on ceremony, 60–61; life of, at Washington, 61–62; policy of, 62; Louisiana purchase, 63–66; justification of, 63; letter to Priestley, 65; popularity of, 67; foreign policy of, 68–69; policy of, towards Anglo-French War, 69; arrest of Burr, 70; embargo policy of, 71; abandonment of embargo, 72; philological work of, 73; support of War of 1812, 74; dislike of, for the Christian religion, 74–75; on Unitarianism, 76; on Missouri Compromise, 76–78; on Monroe Doctrine, 78; and University of Virginia, 79; attitude to religious education, 80; death of, 81; on epitaphs, 82; compared with Calhoun, 84; meeting of, with Calhoun, 87; on Franco-British War, 88; pacifism of, 89; newspaper controversies of, 96; banquet on birthday of, 104; and Calhoun, 151; and slavery, 183; compared with Wilson, 229

Jerome Bonaparte, popularity of, in Rhineland, 291

Johns Hopkins, Wilson gets Doctorate of, 226

Johnson, Andrew, arrests Davis, 223

Johnston, Mr. Alexander, quoted on state sovereignty, 184

Johnston, General, victory of, at Bull Run, 200; and Southern

Index

disorganization, 200; McClellan opposed to, 205
Joline, Wilson's letter to, 249
Jones, and Harvester Corporation, 256
Jouitte, saves Jefferson, 28

KANSAS, squatter sovereignty in, 161–163; John Brown in, 173
Kansas City, Wilson's speech at, 246
Katzenbach, Frank S., candidate for Governorship of New Jersey, 240
Kentucky, resolutions, 56–57; resolutions appealed to, 99; Lincoln from, 174; neutrality of, 199; invasion of, 212
Kerney, Mr. James, quoted on Wilson, 230; quoted on Wilson's nomination for Governorship, 241; visits Wilson at Princeton, 241; advice to Wilson of, 242; on crooks, 244; on *Trenton True American*, 247; on European diplomats, 293
Kinkead, at New York dinner, 240
Kitchin, Claude, at Sunrise Conference, 266

LAFAYETTE, defense of Virginia, 27; in French politics, 34; visits Monticello, 81
Lamont, Thomas W., Government's financial adviser, 276
Lansing, Robert, Secretary of State, 264; and Versailles Conference, 283; dismissed, 301
Lawrence, David, Student-reporter at Princeton, 237
Leavenworth Convention, 169
Lee, Colonel Henry, criticizes Jefferson, 28
Lee, General Robert E., religion of, 158; and secession, 180, 192; and the war, 195; defeats McClellan, 206; invades Maryland, 206–207; at Antietam, 208; victory of, at Fredericksburg, 209; position of, 215; in Maryland, 219; surrenders, 221; Wilson and, 225; Wilson's character-sketch of, 230, 231
Leopard, duel with *Chesapeake*, 71
Lewis, and Clark, expedition of, 67
Lewis, Major, head of Jackson's Kitchen Cabinet, 106
Lexington, battle of, 11
Liberator, abolitionist paper, 108, 112
Liberty, On, by Mill, compared with theories of Jefferson, 23
Lincoln, Abraham, attitude to free speech, 24; contempt of state, 65; compared with Calhoun, 84, 86; answers Calhoun, 120; passim, 153–224; character of, 154–156; and Butler, 156; religion of, 156–157; morals of, 158; early life of, 159; stands for the Senate, 160; joins Republican party, 163; and Dred Scott decision, 167; debates with Douglas, 170–172; and Douglas' dilemma, 172; on John Brown, 174; in Republican Convention, 175; bargains concerning, 176; and Cameron, 176–177; elected President, 178; as President, 179; on secession, 180; on North and South, 181; effect of election of, 182; and the tariff, 182; and the Constitution, 182–183; short-sightedness of, 184; contempt of, for State rights, 185; correspondence of, with Stephens, 188; rejects Crittenden Compromise, 188–189; 1st Inaugural of, 190; and Fort Sumter, 191; policy towards Sumter, 192; Douglas on election of, 194; and the war, 195; character of, 197–198; and neutrality of Kentucky, 199; and Bull Run, 199; and Mason-Slidell case, 201; and Frémont, 202, 203; and Cameron, 203; dismisses Cameron,

333

204; appoints McClellan, 205; and Maryland, 208; and 1864 election, 208–209; and Chicago petition, 209; and emancipation, 210; differences in Cabinet of, 211; at Gettysburg, 212; and conscription, 213; criticisms of, 214; and Vallandigham, 214; and Greeley, 215; and election of 1864, 216; at Hampton Roads Conference, 218; 2nd Inaugural of, 218–220; doubts of, 219; reads Macbeth, 221–222; murder of, 222; Davis arrested for murder of, 223; character of, 223–224; trial for murder of, 225; contrasted with Wilson, 305; and Buchanan, 305

Lincoln, Levi, Jefferson's attorney-general, 60

Lincoln, Mrs. Lincoln's indifference to, 154; at Lincoln's assassination, 222

Lincoln, Nebraska, Bryan retires to, 264

Lind, Wilson's agent in Mexico, 259, 260

Lindabury, Richard V., at New York dinner, 240

Locke, John, Jefferson's debt to, 16; Calhoun's reading of, 87

Lodge's *Works of Alexander Hamilton*, 43

Longfellow, on John Brown, 174

Louis XVI, dons tricolor, 34

Louisiana, sold by Spain to France, 49; purchase of, 63; effect of purchase, 64–67; effect on Jefferson, 67; Burr's designs on, 70; Missouri carved out of, 77; claim that Texas included in, 135; secedes, 189

Lowell, James Russell, quoted, 118, 119; attacks Calhoun, 120; on the Stock Exchange, 179, 189; on Virginia Peace Conference, 192

Ludendorff, General, on Germany's defeat, 280

Ludwig, Herr Emil, *Wilhelm II* of, 271

Lundy, Benjamin, tour of, 113

Lusitania, sinking of, 264; American policy concerning, 270; Prussia and, 275

Luther, Martin, Calhoun compared with, 108

Lyme, Wilson's holiday at, 239

Lyon, General, in Missouri, 199

Lyons, Lord, on Lincoln's Government, 214

MACAULAY, Lord, Wilson compared with, 230

Macbeth, Lincoln reads, 222

Madero, Francesco, assassinated, 257

Madison, accepts Constitution, 41; Jefferson wishes to stand for President, 54; introduces Virginia Resolutions, 57; letter of Jefferson to, 68; succeeds Jefferson, 73; term expires, 76; and War of 1812, 88; succeeded by Monroe, 91

Maine, created a State, 78; and Mexican War, 141

Maistre, Comte de, influence of, in France, 75; quoted on American revolt, 75

Man of Destiny, by Mr. Shaw, quoted, 110

Mann, Horace, quoted on Calhoun, 146

Mansfield, criticized by Jefferson, 75

Manual of Parliamentary Practice, by Jefferson, 55

Marie Antoinette, obstacle to reform, 35

Marshall, Chief Justice, quoted concerning Jefferson's retirement, 51; and midnight judges, 60; Burr's trial before, 70

Marshall, Vice-President, and the succession, 301

Martine, elected Senator, 244

Index

Maryland, religious tolerance in, 24; supports Adams, 54; Southern sympathies of, 199; and the Civil War, 199; invasion of, 206–207; Lincoln and, 208; Lee in, 219

Mason, Senator, reads Calhoun's last speech, 148; captured by the North, 201

Massachusetts, preparations of, for war, 10; war begins in, 11; demands a higher tariff, 97; Calhoun's attitude to, 124

Massachusetts Institute of Technology, invitation of, to West, 233

Matamoras, Mexican troops at, 141

Maurras, M. Charles, 274

Maximilian, in Mexico, 200

McAdoo, influence of, 254

McClellan, General, 205; and Lincoln, 205, 206; political ambitions of, 208; letter of, 209; and conscription riots, 213; opposes Lincoln, 217; and Democratic candidature, 217

McCombs, Wilson's manager, 247; and Wilson's withdrawal, 252; congratulates Wilson, 253; behavior of Wilson towards, 310

McDowell, General, defeated at Bull Run, 200; and McClellan, 205–206

McKinley, and plutocracy, 310

McMaster, Professor J. B., quoted, 61

Meade, General, at Gettysburg, 212; at Appomattox, 221

Megalonyx Jeffersonii, giant sloth, 55

Mexico, Burr's designs on, 70; effect of Monroe Doctrine on, 79; and Texas, 128, 131; desires war with, 136; and Texas, 140, 141; war with U.S.A., 141–142; schemes of Napoleon III in, 201; loss of California, 202; suggested joint attack on, 218; Wilson's policy in, 257–258; Cowdray and, 260; farce of democracy in, 261; Fall's interests in, 302

Mexico, Gulf of, squadron sent to, 131

Michigan, in election of 1844, 137

Milan, Wilson at, 285

Milan Decrees, 71

Mill, John Stuart, compared with Jefferson, 23

Miranda, correspondence of, with Hamilton, 56

Mississippi, commerce on, 49; evils of slavery on, 118; fighting for, 204; Northern mastery of, 205, 212

Mississippi (State), suggested leadership of, in Southern Convention, 147; secedes, 189

Missouri, slavery question in, 77; compromise, 78, 98, 142; Calhoun's understanding of compromise, 143; Lincoln's support of, 160; validity of, questioned, 164; and Dred Scott case, 165; Seward opposes repeal of, 175; coerced into loyalty, 199; Frémont in command in, 202; policy of Frémont in, 203

Mix, Elijah, charges of, against Calhoun, 93

Mobile, capture of, 215

Monaco, sovereignty of, 184

Monroe, President, negotiates Louisiana sale, 63; letter of Jefferson to, 68; succeeds Madison, 73, 76; doctrine of, 78; as President, 91; Adams and Calhoun in Cabinet of, 93; leaves office, 94; doctrine of, in danger, 133; Calhoun in Cabinet of, 142; doctrine of, to be applied to world, 269

Montaigne, criticized by Jefferson, 52

Monterey, American consul at, 202

Montesquieu, Jefferson's support of, 35; on republics, 62

Montgomery, Convention at, 189

Monticello, Jefferson at, 39, 55, 73; Jefferson's closing years at, 76; view of University of Virginia from, 79;

Jefferson's death at, 81; Jefferson and, 83
Morgan, J. P., Harper and Brothers and, 238; Bryan and, 251; power of, 276; and Wilson, 310
Morgenthau, Henry, subsidizes Wilson, 247
Morrow, Dwight, Government's financial adviser, 276
Murfreesborough, Lincoln on, 222
Murray, Earl of, ancestor of Jefferson, 4

NAPOLEON I, and human equality, 16; quoted, 52; compared with Burr, 59; sells Louisiana, 63; will not settle Louisiana frontier, 68; continental system of, 69, 71; compared with Calhoun, 92; attitude of, spoiled, 110; not a militarist, 272; Mr. George and, 289
Napoleon III, Mexican schemes of, 200; and Civil War, 201; opposition of, to passports, 214; failure of, to support Austria, 290
Nashville, Jackson retires to, 123; battle of, 215
Nassau Hall, meeting, 234–236
Nassau, slaves flee to, 126
National Gazette, in Hamilton-Jefferson controversy, 43
National Intelligencer, quoted on 1860 election, 178
Nebraska, Dred Scott in, 164; Bryan delegate from, 250, 251; defeats Clark, 253
New Jersey, supports tariff, 97; and the tariff, 178; Wilson and, 238; bosses in, 238; Wilson Governor of, 243
New Mexico, American demand for, 141; Calhoun's policy concerning, 145; Calhoun and, 150; slavery and, 161; slavery in, 188
New York (City), British occupation of, 27; riots in, 213

New York (State), supports tariff, 97; asserts right of secession, 98; supports Jackson, 103; in election of 1844, 137; asserts right of secession, 179; at Baltimore Convention, 251
New York Times, and Wyman legacy, 237; Wilson's letter to, 306
New York Tribune, quoted, 174; quoted on Cameron, 203; Greeley editor of, 216
Norfolk, Jefferson lands at, 39; Douglas' speech at, 194
North Carolina, *see* Carolina, North
North, Lord, attempt at conciliation of, 11; expletives of, 29
Notes on Virginia, by Jefferson, quoted on religious freedom, 19; discussed, 29–30
Nueces River, Mexico claims as frontier, 141
Nugent, James, in New York politics, 239; at New York dinner, 240

OAXACA, Bazaine at, 202
Ohio, Burr committed in, 70; supports tariff, 97; and Chase, 216
Oklahoma, an Indian reservation, 188
Old Point Comfort, delivery of stones to, 93
Oregon, question of, 138; compared with Texas, 139; British policy towards, 140; bill for organization of, 144; remains unorganized, 144
O'Shaughnessy, Mrs., quoted on murder of Madero, 258
Our American Cousin, Lincoln assassinated while seeing, 222
Oxford, clubs at, 231

PAGE, John, candidate for Governorship of Virginia, 26
Paine, Tom, writes "Common Sense," 12; misses the point, 13; influence of, in French Revolution, 35; on Burke,

Index

36; Jefferson's commendation of *Rights of Man* by, 42; influence of, on Lincoln, 156

Pakenham, Calhoun's correspondence with, 131

Parker, Alton B., temporary chairman of Baltimore Convention, 250

Patriot King, Bolingbroke's, studied by George III, 9

Peel, Sir Robert, Clay compared with, 110

Pennsylvania, supports Jefferson, 54; supports tariff, 97; supports Jackson, 103; sovereignty of, 125; supports Polk, 138; and the tariff, 177, 178

Penrose, Senator Boise, on Record appointment, 256

Pensacola, Jackson's attack on, 105

Perkins, George, Roosevelt's manager, 247; opposes Record, 256; on Jones case, 257

Petersburg, Confederate army at, 218

Philadelphia, Continental Congress at, 12; Convention at, 37

Philadelphia American and Gazette, quoted on 1860 election, 178

Philadelphia North American, quoted on 1860 election, 178

Phillips, Wendell, on secession, 181; on Lincoln, 214

Pickering, opinion of, on Adams, 56; Jefferson's letter to, 76

Pinckney, Thomas, candidate for Presidency, 54; again, 57; Hamilton's intrigue concerning, 58

Pindell, offered St. Petersburg Embassy, 255

Pittsburgh, Wilson at, 232, 236

Plattsburg training-camp, revelations concerning, 278

Plumer, Senator, quoted on Jefferson's hospitality, 61

Pocahontas, Princess, ancestor of Jefferson, 4

Poincaré, M. Raymond, defeated, 125

Poland, Calhoun's interest in history of, 87; problem of, 289

Polk, President, 135; elected, 137; on the tariff, 138; drops Calhoun, 138; policy of, concerning Oregon, 139; bluster of, 141; declares war on Mexico, 141; Calhoun's supposed desire to succeed, 143; term of, ends, 147

Pope, Alexander, Jefferson's admiration for, 79

Pope, General, defeat of, 206

Port Hamilton, slaves flee to, 126

Potomac, capital to be built on, 47; John Brown crosses, 173; Confederates to the South of, 198

Priestley, Dr., Jefferson's letter to, 65

Princeton, explosion on, 128

Princeton, Wilson at, 226; Wilson returns to, 228; Wilson President of, 230; and Oxford, 231–232; inequalities of, 232; Graduate School at, 233–236; Wilson resigns from, 242; Wilson returns to, 268

Procter, William C., offer of, 234; made unconditional, 236

Prussia, barbarian nature of, 274–275; and Austria, 287; created by France, 290

Pueblo, Wilson's breakdown at, 300

Pyne, Moses Taylor, a supporter of Wilson, 230; of West, 233; wealth of, 235

QUERETARO, Maximilian shot at, 200

RANDOLPH, George Wythe, Jefferson's educational course for, 80

Randolph, John, denounces Adams, 56; abusive language of, 96; at Webster-Calhoun debate, 109

Rawle, Judge, quoted on secession, 98, 180

Raynal, Abbé, criticized by Jefferson, 30
Reflections on the French Revolution, by Burke, 36
Revolution in Virginia, The, by Dr. H. J. Eckenrode, criticizes Jefferson, 28
Rhode Island, supports tariff, 97; asserts right of secession, 98, 179; freedom in, 124
Rhodes, Mr. J. F., quoted on Douglas, 162; on Dred Scott decision, 165
Richmond, Burr tried at, 70; Southern graves at, 84; Confederate Congress meets at, 199; McClellan's plans against, 205; danger of, 206, 215; Confederate army at, 218; evacuation of, 220
Rio Grande, incident on, 141
Rochefaucauld, La, criticized by Jefferson, 52
Rockingham, Lord, repeals Stamp Act, 6
Roman Empire, compared with British, 9
Rome, Calhoun's interest in history of, 87; Calhoun as Senator of, 151
Roosevelt, Theodore, attacks plutocracy, 232; campaigns of, 243, 247; progressive candidate, 253; defends German behavior in Belgium, 263; and "Y.M.C.A. banditti," 275; desire of, for a command, 277–279; on Wilson, 282; protest of, against plutocracy, 310
Root, Elihu, and League to Enforce Peace, 296
Ross, at New York dinner, 240
Rousseau, Jean Jacques, and natural rights, 7; and representation, 31
Ruhr, French blunder concerning, 291
Rutledge, Anne, Lincoln's love for, 154
Ryan, Thomas F., Colonel Watterson and, 249; and Bryan, 251

St. Louis, Democratic Convention at, 267, 273
St. Mark's, Jackson's attack on, 105
St. Petersburg, Cameron sent to, 204; Pindell offered Embassy at, 255
San Antonio, 129
San Ildefonso, Treaty of, 49, 63; vagueness of, 68
San Jacinto, battle of, 129
Saratoga, battle of, 26
Sazonoff, M., 274
Schurz, Carl, Indian policy of, 92
Scott, Dred, decision, 145; case, 165; Douglas accepts verdict on, 168; in Lincoln-Douglas debates, 171–172; Southern rights under, 178; Republican refusal to accept, 180; Lincoln's attitude to, 183, 224
Seabury, Samuel, theory of sovereignty of, 8; theory of rights of, 10
Seminole affair, Calhoun's behavior in, 105; Van Buren's behavior in, 123
Seward, and Dred Scott decision, 167; on Douglas, 169; strong candidature of, 175; support of Lincoln, 176; on "irrepressible conflict," 181; and the Constitution, 183; on plebiscite, 189; policy of, 192; why Lincoln preferred to, 198; and Great Britain, 201; advice of, on Emancipation, 210; and Chase, 212–211; at Hampton Roads Conference, 218; Lincoln and, 219
Shantung question, 297, 298
Shenandoah Valley, battle in, 215; political effect of, 217
Sheridan, General, campaigns of, 218
Sherman, General William T., advance of, 215; campaigns of, 218; Lincoln and, 219
Shiloh, Grant at, 204; result, 212
Sidney, Algernon, and natural rights, 16; quoted by Jefferson, 18
Slidell, captured by the North, 201

Index

Smith, Ashbel, Texan Minister in London, 133
Smith, Caleb, bargains with Davis, 176
Smith, James, in New Jersey politics, 239; at New York dinner, 240; visits Wilson at Princeton, 241; Record's questions concerning, 242; and the Senate, 243; Wilson quarrels with, 244
Smith, Mr. Randolph Wellford, quoted on Mexican situation, 260
Smuts, General Jan, at Versailles, 292
South Carolina, *see* Carolina, South
South Carolina Exposition, quoted, 99; reference to slavery in, 112; on Supreme Court, 167
Spain, success of religious intolerance in, 24; enters American War, 27; sells Louisiana to France, 49; attitude of, towards Florida frontier, 68; and Texas, 128
Spanish Empire, compared with British, 9
Springfield, Lincoln practices law at, 160; Lincoln at, 178
State and Federal Government, by Wilson, 239
Statute of Religious Liberty in Virginia, in Jefferson's epitaph, 79
Staunton, Virginia Legislature meets at, 28
Stephens, Alexander, on slavery, 183; Lincoln's correspondence with, 188; Vice-President of Confederacy, 189; and secession, 192; at Hampton Roads Conference, 218; Wilson sees, 225
Stettinius, Edward R., Assistant Secretary of War, 276
Stevens, Thaddeus, 184; on Cameron, 203
Stone, Senator, Clark's floor-leader, 252
Stowe, Harriet Beecher, quoted, 118; and slavery, 182

"Summa Contra Gentiles," of St. Thomas Aquinas, its doctrine of human equality, 16
"Summary View of the Rights of British America, A," pamphlet by Jefferson, 9
Sumner, Charles, 184; Lincoln and, 219

Taft, William Howard, Republican candidate, 253; and League to Enforce Peace, 296
Talleyrand, negotiates with Adams, 56; negotiates about Louisiana, 63; *On the Advantages of Withdrawing from New Colonies in Present Circumstances* quoted, 66
Tampico, American sailors arrested at, 261
Taney, Roger, Dred Scott decision of, 145; and Lincoln, 157; in Dred Scott case, 165; charge of collusion against, 167; and the Bank, 168; administers the oath to Lincoln, 190
Tarleton, General, raids of, 27
Taylor, General Zachary, in command against Mexico, 141; President, 147; Lincoln tries to get Commissionership from, 160
Tennessee, secedes, 199; Confederate retreat to, 212; goes Republican, 304
Texas, independence of, 128; Jackson and, 130; Treaty with, rejected, 135; assistance promised to, 136; annexed, 137; Calhoun's hopes of, 138; and Mexico, 140; frontier question, 140; and the war, 141
Thomas, General, victory of, 215
Tippecanoe, Harrison's victory at, 127
Toussaint l'Ouverture, revolt of, 63
Trenton Evening Times, Mr. Kerney editor of, 241
Trenton True American, Wilson paper, 247
Tripoli, American war with, 63

Trist, Nicholas, at Jefferson's deathbed, 81
Tumulty, Joseph, Wilson's secretary, 254; a Democrat, 275; Wilson's only friend, 297, 302; repudiation of, 305–306
Turgot, schemes of financial reform, 35
Turner, Nat, insurrection of, 113
Tyler, President, 127; cries, 128; on Texan annexation, 135; accepts verdict of election, 137; leaves office, 137
Tyler, Wat, not a Whig, 127

UNCLE Tom's Cabin, by Harriet Beecher Stowe, 182
Underwood, at Baltimore Convention, 250
United States Gazette, involved in Hamilton-Jefferson controversy, 43
Upshur, killed, 128; policy of, 130; negotiations of, with Aberdeen, 132; fear of Great Britain, 132
Utah, slavery in, 161; polygamy in, 165

VALLANDIGHAM, opposition of, to war, 214
Van Buren, Martin, intrigues against Calhoun, 97; Secretary of State, 103; behavior of, to Mrs. Eaton, 104; discredits Calhoun, 105; intrigues with Crawford, 106; President, 123; Texan policy of, 129; discredited, 130; refusal of, to annex Texas, 132; rejected by Democrats, 135
Vane, Jefferson quotes attack of, on Massachusetts, 12
Vattel, quoted on international debt, 48; on treaties, 50
Vera Cruz, Americans occupy, 261
Versailles, Wilson at, 238; Treaty of, 292; U.S. promissory notes at, 294
Vesey, insurrection of, 113
Vicksburg, Southern fortress at, 205; captured, 212; Lincoln, 222

Villa, General, claims succession to Huerta, 262
Virginia, institution of slavery in, 2; leads America, 10; votes for war, 11; constitution of, drafted by Jefferson, 13; failure of religious intolerance in, 24; British attacks on, 27; *Notes on*, by Jefferson, 29; rivalry with Maryland, 54; slavery in western territory of, 78; University of, 79–81; compared with Inquisition, 80; asserts right of secession, 98; Resolutions of, appealed to, 99; insurrection in, 113; Brown's invasion of, 173; asserts right of secession, 179; summons Peace Conference, 192; secedes, 199; rivalry of, with Maryland, 207
Volney, influence of, on Lincoln, 156
Volstead law, Wilson opposes, 303
Voltaire, lost influence of, 22; compared with Jefferson, 29

WALPOLE, Sir Robert, compared with Clay, 88
Ward, Artemus, quoted, 197
Washington, George, supports preparations for war, 11; admires Paine's "Common Sense," 12; strategy of, 27; President, 39; his dislike of party, 45; takes Jefferson's side on French Treaty, 50; allows Jefferson to retire, 51; Hamilton's influence on, 53; death of, 53; opposes Virginia Resolutions, 57; no opposition to, 94; Lincoln compares himself with, 190; Wilson on, 229; Wilson's character-sketch of, 230, 231
Washington (City), built, 60; Treaty of, 127; Peace Conference at, 191; anxiety for safety of, 198; McClellan's desertion of, 205–206; Early's raids on, 215
Washington (State), in Oregon territory, 138

Index

Watterson, Colonel Henry, Wilson's quarrel with, 248–249
Webster, Daniel, Calhoun's defiance of, 90; belief of, concerning the South, 101; gibe at Calhoun, 102; debates with Hayne, 104; debates with Calhoun, 109; quotes Calhoun on law of nations, 126; compared with Calhoun, 149; on Calhoun, 151; support of Clay's compromise, 161; Imperialism of, 185
Weed, Lincoln's letter to, 220
Wesleyan Alumnus, quotation from, 228
Wesleyan University, Middletown, Wilson at, 228
Westcott, and bargaining for votes, 241
West Point, secession taught at, 180; Lee and Grant talk concerning, 221
White, Mr. William Allen, quoted, 236; and Wilson's descent, 241; on Wilson, 282; on Wilson's faith, 287; on Wilson's illness, 302; on Wilson, 303; on Wilson's leaving office, 305
Whitman, Walt, quoted on the war, 195–196
Whitney, Eli, 2
Wichita, Wilson taken ill at, 300
Wilhelm II, by Herr Emil Ludwig, 271
William and Mary College, decadence of, 79
Williamsburg, Virginia Assembly meets at, 19
Wilmot Proviso, 142; opposition to, 142–144; effect of, 161; Calhoun on, 164
Wilson, Henry Lane, American Ambassador in Mexico, 258
Wilson, Rev. Joseph Ruggles, father of Woodrow, 225
Wilson, Mrs., 296; and House, 297
Wilson, Thomas Woodrow, compared with Calhoun, 86; passim, 225–307; as a boy, 225–226; goes to Princeton, 226; style of, 228; writings of, 229–230; President of Princeton, 230; and quadrangle system, 232; and Dean West, 233–236; at Nassau Hall meeting, 234–235, 236; and West's brochure, 236; and Wyman legacy, 237; and Colonel Harvey, 238–239; political ambitions of, 239; at New York dinner, 240; nominated for Governorship of New Jersey, 241; elected Governor, 242; supports Martine, 244; quarrels with Smith, 244; meets House, 245; and Governor's salary, 246; Harvey supports, 248; quarrels with Harvey, 248; quarrels with Watterson, 249; at Baltimore Convention, 250; Bryan and, 250; suggested withdrawal of, 252; elected President, 253; and Edwards, 254; appoints Bryan Secretary of State, 254; as President, 255; Mexican policy of, 257–258; neglect of diplomatic representatives, 259; threat to Huerta, 260; expels Huerta, 261; declares neutrality in European War, 263; and the *Lusitania*, 264; and preparedness, 264; financial influence on, 265–266; renominated, 267; demands of, from Germany, 268; peace formulæ of, 269; difficulties of, 270; foresees calamities, 272; reasons of, for delay, 275; corruption under, 275; and J. P. Morgan, 276; and Roosevelt, 277–279; service of, to Allies, 279; Fourteen Points of, 280–281; demand of, for a Democratic Congress, 282; repudiation of, 282; goes to Paris, 283; at Buckingham Palace, 284; and ignorance of Europe, 286; belief in human nature, 287; M. Clemenceau's contempt for, 288; Polish policy of, 289; ignorance of, 291; and League of Nations,

292; and U.S. promissory notes, 294; and publicity, 295; at Boston, 296; quarrel with House, 297; and Shantung, 297, 298; rejects Root-Taft-Hughes amendments, 298; and the Secret Treaties, 299; illness of, 300; rumored insanity of, 301; and League of Nations, 302; friends' defense of, 303; defeat of policy of, 304; retirement of, 305; dies, 307

Wise, Henry A., policy of, 128

Wood, Fernando, invitation of, to McClellan, 208

Wood, General Leonard, ambitions of, 277–278

Wyman, Isaac C., legacy of, 237

Wyndham, George, attitude of, to public life, 51

YALE, Calhoun goes to, 87

York River, Peninsular Campaign and, 205

Yorktown, battle of, 29, 86

Yucatan, and Mexican War, 141

ZAPATA, General, claims succession to Huerta, 262

OTHER TITLES AVAILABLE FROM ST. AIDAN PRESS

View a sample chapter from each title at www.staidanpress.com.

THE STORY OF THE WAR IN LA VENDÉE AND THE LITTLE CHOUANNERIE
by George J. Hill, M. A.

The brave French Catholics of the Vendée and neighboring provinces rose up in arms when the revolutionary government replaced their priests with clergy who had renounced the Pope. Though they lacked money, allies, and were divided by disputes, they did not cease to fight until they had secured the open practice of their Faith. Here is the story of their devotion and courage against the advocates of liberty, equality, fraternity, and death.

$18.00 — 342 pages. Available at amazon.com.

CATHOLICISM AND SCOTLAND
by Compton Mackenzie

Much has been written about the desperate fight that English Catholics waged to keep the Faith, but Scotland's Catholic history is little known. Have you ever heard of David Beaton, Cardinal Archbishop of St. Andrews, and his struggles? Or of Fr. Ninian Winzet, who boldly challenged Calvinist champion John Knox to a public debate? Read this book and find out about the Scots who sought to defend their country and their Faith from the onslaught of Protestantism.

$12.00 — 138 pages. Available at amazon.com.

DOMINICAN SAINTS
by the Novices of the Dominican House of Studies

Here are related the astonishing lives of fourteen saints of the Dominican Order, including St. Dominic, St. Catherine of Siena, Pope St. Pius V, St. Rose of Lima, St. Vincent Ferrer, and more. An encyclical on the Dominican Order by Pope Benedict XV and a list of all the Dominican Saints and Blesseds (as of 1921) complete this wonderful introduction to the "Dogs of the Lord."

$19.00 — 392 pages. Available at amazon.com.

FICTION

The Queen's Tragedy, by Msgr. Robert Hugh Benson
"Upon the publication of former books of mine several kindly critics remarked that the reign of Mary Tudor told a very different story with regard to the Catholic character. It is that story which I am now attempting to set forth as honestly as I can."
$19.00 — 364 pages. Available at amazon.com.

The Net, by Agnes Blundell
"Roger felt a freezing dew break out upon his forehead. The net was over him it seemed; in vain he told himself that he could establish his identity. His head was worth forty pounds to the vile creatures at the stair foot, and once in their clutches who knew if he could ever communicate with his friends?"
$16.00 — 264 pages. Available at amazon.com.

They Met Robin Hood, by Agnes Blundell
Osmund does a good turn to one of Robin Hood's outlaws and makes friends with the band. But how can outlaws help his family against a friend of Prince John?
$15.00 — 214 pages. Available at amazon.com.

Redrobes, by Fr. Neil Boyton, S.J.
Thirteen-year-old orphan Jacques gets into trouble in Quebec, and decides to run away to Huronia and become an interpreter for his Jesuit guardian, Father John Brebeuf. But his journey along the Iroquois-infested river may not be so easy as he hopes!
$17.00 — 300 pages. Available at amazon.com.

The Anchorhold, by Enid Dinnis
A chaplain's sermon drove Editha de Beauville to give up the world and enter the religious life. But could a strong-willed noblewoman accept and embrace full seclusion in an anchorhold? Read on to learn how she fared, and how her life affected those around her: Sir Aleric, her erstwhile suitor, now a crusader knight; Fr. Nicholas, a young priest who was quite bright, and thought so too; and Fiddlemee, the witty yet wise court jester whose past held a surprising secret.
$14.00 — 196 pages. Available at amazon.com.

The Road to Somewhere, by Enid Dinnis

Richard and Ann discover a real Tudor house in London being sold cheap, complete with leather latch-strings, a tale of hidden treasure, and a wonderful piper. But will the treasure lose them the house and each other, or can it set them on the real road to Somewhere?

$10.00 — 106 pages. Available at amazon.com.

The Shepherd of Weepingwold, by Enid Dinnis

Sir Robert Luffkyn, rich grandson of a peasant, has purchased the manor of Weepingwold from the noble but impoverished de Lessels, intending to make the renamed Luffkynwold a busy center of his tanning trade. He sends Petronilla, last de Lessels, to Gracerood, intending her for its future Abbess, and plucks little Brother Kit from the cloister to become the new parson of the long-abandoned church. How will Father Kit fare with the parish and his own soul? What is Petronilla's true vocation? And is there really a witch in the parish?

$14.00 — 202 pages. Available at amazon.com.

Scouting for Secret Service, by Fr. Bernard F. J. Dooley

Frank and George are going to spend their summer vacation in the Adirondacks, thanks to Frank's uncle Ed. But once they get there, they realize something fishy is going on. Can they trust Pete, their Indian guide, or is he mixed up in it too? And is Frank's mysterious uncle really behind it all?

$14.00 — 188 pages. Available at amazon.com.

The Masterful Monk, by Fr. Owen Francis Dudley

Brother Anselm comes back to England to counter the Atheist's efforts to destroy the influence of Catholic morals. Between his lectures he is drawn into a struggle for the soul of Beauty Dethier, who is Catholic but fascinated by the "freedom" of the world and the Atheist. It will take more than argument to save her from disaster.

$18.00 — 342 pages. Available at amazon.com.

Will Men Be Like Gods? & The Shadow on the Earth, by Fr. Owen Francis Dudley

Father Dudley's first two books on human happiness are published together here—his rare collection of essays together with a novel which introduces his most famous character, the Masterful Monk.

$15.00 — 216 pages. Available at amazon.com.

CANDLELIGHT ATTIC & ODD JOB'S, by Cecily Hallack
Here are seven true stories in honour of the Seven Joys of Our Blessed Lady, and ten more invented ones about the delightful Barnabas Job, to make a comfortable book for those who are afraid of the dark.
$14.00 — 192 pages. Available at amazon.com.

THE HAPPINESS OF FATHER HAPPÉ, by Cecily Hallack
Shingle Bay did not know what to make of Fr. Savinius Happé. He was a cheerful, rotund Franciscan, a famous author of books on everything from Etruscan civilization to Alpine meadows to beetles, and someone who had never quite mastered the English language. His jovial demeanor concealed a wisdom that alternately bewildered, astonished, but ultimately won over the people of Shingle Bay.
$10.00 — 112 pages. Available at amazon.com.

THREE RELIGIOUS REBELS, by M. Raymond, O.C.S.O.
There must be men who give themselves to God, because there is a God who gave Himself to man.
This is the story of three such men—St. Robert of Molesme, St. Alberic, and St. Stephen Harding.
$17.00 — 294 pages. Available at amazon.com.

THE RED INN OF SAINT LYPHAR, by Anna T. Sadlier
Once Saint Lyphar was a happy village in France, ruled by a generous Marquis and taught by the good Curé. Now the Révolution has put the Curé to death, and the villagers are about to rise under the famous leader Jambe d'Argent. But a Revolutionary spy is lurking near the Inn. . . .
$13.00 — 168 pages. Available at amazon.com.

CON OF MISTY MOUNTAIN, by Mary T. Waggaman
"It had been a long night for Con. Just what had happened to him he was at first too dazed to know. Dennis had flung him into the smoking-room with no very gentle hand, turned the key and left him to himself. And, sinking down dully upon a rug that felt very soft and warm after the hard flight over the mountain, Con was glad to rest his bruised, aching limbs, his dizzy head, without any thought of what was to come upon him next."
$14.00 — 190 pages. Available at amazon.com.

www.ingramcontent.com/pod-product-compliance
Lightning Source LLC
Chambersburg PA
CBHW030818090426
42737CB00009B/772